Writing the
Arab-Israeli Conflict

Writing the
Arab-Israeli Conflict

Pragmatism and
Historical Inquiry

Jonathan B. Isacoff

LEXINGTON BOOKS

A Division of
ROWMAN & LITTLEFIELD PUBLISHERS, INC.
Lanham • Boulder • New York • Toronto • Oxford

LEXINGTON BOOKS

A division of Rowman & Littlefield Publishers, Inc.
A wholly owned subsidary of The Rowman & Littlefield Publishing Group, Inc.
4501 Forbes Boulevard, Suite 200
Lanham, MD 20706

PO Box 317
Oxford
OX2 9RU, UK

British Library Cataloguing in Publication Information Available

Library of Congress Cataloging-in-Publication Data

Isacoff, Jonathan B., 1970–
    Writing the Arab-Israeli conflict : pragmatism and historical inquiry / Jonathan B.
Isacoff.
      p. cm.
    Includes bibliographical references and index.
    ISBN-13: 978-0-7391-1272-4 (cloth : alk. paper)
    ISBN-10: 0-7391-1272-4 (cloth : alk. paper)
    ISBN-13: 978-0-7391-1273-1 (pbk. : alk. paper)
    ISBN-10: 0-7391-1273-2 (pbk. : alk. paper)
    1. Arab-Israeli conflict—Historiography. 2. History—Methodology. I. Title.
DS119.7.I73 2006
    956.04—dc22
                                                            2006000374

Printed in the United States of America

∞™ The paper used in this publication meets the minimum requirements of American
National Standard for Information Sciences—Permanence of Paper for Printed Library
Materials, ANSI/NISO Z39.48-1992.

Contents

Introduction

President Bill Clinton aptly remarked that no party to the Arab-Israeli conflict holds a monopoly of either virtue or suffering. However, does anyone hold a monopoly of historical truth about the conflict? It hardly takes a regional expert to perceive that the way the "story" of the Arab-Israeli conflict is told is vastly dependent upon the perspective of the storyteller. This does, however, create somewhat of a quandary for the would-be objective political scientist: to whose story do we listen? How do we know that one story is not just as good as the next? Observant researchers will note that during the past decade, the Arab-Israeli conflict has in a sense split into at least two conflicts: one represented by the older, more Zionist-inspired history of the dispute and the other embodied in the sharply contrasting narrative of the Israeli "new historians." While each body of historical scholarship purports to explain the underlying causes and provide a "true" account of the conflict, the old and the more recent Israeli histories in fact allude to two completely distinct case studies that might be constructed by a political scientist examining the subject.

This book suggests that the type of historical problem just mentioned is common in all the subfields of political science. While much attention has been paid to avoiding selection bias in quantitative political science scholarship, significantly less energy has been devoted to the problem of how to determine when an entire historical narrative, encapsulated in multiple sources, is itself biased. How do we know that what we are reading is untainted by political and ideological sentiments? Does the truth of history really come down to who tells the best stories? In order to begin to respond to these questions, a good story is indeed in order.

Having utterly failed to predict the fall of the Soviet Union, political scientists during the early 1990s were in a near frantic state, trying to make sense out of world politics following a half-century of Cold War. One of the first and most cited "realist" contributions to the debate over the end of the Cold War, Christopher Layne's "The Unipolar Illusion," suggested that the time was ripe to test and validate the long-standing realist claim that "In international politics, overwhelming power repels and leads other states to balance against it."[1] Layne concluded that unipolar moments are fleeting interludes that rapidly dissolve as states mechanistically struggle to balance against hegemony. A year later, the diplomatic historian Paul Schroeder published an essay responding to Layne's arguments and their applicability within the broader context of European history. Regarding the cogency of structural realism, Schroeder wrote that

> a normal, standard understanding of neo-realist theory, applied precisely to the historical era where it should fit best, gets the motives, the processes, the patterns, and the broad outcomes of international history wrong, and predicts things of major theoretical and historical importance which on closer examination turn out not to be so.[2]

With respect to Layne's approach toward the matter of historical inquiry, Schroeder remarked that Layne came close to "an extreme form of the old, discredited principle of the primacy of foreign policy which not even its nineteenth-century exponents such as Leopold von Ranke would have defended." Schroeder concluded that in the most basic of terms, Layne's "argument is not factually sound."[3]

At a first glance, the preceding exchange appears to be an interdisciplinary squabble between a theory-minded social scientist and a historian with a different view on historical causation. However, it is more than just that: the Layne-Schroeder dialogue highlights a deeper, more fundamental problem: How do we come to understand what we think happened in the past? As anyone who has read a little history can tell, historians and political scientists have somewhat divergent ways of responding to the preceding question. Whereas historians tend to examine small samples of problems in great and intricately contextualized detail, political scientists often seek a balance between historical nuance and theoretical parsimony. But the problem of understanding the past is more complex than merely determining an appropriate sample size and articulating key variables. At the heart of the debate among historians and political scientists is a crucial epistemological problem: how do we ground our claims to knowledge about that past? This book responds comprehensively to that problem.

The timing of this study is in a number of ways quite appropriate. There has been a surge in interest among political scientists in historical questions as evidenced by the addition of the new "International History and Politics" section, which joins the more established "History and Politics" section of the American Political Science Association (APSA). In addition, with regard to the study of war and peace, for example, many of the most significant and widely-cited studies are inherently historical in their method and approach, despite great differences in "paradigmatic" perspective.[4] The authors of these recent studies disagree vehemently on theoretical matters; some are staunch liberals, others entrenched realists, and yet others, constructivists. Despite their disagreements within the realm of political science, these scholars generally agree methodologically that historical "process tracing," or retracing historical sequences of events encapsulated in case studies, is the preferred manner in which to assess theoretical claims. That is, whether acknowledged or not, each of these authors shares a fundamental concern with history.

There are at least two additional reasons why the timing of this book is particularly opportune. The first is that the growing importance of social constructivism and postpositivist critical scholarship has brought about an increased interest in metatheoretical questions in political science, especially with regard to international relations (IR) theory. The most discussed and ambitious text in this vein is Wendt's recent *Social Theory of International Politics*, which seeks an alternative epistemology for what we have come to know as the international system and its structural characteristics.[5] The second and more important reason is that despite the upsurge of interest in metatheory raised by Wendt and others, constructivism, at least in its international relations scholarly aspect, has yet to explore the vastly significant problem of how we acquire knowledge of the past events to which we refer in order to test theoretical claims, whether those claims are positivist or constructivist. This problem is crucially important in that history, in the form of historical case studies about wars, crises, and other noteworthy events, forms the basic building blocks of all empirical political science research, quantitative as well as qualitative.[6] While I argue that the examination of how we ground the basis for historical knowledge and justify our claims to that knowledge is an understudied problem for political science, others have in various ways touched upon the problem in the past.

Interest in this area was high in mid-twentieth century America. In 1946, for instance, the Committee on Historiography of the Social Science Research Council (SSRC), chaired by Charles Beard, set out to assess the state of knowledge at the intersection of history and the social sciences and to offer recommendations for further investigation. The Committee was comprised almost exclusively of historians; discussion of social science as it is currently conceived is scarce in the report. Nonetheless, at least four of the Committee's twenty-one propositions are relevant to the themes of this book. In particular, the Committee proposed: (1) that "all the data used in the social

sciences . . . are drawn from records of experience in, or writing about the
past;" (2) scholars should make evident that their work "is in fact an interpretation or emphasis and is to be regarded as limited by the very nature of
the interpretation or emphasis;" (3) "In a scientific methodology clear distinctions must be maintained between the unrecoverable totality of the past,
the records of the past, and written or spoken history;" and (4) "Every written history . . . is a selection of facts made by some person or persons and is
ordered or organized under the influence of some scheme of reference, interest, or emphasis—avowed or unavowed—in the thought of the author or authors."[7] These points are instructive in that the SSRC group consciously and
explicitly stressed the role of human interpretation and understanding about
the past. In more contemporary parlance, the SSRC report lent credence to a
more interpretivist and less scientific approach toward questions of history.
That such an emphasis would come from professional historians, as opposed
to political scientists, is an observation that will be touched upon in more detail in the following chapters of this book.

Eight years later, under the leadership of the new chair, Thomas Cochran, the
SSRC Committee published a second report, which self-consciously strove,
"Unlike its predecessor, [to be] primarily concerned with substantive issues of
method and analysis."[8] Toward that effect, the report is positively predisposed
toward collaborative scholarship and a convergence of concepts and methods
between history and the social sciences. However, the directional thrust of the
report deals more with what the historian can learn from the social sciences, as
opposed to vice versa. Thus, the report asserts that "The historian can gain a
working knowledge of the social sciences only from wide reading, discussion,
and application of specific concepts to historical materials."[9]

During the late 1960s, the SSRC work on history was taken up by a new
committee, The Problem and Policy Committee. Working in conjunction with
the Committee on Science and Public Policy of the National Academy of Sciences, the joint group published a report stressing that the major distinctions
between social scientific history, which is problem-oriented and "assumes
that there are uniformities of human behavior that transcend time and place
and can be studied as such," versus the humanist approach, which "views any
such extraction of human experiences from its matrix of time and place as an
insult to the integrity of the historical process."[10] While acknowledging that
there is a distinction between the more scientific versus the more humanistic
approaches to history, the 1960s report, like its predecessor, sidestepped the
issue of if and how these two approaches might be bridged or reconciled.

During the 1970s and 1980s, the most prolific work on historical inquiry
was to be found in macro-historical sociology and American political development (APD). The former, which had an immense impact on political sci-

ence, focused on long-term historical patterns, such as industrialization, class mobilization, and state formation, over large swaths of time.[11] Subsequent scholarship in historical sociology defined the contours of the relationship between history and sociology with regard to methodological and empirical questions, although not on an epistemological level regarding the ability to ground claims to historical knowledge.[12] Similarly, a significant number of APD scholars have reemphasized historical scholarship via the "new institutionalism," which focuses on the historical development of major institutions as key shapers of behavior and processes in American politics.[13] Rogers Smith, for instance, argues for exploring "the power of different accounts" of history and accumulating "the evidence for particular conceptions that those comparisons provide." This would involve presenting "different types of structures and institutions" as potentially constitutive of human behavior and identity.[14] The new institutionalism has also gained a smaller, if not less notable, foothold in the subfield of comparative politics, especially in the study of economic institutions in historical perspective.[15] The work of the past three decades in both historical sociology and APD has been referred to by some as the "historic turn in the human sciences," which has brought together scholars from a diversity of fields who share a common and interdisciplinary concern with history.[16]

Ostensibly, scholars interested in the Arab-Israeli conflict might want to know about the state of historical research in the study of war and peace, which has been dominated, at least in the Anglo-American world, by the political science subfield of IR. Here, we find a much more abbreviated genealogy of historical research than is the case either in sociology or in the other subfields of political science. To the extent that questions of historical inquiry and interpretation have been discussed in IR, it has typically been via debates that are themselves apart from the question of history. Thus, during the 1960s, IR scholarship was defined by the schism between traditional versus scientific approaches toward the study of world politics. At the heart of the former was the English School of International Relations, whose most famous and outspoken advocate, Hedley Bull, characterized the classical school as

> the approach to theorizing that derives from philosophy, history, and law, and that is characterized above all by explicit reliance upon the exercise of judgment. . . . The practitioners of the scientific approach, by cutting themselves off from history and philosophy, have deprived themselves of the means of self-criticism, and in consequence have a view of their subject and its possibilities that is callow and brash.[17]

While historical analysis is clearly a vital subcomponent of Bull's classical approach, his primary focus is on the possibilities of scientific analysis in IR, or the lack thereof.

Bull's most famous and eloquent opponent, Morton A. Kaplan, not surprisingly, took a very different view on the matter. Strongly rebutting the notion that IR traditionalists command a monopoly of sensitivity to historical context, Kaplan argued that scientific IR scholars use "history as a laboratory for their researches." Thus, history provides the raw empirical data upon which "disciplined and articulated theories and propositions . . . can be investigated."[18] This claim carries with it a host of important implications for historical inquiry, the latter of which are the subject matter of chapter 4 of this book. But those implications themselves are not addressed in the debate between Bull and Kaplan and their respective supporters. Even subsequent scholars unsympathetic to the English School agree that the scientific turn in IR diverted attention away from historical problems. Thus, "to begin with history," writes R. B. J. Walker, "is to encounter problems that are usually encountered under the heading of the philosophy of history. Given the difficulty of some of these problems, it is perhaps not entirely surprising that they are so often marginalised and resolved in favour of ahistorical accounts of continuity and structural form."[19]

By the late 1970s, the ongoing debate between traditionalists and adherents of scientific IR had evolved into a new form across the Atlantic with the emergence of J. David Singer's Correlates of War (COW) project founded at the University of Michigan. A stimulating discussion of the debate among historians and quantitative IR scholars is encapsulated in the 1977 symposium sponsored in the *Journal of Conflict Resolution*.[20] A similarly rich dialogue, in this instance among diplomatic historians and qualitative IR scholars, was undertaken during 1997, first in the journal *International Security* and later in an edited volume published by MIT Press.[21] What is interesting about these symposia is that while they make important contributions to the study of IR methodologically, they essentially skirt the core question of how to ground claims to historical knowledge, which is the narrative stuff out of which historical IR research is made. The most resonant theme among the contributors to the *IS* symposium, which included both Layne and Schroeder, was the notion that there is and should continue to be a strong sense of empirical solidarity among diplomatic historians and IR scholars. Indeed, one paper referred to the two groups as nothing less than "brothers under the skin."[22] But despite the general good will expressed among the participants, the most glaring aspect of the *IS* symposium was what was *not* discussed almost without exception; namely, the fundamental epistemological problem of grounding the basis for historical knowledge and developing frameworks to attain access to that knowledge. The fact that positivism—which has long been dominant in both IR and diplomatic history—has been heavily critiqued during recent decades was acknowledged by a sole author who devoted a single sentence to this point.[23] None of the contributors discussed the fact that there are richly developed alternatives to positivism within the literature on historical inquiry.

One of the rare IR texts to address these issues is Thomas Smith's ambitious *History and International Relations*, which provides an intellectual analysis of history and the study of world politics.[24] Smith highlights a number of historical problems typical to IR scholarship, including selection bias, anecdotalism, ahistoricism, and theoretical filtering.[25] Smith responds with a stimulating and novel discussion of several key figures in twentieth-century history and IR in which he asserts that the claims of social constructivists and postmodernists deserve to be taken seriously. Toward that effect, his narrative suggests a skepticism about the more scientific approaches toward IR. Smith thus provides an important service in the sense of laying the problem of conceptualizing history on the table and demonstrating its relevance in a number of IR literatures. But in the end, Smith too skips over the question of how to ground claims to historical knowledge in a way that would avoid the difficulties encountered by the various scholars he analyzes.

Ian Lustick, in contrast, attempts to tackle this problem, although his approach is more methodological than theoretical. Rather than take for granted the positivist view in which history is raw, undifferentiated data, Lustick argues that history should be understood as represented by a variety of different implicit theoretical perspectives embedded within historical texts.[26] In epistemological terms, this calls for abandoning the notion that the single, correct, and human-independent "truth" of historical events could be captured by scratching ever closer to that truth, at least so far as political science research is concerned. While the correct truth may very well be out there, all political scientists have to rely on are historical texts, and once this is acknowledged, then the division between historical fact and interpretation has been irrevocably crossed. In response to this realization, Lustick identifies a number of methodological ways of thinking that can help scholars to devise more sophisticated and nuanced historical case studies.

This book seeks to pick up the matter where Smith and Lustick have left off by developing not only methods that scholars can use in their everyday practices, but also an epistemological foundation on which scholars can ground their claims. I begin with the most basic of questions: why do history and historical inquiry matter to political science? The response offered here is simple: the vast majority of original research in political science is directly or indirectly historiographical. Qualitative research generally adopts the form of studies that test theoretical propositions in view of a handful of historiographical reconstructions (case studies) of relevant examples of a given phenomenon. In the quantitative methods, scholars do the same using hundreds of such cases coded by assigning numerical values to indicate measurements of the presence or lack of certain variables. In so doing, however, quantitative scholars invariably must, in order to code or recode their data, refer to data sets, such as those originating in the Correlates of War (COW) project, which were themselves originally assembled by reviewing historiographical reconstructions. In short, then, there could be no research in political science, whether qualitative or quantitative, without historiographical reconstruction. However, simply focusing on issues to which we can ascribe the label "historical" does not in itself respond to the overarching question of how claims to knowledge about the past can be grounded and supported. That is, how do we *really* know what we think happened in the past?

In response to this problem, I begin by elaborating on the basic nature of historical inquiry. The problem of historical inquiry alludes to the difficulty inherent in seeking to ground the basis for historical knowledge of the past. In the *Idea of History*, R. G. Collingwood suggests the problem of historical inquiry in his famous claim that "All history is the history of thought. . . . But how does the historian discern the thoughts that he is trying to discover? There is only one way in which it can be done: by re-thinking them in his own mind."[27] This notion is radical in suggesting that historical inquiry is not akin to scientific inquiry. Whereas with the latter, the investigator inquires into a tangible physical object separated from the inquirer only by space, the object of historical inquiry is not in actuality physically existent—its spatial instantiation is permanently separated by time. Collingwood elaborates on this fundamental epistemological problem when he says that "Historical knowledge is the knowledge of what mind has done in the past, and at the same time it is the redoing of this, the perpetuation of past acts in the present. Its object is therefore not a mere object, something outside the mind which knows it; it is an activity of thought, which can be known only in so far as the knowing mind re-enacts it and knows itself as so doing."[28] Collingwood's articulation of the temporal separation of past events is a problem that most philosophers of history acknowledge. His solution, however, is only one of several alternatives on the matter and in fact, it is not the one that most political scientists choose.

In chapter 1, three possible approaches to historical inquiry are introduced and elaborated upon. The first, and that with which mainstream political science scholarship is most comfortable, is positivism. Positivism views historical inquiry as similar to archeology. While the events of the past cannot in any literal sense be replicated or witnessed, we are left with shards of evidence: documents, records, firsthand observations, and so forth from which an objective account of what happened in the past can be reconstructed. Employing the documentary and other materials inherited by historians over

time, bits and pieces of evidence can be fitted together to produce a sum total that can be accurately and fairly called a true historical account.

This understanding of historical inquiry has come under sustained critique
during recent decades from a number of critical perspectives alternatively
known as postmodernism or poststructuralism.[29] While these critiques are by
no means unified, they are generally agreed on at least two matters: firstly,
they each express a strong dissatisfaction with historical positivism and, sec-
ondly, they agree that there is not and indeed there *cannot* be only one objectively true narrative that reflects the past in mirrorlike fashion. Thus, critics
of positivism argue that it is impossible to explain the unity of the historical
past in light of the multiplicity of interpretations that invariably claim to represent that past. This problem requires a basis for arbitrating among and judging differing interpretations as either good or bad. Postmodernism responds
with an adamant skepticism toward all potential arbitrating mechanisms,
viewing them to be facades for oppressive relations and empowered interests.
There is certainly a strong intuitiveness to this position, as exemplified in the
old saying, history is always written by the victors. Similarly, national histories are typically written to reflect the historical reconstruction favored by and
favorable to the dominant classes and groups within nation-states. But to
abandon all arbitrating mechanisms to judge good history from bad, accurate
from inaccurate, is a disturbing prospect for many people and especially for
mainstream social scientists. Postmodernism does not have a coherent response to this problem of rejecting existing means of arbitration and judgment other than to suggest that perpetual criticism is preferable to the positivist alternative.

Is there no middle ground between these positions? This study argues that
the pragmatist thought of John Dewey creates precisely such an epistemological space. Dewey agrees with both Collingwood and the postmodernists that
there is no scientific way in which to reconstruct an account that mirrors past
reality. But he disagrees that we must be left with no means by which to distinguish good history from bad. Rather, Dewey views historical inquiry and
all inquiry for that matter as resulting from the basic human need to respond
to problematic situations. Thus, it is only natural for humans to be concerned
with the past at all insofar as doing so addresses problems humans have in the
present. While there is an ethics associated with this position, the claim is not
itself normative—that is, it is not necessary *per se* that we *should* look to the
past to make the present better. Rather, Dewey's point is an empirical one—
people learn from past mistakes as a means of coping with present reality.
Given this knowledge, however, it logically follows that if we do, in fact,
want to improve our present and future conditions, it would only be practical
to see how we might interpret the past in order to so. The way in which this

occurs is the way in which historical inquiry is institutionalized into a set of practices and procedures.

Chapter 1 establishes the theme of the entire book, arguing that Dewey's position is the most coherent and promising of the three alternatives, positivism, postmodernism, and pragmatism. Chapter 1 concludes by discussing some of the important ethical implications of the debate over historical inquiry and interpretation. In particular, the Deweyan approach toward history allows us to see that the production of historical knowledge is itself a socially constructed practice that arises from the need and desire of certain groups to understand the past in ways that might help to give rise to a different future. This assumption is tested by examining the ways in which the Arab-Israeli conflict has been written by various generations of historians. The contrasting narratives of the older and more recent, critical Israeli historians as well as the implications of those themes for political science are the subjects of chapters 2, 3, and 4.

The Arab-Israeli conflict is an especially useful case for history and political science for at least two reasons. First, the Arab-Israeli conflict generally speaking is a subject of widespread interest. It has associated with it a broad and interdisciplinary body of scholarly literature on topics such as the causes of war, international law and sovereignty, international bargaining and mediation, and identity politics and ethnic conflict—topics that matter to a large and diverse audience both within the academy and the policymaking community. Second, Israeli historiography is in a sense an ideal-type instance of historical revisionism involving a distinctive "old" literature that can be identified and compared diachronically with a more recent and decidedly more critical body of scholarship. A note on terminology is especially important here: in the literature, this body of scholarship is typically referred to as the Israeli "new history." This is problematic, however, in that many of the "new historians" cover historical events and issues that overlap in some measure with their earlier counterparts. Alternatively, not all contemporary Israeli historians are "new historians," and some are decidedly anti-new-history. Thus, in this book, I will refer to the "new historians" instead as "critical historians." This makes clear that I am dealing with those historians who are both contemporary *and* critical of the earlier Israeli narrative of the Arab-Israeli conflict.[30]

The Israeli critical historians have produced a remarkably broad and deep wave of new and provocative studies examining the early history and prehistory of the State of Israel and the origins of the Arab-Israeli conflict. Two factors in particular appear to be driving this revisionist movement: the release of new Israeli archival data pertaining to the Arab-Israeli war of 1948–1949 and a fundamental shift in the politics of public discourse within Israel about the country's founding history and mythology.[31] Taken together, these factors have brought about a major questioning and in some instances an all-out assault on a number of grand myths regarding early and mid-twentieth-century Israeli and Arab-Israeli history.[32]

The great divide between the old and the critical Israeli historiography on the 1950s is analyzed in chapter 2. One of the striking features of this gap is that the first generation of Israeli historiography on the 1940s and 1950s was generally written by public officials and aspiring state-builders, the most notable of whom was founding Prime Minister David Ben-Gurion. All of these early historical writers had a substantial stake in portraying the birth of Israel and the Arab-Israeli conflict in ways that would legitimate and reinforce the Zionist state-building project. Thus, the early historiography of the 1950s portrays Israel as a weak, benevolent state struggling to meet its basic security requirements in a viciously hostile regional environment. The Arab states are portrayed as monolithically powerful entities whose primary objective was to destroy the nascent Israeli state. Three factors in particular: the *fedayeen* terrorist raids into Israel, the blockade on Israeli shipping in the Straights of Tiran, and the Czech arms deal of September 1955 are emphasized as indicative of Arab power and intent.

The Israeli critical historians call much of the prior interpretation of the Arab-Israeli conflict into question. Israel was neither as weak nor as benevolent as the early state leaders portrayed it to be. Nor were the Arabs unprovoked by aggressive Israeli military actions. Most revealing in the critical history is the notion that the belligerent, activist policies of Israel during the 1950s have their roots in a domestic political competition between David Ben-Gurion and his primary rival, Moshe Sharett, which had as much to do with long-term visions of Israel state-building as it did with the Arab problem. So in this sense, there is no single historiography of the Arab-Israeli conflict of the 1950s. Rather, there are at least two vastly divergent accounts.[33] Having identified this prolific instance of historical revisionism, the question remains regarding its implications for political science theories of war and peace.

Chapter 3 examines in detail the way in which the causes and dynamics of the 1956 Arab-Israeli war have been reconstructed as a case study within qualitative political science scholarship on war and peace. The chapter thus summarizes a number of articles and book chapters pertaining to the 1956 war, analyzing both the way in which the studies present the case and the theoretical claims that are tested in light of the case. The chapter then examines how the studies fare when taking into account the critical Israeli interpretations in the case. Thus, two claims are assessed simultaneously. The first and weaker claim is that the political science literature is empirically out of step with the most recent understandings of the 1956 Arab-Israeli war. To an extent, this first problem is not especially surprising: after all, political scientists cannot be expected to have information available to them that is not yet in existence. Yet, this is not the end of the matter. Regardless of what information is or is not available to scholars, the political science literature has in general placed too much reliance on the assumption that the grounding of historical case studies will remain static. That is to say, political science scholarship tends to treat historical case studies as if they were discrete, unified data that are not likely to change or are even capable of changing. This suggests a second and stronger claim, which is that the over-reliance on static cases has led political scientists to make theoretical claims that fail to hold when the stasis of historical meaning underlying them is called into question. The chapter thus uses the Israeli critical history as a vehicle to determine the extent to which theoretical political science claims regarding war and peace will hold when the test case—namely, the 1956 Arab-Israeli war—is revised.

Chapter 4 examines the treatment of the second Arab-Israeli war in quantitative international relations scholarship. In particular, the chapter examines the coding of the case in three prominent IR data sets, the Militarized Interstate Dispute (MID) Version 2.1 data set, the Correlates of War (COW) International and Civil War data set, and the Interstate Crisis Behavior (ICB) Project data set. The chapter suggests that quantitative IR scholarship is even more reliant than is its qualitative counterpart on the notion that cases are points of data that can be construed in a manner similar to that of physical evidence. Thus, quantitative IR scholarship emulates the physical science/laboratory method in that it seeks to establish the unity of its data much as the chemist establishes that carbon is carbon. Once the essence of the data is established and known, it is not deemed likely to change.

However, I argue that historical data is fundamentally unlike carbon insofar as it is quite likely to change in its very essence, and thus, scientific investigation on the basis of an assumed static data set is a doubtful proposition. The chapter suggests that some of the data in the three sets examined are highly questionable according to any rendering of the case, whether old or critical. Even when the data are not problematic, however, they tend to be presented in an ambiguous and incomplete fashion that is generally unhelpful toward a basic understanding of the case. Finally, the analysis of the three data sets reveals a low level of interdata set reliability. That is, the data sets fail to agree with each other regarding basic facts, such as the entry and exit dates into the conflict and the number of battlefield deaths. This suggests that data sets, like the historical narratives that were used to compile them, suffer from a basic and underlying problem insofar as there is a lack of any independent arbitrating mechanism to determine good from bad data.

The problem of grounding historical knowledge on contested subjects would not be troubling were it limited solely to the study of the Arab-Israeli conflict; after all, the Middle East has been and continues to be a particularly impassioned and controversial subject of inquiry. Chapter 5 thus examines recent historical debates of the American decision to escalate to full-scale war in Vietnam. The most recent historical literature on Vietnam has strongly challenged the extant notion that international systemic factors played a significant role in the American decision to escalate the conflict during 1964–1965. Rather, contemporary American historians have focused in particular on the central role of President Lyndon B. Johnson and Secretary of Defense Robert McNamara and "pushing" the United States toward war. This becomes problematic, however, when one contrasts the more recent interpretations with the historical assumptions about Vietnam contained with the political science literature on the war. Chapter 5 assesses a portion of the literature in order to demonstrate that a good deal of the political science scholarship on Vietnam has not very well withstood the "test of time."

While keeping up to date with history is certainly important in itself, to what extent does the particular mode of historical inquiry used in political science further or impede research in the field? In chapter 6, again focusing on the case of Vietnam, I argue that with or without the newer historiography at their disposal, political scientists were quick to impute a preconceived systemic orientation to history regardless of the evidence, or lack thereof, for such a perspective. Focusing in particular on Jack Snyder's important work, *Myths of Empire*, the chapter finds that in some instances, the historical "data" is so stylized that it agrees neither with the old nor the more recent historiography on Vietnam. In the case of *Myths of Empire*, the work's theoretical claims appear to be seriously at odds with the implicit theoretical arguments of the very historical sources referenced in the study. This suggests that the problem of historical inquiry has wide-ranging implications for both empirical and theoretical scholarship in political science.

These six chapters taken together produce three major conclusions and one significant problem. First, political scientists should be quite concerned with the problem of grounding claims to historical knowledge, much more so than they have been until this juncture. Second, historiography is a socially constructed, contested, and continuously changing phenomena. Efforts to undertake historical inquiry that assume a stasis of historical meaning not only fail to properly appreciate the nature of the material with which they are working; they are apt to go awry. Third, historical revisionism, as a result of the constructed nature of historical phenomena, is a crucial matter with which political scientists as well as historians should be vitally concerned.

The preceding conclusions lead to a very significant and admittedly complicated challenge: how can political science acknowledge and cope with the problem of historical inquiry and interpretation? A response to that question is the subject matter of chapter 7. The chapter begins by assessing the extent to which the problem of historical inquiry has been addressed in the state of the art of contemporary political science methodology. I conclude that even widely-respected texts such as King, Keohane, and Verba's *Designing Social Inquiry* and Van Evera's, *Guide to Methods for Students of Political Science* fundamentally avoid the problem of historical inquiry as it pertains to and affects political science research.[34] The chapter thus asks the question, assuming that we adopt a pragmatist historical approach of the type elaborated upon in chapter 1 of this study, what practical measures can political scientists take to alleviate the problem of historical inquiry? Chapter 7 proceeds to elaborate upon a number of steps that will help scholars to locate and more effectively employ historical literatures in research. The chapter also addresses the matter of problem orientation and historical political science, arguing that to an extent, the particularistic normative perspective of the researcher affects the type and use of historical sources employed in research. But despite this seeming bias, I argue that there are ways that political scientists can incorporate alternative historical perspectives so as to reduce bias and produce more sophisticated historical accounts. Chapter 7 concludes by discussing some of the ways in which quantitative historical researchers might respond to the problem of grounding history in order to account for horizontal diversity, or differing interpretations over space, as well as vertical diversity, or changes in historical narratives as they are revised over time.

NOTES

1. Christopher Layne, "The Unipolar Illusion," *International Security* 17, no. 4 (Spring 1993), reprinted in Sean M. Lynn-Jones and Steven E. Miller, eds., *The Cold War and After* (Cambridge: MIT Press, 1993), and Kenneth N. Waltz, "America as a Model for the World? A Foreign Policy Perspective," *PS* (December 1991): 669, cited in Layne, "The Unipolar Illusion," 246.

2. Paul Schroeder, "Historical Reality vs. Neo-Realist Theory," *International Security* 19, no. 2 (Summer 1994): 147.

3. Schroeder, "Historical Reality," 143, 144.

4. For prominent examples from the realist perspective, see Robert Gilpin, *War and Change in World Politics* (New York: Cambridge University Press, 1981); Stephen M. Walt, *The Origins of Alliances* (Ithaca: Cornell University Press, 1987), and Walt, *Revolution and War* (Ithaca: Cornell University Press, 1996). For neoliberals' examples, see Jack Snyder, *Myths of Empire* (Ithaca: Cornell University Press, 1991); T. V. Paul, *Asymmetric Conflicts: War Initiation by Weaker Powers* (Cambridge

University Press, 1994); Thomas Risse-Kappen, *Cooperation Among Democracies* (Princeton: Princeton University Press, 1995); and G. John Ikenberry, *After Victory: Institutions, Strategic Restraint, and the Rebuilding of Order after Major Wars* (Princeton: Princeton University Press, 2000). For constructive examples, see Martha Finnemore, *National Interests in International Society* (Ithaca: Cornell University Press, 1996); Elizabeth Kier, *Imagining War: French and British Military Doctrine between the Wars* (Princeton: Princeton University Press, 1998); Rodney Bruce Hall, *National Collective Identity: Social Constructs and International Systems* (New York: Columbia University Press, 1999); and Ward Thomas, *The Ethics of Destruction* (Ithaca, NY: Cornell University Press, 2001).

5. Alexander E. Wendt, *Social Theory of International Politics* (Cambridge: Cambridge University Press, 1999). Wendt's book is in large measure a social theoretic critique of Kenneth N. Waltz's classic text of structural realism, *Theory of International Politics* (Reading, MA: Addison-Wesley, 1979).

6. While quantitative IR proceeds along a different set of operating assumptions from that of qualitative process tracing, it is no less reliant than is its qualitative counterpart on historical case studies, which provide the basis for coded empirical data. This holds true for all of the major IR data sets, including the various Correlates of War (COW) projects, the Militarized Interstate Disputes (MID) data sets, and the International Crisis Behavior (ICB) Project data, each of which is discussed in chapter 4.

7. Social Science Research Council (SSRC), *Theory and Practice in Historical Study: A Report of the Committee on Historiography*, Bulletin 54 (New York: Social Science Research Council, 1946): 134–35.

8. Social Science Research Council (SSRC), *The Social Sciences in Historical Study*, Bulletin 64 (New York: Social Science Research Council, 1954), 18. Brackets added.

9. SSRC, *The Social Sciences in Historical Study*, 34.

10. Charles Tilly and David S. Landes, eds., *History as Social Science* (Englewood Cliffs, NJ: Prentice-Hall, 1971), 9–10.

11. The landmark work in this vein is Barrington Moore's *Social Origins of Dictatorship and Democracy: Lord and Peasant in the Making of the Modern World* (Boston: Beacon, 1966). Of especial note is the fact that sociologist Theda Skocpol was elected President of the American Political Science Association (APSA) on the basis of her work in this field. See also Charles Tilly, "War Making and State Making as Organized Crime," in Peter Evans et al., *Bringing the State Back In* (Cambridge: Cambridge University Press, 1985); and Charles Tilly, *Coercion, Capital, and European States* (Cambridge, MA: Blackwell, 1992).

12. See Charles Tilly, *As Sociology Meets History* (New York: Academic Press, 1981), esp. 1–44; Theda Skocpol, "Sociology's Historical Imagination," in Skocpol, ed., *Vision and Method in Historical Sociology* (New York: Cambridge University Press, 1984), esp. 1–7; Skocpol, "Emerging Agendas and Recurrent Strategies in Historical Sociology, in *Vision and Method*, esp. 356–63; and Skocpol and Margaret Somers, "The Uses of Comparative History in Macrosocial History," in Skocpol, *Social Revolutions in the Modern World* (New York: Cambridge University Press, 1994).

13. See Karren Orren and Stephen Skowronek, "Beyond the Iconography of Order: Notes for a 'New Institutionalism,'" in Lawrence C. Dodd and Calvin Jillson, eds., *The Dynamics of American Politics* (Boulder, CO: Westview, 1994); and contributions to the forum on the new institutionalism in *Polity* 28, no. 1 (Fall 1995).

14. Rogers Smith, "Science, Non-Science, and Politics," in McDonald, ed., *The Historic Turn*, 142.

15. See Kathleen Thelen and Sven Steinmo, "Historical Institutionalism in Comparative Politics," in Steinmo, Thelen, and Frank Longstreth, eds., *Structuring Politics* (New York: Cambridge University Press, 1992), esp. 1–7, 10–13.

16. For an interdisciplinary dialogue on this theme, see the proceedings of the conference held at the University of Michigan published in Terrence J. McDonald, ed., *The Historic Turn in the Human Sciences* (Ann Arbor: The University of Michigan Press, 1996).

17. Hedley Bull, "International Theory: The Case for a Classical Approach," in K. Knorr and J. N. Rosenau, eds., *Contending Approaches to International Politics* (Princeton University Press, 1969), 20, 37.

18. Morton A. Kaplan, "The New Great Debate: Traditionalism vs. Science in International Relations," in K. Knorr and J. N. Rosenau, eds., *Contending Approaches to International Politics* (Princeton University Press, 1969), 56.

19. R. B. J. Walker, *Inside/Outside: International Relations as Political Theory* (New York: Cambridge University Press, 1993), 100.

20. See contributions by Alan Alexandroff, Richard Rosecrance, Arthur Stein, Paul W. Schroeder, and Melvin Small, in *Journal of Conflict Resolution* 21, no. 1 (1977). For an excellent discussion of the use of history in the COW project, see J. David Singer, "The Incomplete Theorist: Insights without Evidence," in *Contending Approaches to International Politics*, 63–86.

21. See "Symposium," *International Security* 22, no. 1 (1997), and Colin Elman and Miriam F. Elman, eds., *Bridges and Boundaries* (Cambridge, MA: MIT Press, 2001).

22. See Stephen H. Haber, David M. Kennedy, and Stephen D. Krasner, "Brothers under the Skin: Diplomatic History and International Relations," *International Security* 22, no. 1 (Summer 1997).

23. Jack S. Levy writes that "In history . . . the influence of postmodernism and the 'linguistic turn' has led many scholars to reject empirical criteria and see history as fiction or rhetoric, concerned with the historicity of texts and the textuality of history." Levy, "Too Important to Leave to the Other," *International Security* 22, no. 1 (Summer 1997), 28–29.

24. Thomas W. Smith, *History and International Relations* (London: Routledge, 1999).

25. Smith, *History and International Relations*, 3–4.

26. Ian S. Lustick, "History, Historiography, and Political Science: Multiple Records and the Problem of Selection Bias," *American Political Science Review* 90, no. 3 (September 1996), see esp., 616.

27. R. G. Collingwood, *The Idea of History* (New York: Galaxy, 1963 (1946)), 215.

28. Collingwood, *The Idea of History*, 218.

29. There is some utility in distinguishing between "postmodernism," or a reaction to and critique of modernity, and "poststructuralism," the same with regard to structural theory. That said, I will employ solely "postmodernism" for the purposes of this book both in reflection of its semantic prevalence in the literature and for the sake of simplicity.

30. For important overviews of the Israeli critical history, see Steven Heydemann, "Revisionism and the Reconstruction of Israeli History," in Ian S. Lustick and Barry Rubin, eds., *Critical Essays on Israeli Society, Politics, and Culture* (Albany, NY: SUNY Press, 1991); Jerome Slater, "The Significance of Israeli Historical Revisionism," in Walter P. Zenner and Russell A. Stone, eds., *Critical Essays on Israeli Social Issues and Scholarship* (Albany, NY: SUNY Press, 1994); Avi Shlaim, "The Debate about 1948," *International Journal of Middle East Studies* 27, no. 3 (1995); contributions to the special issue, "Israeli Historiography Revisited," *History and Memory* 7, no. 1 (Spring/Summer 1995); Israel Studies, Ian S. Lustick, "Israeli History: Who is Fabricating What?" *Survival* (Autumn 1997): 157–62; Daniel Levy, "The Future of the Past: Historiographical Disputes and Competing Memories in Germany and Israel," *History and Theory* 38, no. 1 (February 1999); and Ilan Pappé, ed., *The Israel/Palestine Question* (London: Routledge, 1999). See also "History Textbooks Replace Myths with Facts," *New York Times*, August 14, 1999, A1; and "Israel: The Revised Edition," *New York Times*, November 14, 1999, Section 7, 6.

31. See "History Textbooks Replace Myths with Facts," *New York Times* and "Israel: The Revised Edition," *New York Times*.

32. Simha Flapan was the first critical historian to devise a "list" of myths. In *The Birth of Israeli: Myths and Realities* (New York: Pantheon, 1987), he lists seven: (1) "that the Zionists accepted the UN partition resolution and planned for peace; (2) that the Arabs rejected the partition and launched the war; (3) that the Palestinians fled voluntarily intending reconquest; (4) that the Arab states had united to expel the Jews from Palestine; (5) that the Arab invasion made war inevitable; (6) that a defenseless Israel faced destruction by the Arab Goliath; and (7) that Israel subsequently sought peace but no Arab leader responded." Cited in Shlaim and Rogan, eds., *The War for Palestine*, 3. Other important critical historians have focused on a similar set of myths. Ilan Pappé cites four: (1) that the Israeli forces in 1948 were heavily outmanned and strategically "inferior" to those of the Arabs; (2) that the "world" was "against" Israel during 1948; (3) that the Palestinian refugee crisis was caused by Arab, not Israeli, policies; and (4) the myth "of Arab intransigence in the face of repeated Israeli peace gestures during and after the war." Pappé, "Critique and Agenda: The Post-Zionist Scholars in Israel," *History and Memory* 7, no. 1 (Spring/Summer 1995): 76–78. Similarly, Jerome Slater notes three myths that have been challenged by the Israeli critical historiography: (1) that "Jews were innocent, largely non-violent victims of fanatical Palestinian violence and terrorism;" (2) that "Israel has been a defensive, status-quo state which seeks only peace and security and has always been prepared for any reasonable compromise—particularly territorial compromise or partition—to achieve it;" and (3) "that Arabs have never reconciled themselves to the existence of Israeli, have refused all compromise, and with the single exception of Egypt since the

mid-1970s, have sought the destruction of Israel." Slater, "The Significance of Israeli Historical Revisionism," 180–81, 186.

33. This book focuses primarily on changes in Israeli historiography as produced by Israelis. However, there are at least two additional places one might look for the historiography of the Arab-Israeli conflict in the 1950s. One is the Hebrew/English language literature of the intervening years between the 1967 war and the onset of the critical history movement of the early 1990s. Four works are particularly notable: Wm. Roger Louis and Roger Owen, eds., *Suez 1956: The Crisis and Its Consequences* (Oxford: Clarendon, 1989); Selwyn Ilan Troen and Moshe Shemesh, eds., *The Suez-Sinai Crisis 1956* (New York: Columbia University Press, 1990); Keith Kyle, *Suez* (New York: St. Martin's, 1991); and Mordechai Bar-On, *The Gates of Gaza* (New York: St. Martins, 1994). There are also a number of Arabic sources on the Arab-Israeli conflict that while not focusing on the 1950s specifically, nonetheless provide a crucial alternative perspective on many relevant issues and themes. These include: Walid Khalidi, ed., *From Haven to Conquest: Readings in Zionism and the Palestine Problem until 1948* (Washington, DC: Institute for Palestine Studies, 1987 (1971)); Walid Khalidi and Jill Khadduri, eds., *Palestine and the Arab-Israeli Conflict: An Annotated Bibliography* (Beirut: Institute for Palestine Studies, 1974); Walid Khalidi, ed., *All That Remains: The Palestinian Villages Occupied and Depopulated by Israel in 1948*, research and text, Sharif S. Elmusa, Muhammad Ali Khalidi (Washington, DC: Institute for Palestine Studies, 1992); Walid Khalid, *Al-Sihyunniyya fi mi'at 'am, 1897-1997* [A Century of Zionism (Beirut, 1998)]; and Muhammad Hasanayn Haykal, *Al-Urush wa'l-juyush: kadhalik infajara al-sira'a fi filastin*, vol. 1 [Thrones and Armies: Thus Erupted the Struggle in Palestine (Cairo, 1998). Fred J. Khouri's *The Arab Israeli Dilemma*, 3rd edition, (Syracuse: Syracuse University Press, 1985), though published in English, provides a similar perspective to that of the mainstream Arabic literature on the Arab-Israeli conflict.

34. Gary King, Robert O. Keohane, Sidney Verba, *Designing Social Inquiry* (Princeton: Princeton University Press, 1994); and Stephen Van Evera, *Guide to Methods for Students of Political Science* (Ithaca: Cornell University Press, 1997).

Chapter One

The Historical Imagination of John Dewey

I. INTRODUCTION

Empirical political science literature, whether qualitative or quantitative, is reliant upon history as the essential matter out of which it is comprised. As discussed in the introductory chapter, interest in historical questions in political science is quite high, yet despite this surge of interest, much historical political science scholarship, especially in the international relations (IR) subfield, is curiously unreflective with regard to the manner in which historical inquiry is done. This chapter argues that underlying all historical inquiry is the basic question asked several decades back by E. H. Carr: what *is* history? More specifically, this chapter introduces and responds to the fundamental problem of grounding claims to historical knowledge. In recounting past events, is one story really just as good as the next? In order to devise a meaningful response to this problem, it is necessary to step outside of the boundaries of empirical political science, where treatment of the matter is underdeveloped, and into the philosophy of history, where the literature is rich with contributions regarding the problem of grounding historical knowledge.

During the past fifty years, debates in the philosophy of history have pivoted on a seemingly timeless and insoluble dichotomy between historical positivism and historical relativism. As the discussion of the literature generally portrays the matter, a pendulum was set in motion in the 1830s with the establishment of Rankeian positivism, which emphasized "feeling for and a joy in the particular in and by itself," or what many have since referred to as the past "as it really was."[1] Since the nineteenth century, positivists and relativists have each sought to prevail upon one another on the question of whether history should be either objectively or subjectively grounded. Contemporary anthologies and texts on historiography and philosophy of history accordingly portray the issue of historical ontology-epistemology as a dichotomy between postmodern relativists and their positivist-traditionalist critics. Carr's classic *What is History*, for instance, points out the unassailability of Lord Acton's positivism at the century's end. But by the 1950s, the diametrically opposing relativist views of Sir George Clark had replaced Acton's position as the conventional wisdom, at least in England. As Carr, poking fun at the objectivity-relativity pendulum, puts it: "When the pundits contradict each other so flagrantly the field is open to enquiry. I hope that I am sufficiently up-to-date to recognize that anything written in the 1890s must be nonsense. But I am not yet advanced enough to be committed to the view that anything written in the 1950s necessarily makes sense."[2]

More recently, Keith Jenkins contrasts postmodern relativists and their positivist-traditionalist critics. Part I of his *The Postmodern History Reader* is accordingly divided into binary oppositional categories aptly labeled, "For Postmodern Histories" and "Against Postmodern Histories."[3] Similarly, Georg Iggers has structured his *Historiography in the Twentieth Century* into three parts: (1) the emergence of history as a professional discipline; (2) the scientization of history; (3) the postmodern challenge. For Iggers, both pre- and postscientific history are positivist in that they "operated with a notion of unilinear time, with the conception that there was continuity and direction in history, that in fact there was such a thing as *history* in contrast to a multiplicity of histories."[4] Thus, both Rankeian and twentieth-century scientific positivism are distinguished quite clearly from what Iggers terms "the postmodern challenge."

The only study to address specifically the relationship between history and IR, Thomas Smith's *History and International Relations* traces the positivism-relativism dichotomy along the lines of two principal figures and their respective epistemologies, namely, Leopold von Ranke's history "as it really was," or what Smith terms the "correspondence" approach, versus Michael Oakeshott's more relativistic constructionism.[5] Finally, no work emphasizes the relativist-positivist dichotomy more cogently or extensively as does Peter Novick's landmark *That Noble Dream*. In his text, Novick presents the positivist-relativist debate as pivoting on the core positivist notion of objectivity. Thus, Novick examines the history of the American historical profession as seen through the positivist-relativist pendulum regarding objectivity, which can be traced in terms of "objectivity enthroned," "objectivity besieged," "objectivity reconstrued," and "objectivity in crisis."[6] What is interesting and noteworthy about the debate over historical ontology and epistemology is that there is no putative alternative to objectivist positivism and subjectivist relativism.

In the following sections of the chapter, I make the case for the historical imagination of John Dewey. John Dewey's theory of knowledge contains an especially coherent historical ontology and epistemology that is of significance to political scientists interested in historical questions. Thus, it is perhaps both more useful and more accurate to speak not in terms of a dichotomy but instead of a *trichotomy* on the debate over historical knowledge and our theories about history. Before proceeding to an in-depth discussion of Dewey's pragmatist history, it is necessary first to examine positivism and postmodernism, as these approaches are fundamental to understanding how many scholars ground historical knowledge.

Section II of this chapter sets the stage for understanding the Deweyan approach by looking first at positivist and postmodernist perspectives. Section III, in turn, explains why of the many possible approaches to the problem of historical inquiry, Deweyan pragmatism is preferable to the alternatives. Section IV discusses the ethical implications of Dewey's approach toward history. The chapter concludes by elaborating briefly upon the topic of chapters 3 through 6 of the book, namely, the problem of historical revisionism in empirical practice.

II. POSITIVIST CLAIMS AND POSTMODERN RESPONSES

In order to address the problem of grounding claims to historical knowledge, this section discusses the manner in which historical positivism offers an ontological basis for the historical past as well as an epistemological basis for what can and cannot be known about the past. While positivism has been dominant in many social sciences and in particular, in academic IR, it is clear to any who have studied history that the notion of solidly grounding knowledge claims as per historical positivism has been aggressively critiqued by various *postist* approaches during recent decades. Thus, I also examine at some length the postmodern response to the problem of history with a mind toward the strongest possible case to be made for positivism and for its postmodern alternatives.

1. Positivism

Positivism has been the dominant metatheoretical position of the Anglo-American tradition of historiography and the social sciences. I refer here to historical ontology as the past as it exists in itself. Thus, the ontological past is the literal object of historical inquiry. Positivists contend that there are both physical and historical worlds that definitively exist or existed and these in turn possess describable features. Positivists also argue that the ontological features of the world are of fundamental importance because it is fully possible to attain "true" knowledge of the world.[7] To clarify this position, Rorty suggests that positivism envisions a "mirror" within all human beings that reflects the external world. "Without the notion of mind as mirror, the notion of knowledge of accuracy of representation would not have suggested itself. Without this latter notion, the strategy common to Descartes and Kant—getting more accurate representations by inspecting, repairing, and polishing the mirror—would not have made sense."[8]

Hilary Putnam makes a similar point in suggesting that positivism assumes humans' ability to attain a "god's-eye standpoint" of ontological reality including the reality of what actually happened in times past.[9] Historical epistemology is the theory of knowledge that allows us to comprehend the ontological past. Among the key ideas of historical positivism regarding epistemology are that inquiry should be scientific; that there is an *a priori* scientific method; that the basic scientific method is the same for both the natural and social sciences.[10] "Whatever their disagreements," Murray Murphey asserts, "historians as a group are agreed that history is a discipline which seeks to establish true statements about events which have occurred and objects which have existed in the past."[11] Let us examine in more depth the core assumptions of historical positivism.

While there are more than a fair number of scholars of importance to the development of historical positivism, the remainder of this section focuses in particular on two, C. Behan McCullagh and Murray Murphey, both of whom are cited prominently and whose work is emblematic of contemporary historical positivism. One reviewer describes McCullagh as "penny-plain, down-to-earth and careful. It will give more satisfaction to an analytical philosopher, and to most practising historians."[12] Another reviewer notes that "McCullagh is not writing about truth in history: he is out to establish nothing less than the truth of history."[13] Murphey's work has prompted much discussion, including the proceedings of "The Murphey Symposium: Murray G. Murphey and the Philosophical Foundations of American Studies," published in *American Studies* in 1996.[14] Both McCullagh's work and Murphey's positions are similar to other well-known historical positivists, such as Gertrude Himmelfarb, but the former two scholars tend to be less polemical and perhaps less controversial in their presentation.[15] In addition, McCullagh's discussion is especially useful as he responds directly to one of the most important of the postmodernists, Jean Francois Lyotard, who is discussed in the following section.

C. Behan McCullagh lists four positivist assumptions required in order to have confidence in the truth of historical claims:

1. "That the world exists and has existed independent of any beliefs about it."
2. "That perceptions, under certain conditions, provide an accurate impression of reality."
3. "That reality is structured according to most of the concepts by which we describe it."
4. "That our rules of inference are reliable means of arriving at new truths about reality."[16]

These assumptions are in turn backed by a set of standardized rules of inference for "argument to the best explanation," a process by which a scientific observer can attain truth based on correlation to the ontological world. According to McCullagh, the conditions for rationally justifying truth are:

1. The statement, together with other statements already held to be true, must imply yet other statements describing present, observable data.
2. The hypothesis must be *of greater explanatory scope* than any other incompatible hypothesis about the same subject; that is, it must imply a greater variety of observation statements.
3. The hypothesis must be *of greater explanatory power* than any other incompatible hypothesis about the same subject; that is, it must make the observation statements it implies more probable than any other.
4. The hypothesis must be *more plausible* than any other incompatible hypothesis about the same subject; that is, it must be implied to some degree by a greater variety of accepted truths than any other, and be implied more strongly than any other; and its probable negation must be implied by fewer beliefs, and implied less strongly than any other.
5. The hypothesis must be *less ad hoc* than any other incompatible hypothesis about the same subject; that is, it must include fewer new suppositions about the past that are not already implied to some extent by existing beliefs.
6. It must be *disconfirmed by fewer accepted beliefs* than any other incompatible hypothesis about the same subject; that is, when conjoined with acceptable truths it must imply fewer observation statements and other statements which are believed to be false.
7. It must exceed other incompatible hypotheses about the same subject by so much, in characteristics 2 and 6, that there is little chance of an incompatible hypothesis, after further investigation, soon exceeding it in these respects.[17]

Thus, McCullagh defines a correlation theory of truth according to which "a description of the world is true if possible experiences of the world correspond to those implied by the world view of which it is part.... Our explanations are

true if they cohere with our other beliefs about the world, and if all the observations they entail would be verified in the experience of anyone who tested
them."[18] McCullagh's positivist ontology and epistemology are predicated on
the claim that "At all events, belief in the truth of our best explanations is indeed an act of faith. . . . It is a convention we all accept that sound inductive
inferences regularly lead us to truths about the world, and it is a convention we
take seriously on faith."[19] McCullagh therefore advocates retaining faith in the
positivist assumptions listed above and justifies "that faith on practical
grounds. As a framework of belief and knowledge, those assumptions have enabled us to relate very successfully to our physical environment, to predict and
control to our advantage, and to delight in it with awe and wonder." McCullagh continues:

> Faith in empiricist assumptions is not enough, I believe, for a happy life. The re-
> ality of human consciousness and the triune God must also be acknowledged.
> But empiricism is a part of our cultural inheritance which has been of such spec-
> tacular value in helping us to understand and control nature that it would seem
> foolish to abandon it. There is no better framework of beliefs about the world
> which we could adopt instead. It is not sensible to reject empiricist assumptions
> because of evidence that they are false when they have served us so very well
> in the past, and when we have nothing better to put in their place. In a philo-
> sophical context we may acknowledge that empiricist assumptions are inconsis-
> tent with the empirical facts of cognitive relativism. But for other practical pur-
> poses we should accept them as true just the same.[20]

Contemplating the alternative to the position articulated above, McCullagh
asks us to "Imagine the terror of living in a world without any idea of the
causal processes at work in it. The sort of knowledge Lyotard advocates, con-
fined as it is to knowledge of particulars which have no general significance
at all, would leave everyone prey to the forces of nature and society, with no
general knowledge with which to predict and control them. . . . General
knowledge of our traditions and institutions is essential for a proper appreci-
ation of their value."[21] The justification for positivist ontology and epistemology McCullagh provides is admittedly problematic insofar as it requires
faith and "cultural inheritance" in order to maintain true knowledge of ontological reality as it exists independent of human experience. In response to
this critique, McCullagh concedes that "Since we have no independent way
of discovering what 'something' is, we simply take the descriptions which we
judge to be reliable and true and act as if the world is as we describe it
. . . scientific theories . . . seem better described as representations of reality,
of whose real nature we remain mostly ignorant, rather than a mirror of its essential nature."[22]

Like McCullagh, Murray Murphey contends that studying the past is an essentially empirical endeavor and one that operates according to a set of positivist assumptions. Murphey's basic positivist assumptions are:

1. There is a real world of which true knowledge is possible.
2. There are other persons who have minds.
3. It is possible for one person to know what another person thinks.
4. A language spoken by one person can be correctly interpreted by someone from outside that linguistic community, and a text in one language can be translated into an approximately equivalent text in another language of comparative resources.
5. There exists a past in which human beings lived and acted.
6. We can have some accurate knowledge of the past.
7. Members of one culture can understand members of other cultures, including members of antecedent states of their own culture.
8. Human action is causally explainable.[23]

The evidential basis for that which we study includes "those entities, events, relationships . . . we believe to have existed in the past, are postulates to account for the evidential base. . . . They are real if our theory is true, and truth is attainable in the study of the past, given adequate evidence, just as it is in other fields."[24]

Recognizing the inherent problem of basing ontological reality on the given epistemology *du jour*, Murphey asserts that one could object that positivism might appear to make that which is real dependent on that which we think. In response, he argues, "If our true theory holds that the real is independent of our knowledge about it, then since the real is what the true theory says it is, reality is indeed independent of what we think about it."[25] Thus, if our theory of truth posits an human-independent reality, then that reality can be said to exist unproblematically.

2. Postmodernism

In contrast to the positivist approaches toward history just discussed, postmodernist approaches seek to reveal that historical knowledge, like all forms of knowledge, is filtered through human cognitive capacities, perceptions, and imagination. Thus, "there are multiple ways of interpreting what others have written and said." Certainty of meaning is thus difficult, if not impossible to attain "because people, scholars included, say many and often contradictory things—often within the same article."[26] For Jean-Francois Lyotard, postmodernism can be defined in the most basic sense as "incredulity toward

metanarratives." According to Lyotard, the metanarratives of modernity—
Enlightenment, progress, Marxism, capitalism, development—are "being dis-
persed in clouds of narrative elements. . . . Conveyed within each cloud are
pragmatic valences specific to its kind. Each of us lives at the intersection of
many of these. However, we do not necessarily establish stable language
combinations, and the properties of the ones we do establish are not necessarily communicable."[27] Postmodernists thus don't so much offer a positive
theory of knowledge as instead provide a skeptical reaction to modernity, including the methodologies and epistemologies of modern social inquiry. If
postmodernism is understood to be generally critical toward generalizations
and toward the grand narratives of modernity, then language and discourse
become the primary objects of analysis. To this it might be added most postmodernists are uninterested in discussing ontological reality, either because
there is no such state of being or because it is epistemologically unknowable
and therefore devoid of meaning.

According to postmodernists such as Lyotard, the fixity of meaning implied by the grand narratives is broken apart into a multiplicity of potential
histories, and the potential for intersubjective agreement over any of these is
questionable. Whereas positivism is comfortable with historical metanarratives that imply "a philosophy of history . . . used to legitimate knowledge,"
postmodernism raises questions "concerning the validity of the institutions
governing the social bond: these must be legitimated as well."[28] Thus, postmodernism seeks to expose the lack of a human-independent arbitrating
mechanism or procedure to determine precisely what constitutes "legitimate"
historical knowledge and what does not. Knowledge is not a "mirror of nature" but rather the product of human-dependent arbitration—"legislation," in
Lyotard's terms—regarding the terms of legitimate discourse.

Positivist, or scientific inquiry, relies on "rules of the game" that are inherently self-referential in their authoritativeness and ultimately, imperialistic.
The "rules of the game of science, are immanent in that game . . . they can
only be established within the bonds of a debate that is already scientific in
nature." Thus,

> there is no other proof that the rules are good than the consensus extended to
> them by the experts. . . . The scientist questions the validity of narrative state-
> ments and concludes that they are never subject to argumentation or proof. He
> classifies them as belonging to a different mentality: savage, primitive, under-
> developed, backward. . . . Narratives are fables, myths, legends, fit only for
> women and children. This unequal relationship is an intrinsic effect of the rules
> specific to each system. . . . It is the entire history of cultural imperialism from
> the dawn of Western civilization. It is important to recognize its special tenor,

which sets it apart from all other forms of imperialism: it is governed by the demand for legitimation.[29]

Thus, the positivist need for fixity of meaning is limitless. Bases of knowledge that deviate from the "rules of the game" are flawed and illegitimate. In this matter, according to Lyotard, positivism brooks no rivals.

Postmodernists also suggest an important distinction between history, or historical narrative, and the past. Unlike the referent objects of science, which are separated from the inquirer in terms of space but not of time, the past is forever locked away in a realm that even positivists acknowledge cannot be physically accessed.[30] In order to capture this distinction between the past versus the texts we use to refer to it, one might allude to Derrida's "originary" violence, which is the notion that there is an inescapable and logical rupture between the ideality or purity of a term, such as a historical event, and the empirical inscription of the term, namely, the textual recording of history.[31]

Some postmodernists have additionally sought to dissolve the boundary between history and literature. Hayden White, the first historian to adopt the mode of literary theory, points out that there are two aspects of interpretation present in every historical work. The first is the plot structure in which "the historian constitutes a story out of the chronicle of events." The second is the choice of an explanatory paradigm in which the historian selects a distinct "narrative technique" that "progressively identifies the *kind of story*" being told. Thus, for example, White argues that whereas Michelet recounts the history of pre-1789 France as a "romance," Tocqueville, by contrast, textualizes the same history as a "tragedy."[32] The crucial point, then, "is that most historical sequences can be emplotted in a number of different ways, so as to provide different interpretations of those events and to endow them with different meanings. . . . *How* a given historical situation is to be configured depends on the historian's subtlety in matching up a specific plot structure with the set of historical events that he wishes to endow with a meaning of a particular kind. This is essentially a literary, that is to say fiction-making operation."[33]

Further elaborating on this point, Frank Ankersmit offers the concept of "narrative substances," which clarifies how and why historical facts get translated into what we perceive as "history." Narrative substances—"names and descriptions created to signify the past and events within it, but which are not directly traceable to that past"—are a key to the way we understand matters as being historical. For instance, Ankersmit would ask, what is the Renaissance or the Industrial Revolution? These concepts have no physical and historical instantiation in nature much less in history. Rather, they are post hoc conceptualizations that do not and cannot exist outside of a text. They are thus

"imaginary, organizing notions that make heuristic sense of statements in
texts which individually, as statements, refer outside of themselves but which,
as narrative substances, do not do so."[34]

Another common postmodernist theme regards the false distinction between the analytical/scientific and normative aspects of inquiry. Jenkins, for
instance, asserts that "The idea of writing an objective, neutral, disinter-
ested text, where explaining, describing, and 'introducing' something is
done for a position that isn't ostensibly a position at all, is a naïve one."[35]
If the normative-analytical dichotomy is suspended, then all modes of inquiry contain an ethical dimension. Since historical inquiry entails choices
of which sources to include/exclude as well as the choice of narrative for-
mat and mode of employment, those choices, whether self-conscious or not,
are guided by ethics. That is to say that all informed choices, including
choices of historical interpretation, require valued judgments and thus they
are inherently ethical choices. Even consulting a neutral methodological
framework to arbitrate the matter of which texts/sources to include/exclude
represents an ethical judgment that the methodology selected is good or
successful.

According to the postmodernist perspective on this point, texts can thus be
deconstructed in order to reveal and expose their embedded ethico-normative
dimensions. Some postmodernists have also sought to reveal the ubiquity of
ethics by arguing that it is the process of agonizing over a decision in the face
of total undecidability that constitutes the ethical.[36] "Undecidability," says
Derrida, "is not a moment to be traversed and overcome. Conflicts of duty—
and there is only duty in conflict—are interminable and even when I take my
decision and do something, undecidability is not at an end. I know that I have
not done enough and it is in this way that morality continues, that history and
politics continue. There is politicization or ethicization because undecidability is not simply a moment to be overcome by the occurrence of the decision."[37] This is of in some sense the inverse of traditional Western understandings of ethics, which allude to the importance of following moral codes
(for instance, religious, national, legal) that dictate appropriate conduct.
While postmodern ethics is generally concerned with the process rather than
the outcome of decisions, some postmodernists occasionally reveal more.
Thus, Derrida asserts that "Deconstruction is hyperpoliticizing in following
paths and codes which are clearly not traditional, and I believe it awakens
politicization in the way I mentioned above, that is, it permits us to think the
political and think the democratic by granting us the space necessary in order
not to be enclosed in the latter."[38] If this view is to be taken seriously, then
one can only but think that Derrida values democracy over other ostensible
alternatives.

III. DEWEY'S THEORY OF HISTORICAL KNOWLEDGE

Like many of the postmodernists, John Dewey's pragmatism is generally unconcerned with ontological matters outside of human experience. Whatever the features of the "real world" may be, it is through experience that we have knowledge of them. So Dewey's ontology quickly collapses into his epistemology; that is, the notion of the independent world is dependent on the means we have of acquiring knowledge of it. Unlike the Lockeian empiricists of the Enlightenment with whom he shares a common genealogy, however, Dewey was quite skeptical that empirical knowledge could perfectly mirror the ontological basis of nature. Thus, Dewey, along with other pragmatists, suggests that positivism conflates the physicality of objects with evidence for their *a priori* ontological existence. As Willard Quine puts it, "The myth of physical objects is epistemologically superior to most in that it has proved more efficacious than other myths as a device for working a manageable structure into the flux of experience."[39] Deweyan pragmatists emphasize that meaning is developed through complex interaction between mind and the environment.[40] This social constructivist understanding is one that had radical implications for American philosophy. Dewey believed it was "time not to offer new solutions to traditional epistemological problems, as the realists proposed, but to raise corrosive questions about the genuineness of the problems themselves."[41]

Dewey's solution to intractable debates in analytic philosophy was to obliterate the distinction between the world of mind and the independent world and to replace it with a world of experience in which mind and environment are locked into a permanent relationship of interaction. Thus, whether or not it is possible to hold the mind to be independent of the world or vice-versa becomes a moot point: the two must always be taken into account in order to understand how knowledge is formed and how it functions. In the human experienced world, knowledge "arises when things are reconstructed by reflective thinking with new meaning and then verified as capable of directing us to our goals."[42] Dewey's understanding of human experience is thus a constructivist one: "[e]verything which is distinctively human is learned, not native, even though it could not be learned without native structures which mark man off from other animals. To learn in a human way and to human effect is not just to acquire added skill through refinement of original capacities."[43]

Dewey's full theory of knowledge is a bit more complex. John Shook lists eighteen principles of Dewey's epistemology, several of which stand out as especially significant. First, Dewey asserts that it is impossible and thus fruitless to explain how meaning as a totality exists. By its nature, any explanation can only proceed from meaningful things to other meaningful things. It is not possible to produce a meaningful understanding from a thing that is in-comprehensible. Meaning, in turn, can only be understood in terms of a sec-ond proposition, which is that humans employ critical intelligence to use meaningful things as means to further human activities. The key point Dewey is making is that critical intelligence allows humans to engage in "reflective inquiry," the process by which people impute meaning to the things they en-counter via experience. By constructing meaning through experience, humans are able to resolve problematic situations; that is, they are able to cope with the difficulties posed by certain things they encounter in the course of life. This notion that meaning is attributed to the empirical world in order to re-spond to the practical problem of operating in it is among the cornerstone principles of pragmatist thought.[44] Dewey's "functional coherence" concep-tion of truth thus argues that ideas are "hypotheses or plans of action, the truth of which rested on their ability to 'work' in experience." Truth depends "not on the accuracy with which an idea copied an antecedent reality or on its co-herence with other truths but on its capacity to guide thinkers toward a suc-cessful or satisfactory solution to a problematic situation. In this sense, the truth of a proposition was not found but 'made' through the process by which it was verified."[45]

Dewey's epistemology suggests a distinctively pragmatist mode of histor-ical inquiry, although one that is familiar to other notable philosophers of his-tory. Thus, Dewey would agree with Oakeshott on the point that "An event independent of experience, 'objective' in the sense of being untouched by thought or judgment, would be unknowable; it would be neither fact nor true nor false, but a nonentity." As such, "history cannot be 'the course of events' independent of our experience of it, because there is nothing independent of our experience—neither event nor fact, neither past nor future."[46] Let us look more carefully at Dewey's views on historical inquiry.

According to Dewey, "Inquiry is a mode of activity that is socially condi-tioned and that has cultural consequences.... Neither inquiry nor the most ab-stractly formal set of symbols can escape from the cultural matrix in which they live, move and have their being."[47] Inquiry arises in response to the need to resolve problematic situations. Thus, all inquiry begins in doubt, in the need to understand the "why" of environmental conditions. But inquiry, if successful, "terminates in the institution of conditions which remove need for doubt. The latter state of affairs may be designated by the words *belief* and *knowledge*." In place of those words, which are admittedly polemical, Dewey preferred to speak in terms of "warranted assertibility."[48] Historical inquiry, in Dewey's view, entails the fixing of order to interminable processes for the purpose of practically understanding temporality. For Dewey, events have no beginning or end of which we can be certain, so when we speak of historical events, we are in fact rendering judgments in order to attribute meaning to specific points in time. "Judgment," Dewey says,

> is transformation of an antecedent existentially indeterminate or unsettled situation into a determinate one. . . . To judge is to render determinate; to determine is to order and organize, to relate in definite fashion. Temporal order is instituted through rhythms which involve periodicities, intervals, and limit; all of which are inter-involved. Absolute origins and absolute closes and termini are mythical. Each beginning and each ending is a delimitation of a cycle or round of qualitative change. A date, a moment or point of time, has no meaning except as such a delimitation.[49]

When we inquire into temporal questions that involve matters such as "from where" and "to where," narrative descriptions ensue that address the problematic quality of human situations. Thus, questions such as the rising and setting of the sun produce narratives—"the sun rose," "the sun set"— that fix events in time that are in fact part of an unending process. But the fixity is necessary in order to resolve a practical problem, namely accounting for human time (i.e., a day). Indeed, events are not in nature. Rather, "*Event* is a term of judgment, not of existence apart from judgment. The origin and development of the Appalachian Mountain Range is an event, and so is the loosening and rolling of a particular pebble. . . . That these are distinguished as particular events involves human judgment as to their "event-ness."[50] This seemingly simple point suggests the somewhat radical notion that historical reality is characterized only by process and as such is fundamentally indeterminate. The ordering of history into time is thus a human invention developed in response to the practical problem of fixing matters so as to make sense of human temporality. For Dewey, "the writing of history is an instance of judgment as a resolution through inquiry of a problematic situation."[51] The problem is humans' desire to understand the past as a means of coping with the present. If knowledge of the past weren't problematic, it would be taken for granted, embedded in consciousness.

On the claim that all historical inquiry is guided by present concerns, Dewey is quite clear: "There is no material available for leading principles and hypotheses save that of the historic present. As culture changes, the conceptions that are dominant in a culture change. Of necessity new standpoints for viewing, appraising and ordering data arise. History is then rewritten. Material that had formerly been passed by, offers itself as data because the new conceptions propose new problems for solution, requiring new factual material for statement and test."[52] Thus, present ideas and practices inherently condition the determination of what is worthy of historical discussion and what is not, as well as the very standards of conducting inquiry. On this point, Dewey is in basic agreement with the postmodernists:

> *All historical construction is necessarily selective.* Since the past cannot be re-produced *in toto* and lived once again, this principle might seem too obvious to be worthy of being called important. But it is of importance because its ac-knowledgement compels attention to the fact that everything in the writing of history depends upon the principle used to control selection. This principle de-cides the weight which shall be assigned to past events, what shall be admitted and what omitted; it also decides how the facts selected shall be arranged and ordered. Furthermore . . . we are committed to the conclusion that all history is necessarily written from the standpoint of the present, and is, in an inescapable sense, the history not only of the present but of that which is contemporaneously judged to be important in the present.[53]

From this basis, Dewey proceeds to articulate a powerful constructivist theory of historical inquiry, revisionism, and ethics. Political and social changes of the present give "a new turn to social problems" and "throw the significance of what happened in the past into a new perspective. They set new issues from the standpoint of which to rewrite the story of the past." Thus, reinterpretations of the past are brought about by the need and desire to contend with the practical problems of the present. Accordingly, historians, "In using what has come to them as an inheritance from the past . . . are com-pelled to modify it to meet their own needs, and this process creates a new present in which the process continues. History cannot escape its own process. It will, therefore, always be rewritten."

This in turn has a profound impact not only on historical understandings, but also on the very social conditions of the present and future human environment. Thus, "as judgment of the significance of past events is changed, we gain new instruments for estimating the force of present conditions as potentialities of the future. Intelligent understanding of past history is to some extent a lever for moving the present into a certain kind of future." Human interpretation of the past, then, involves potential path dependencies, although these are by no means *a priori.* To the contrary, the contingently particular way in which hu-mans interpret and reinterpret the past will create contingently different pres-ents and futures; human history is thus in no way inevitable or preordained.[54]

IV. DEWEY BEYOND POSITIVISM AND POSTMODERNISM

Whereas the preceding section laid out some of the most significant aspects of Dewey's thought on history, this section argues that upon more careful scrutiny, his pragmatist history accounts for many of the problems overlooked by the positivist and postmodernist approaches. In so doing, Deweyan pragmatism offers a more coherent means of grounding claims to historical knowledge. The primary problem with historical positivism is that when assessed in a more stringent light, it implodes under the weight of its own unsupportable assumptions. Postmodern critiques of positivism are effective insofar as they go, but on the matter of historical inquiry, they raise more problems than they resolve.

Positivism, if it is to succeed in its purpose, must provide for both a fully developed ontological reality and an epistemology that allows for human knowledge of reality, whether present or past, as it actually is/was. However, we recall that in order to ground these propositions, positivists such as McCullagh ultimately require an appeal to faith in the veracity of the positivist view: "[at] all events, belief in the truth of our best explanations is indeed an act of faith. . . . It is a convention we all accept that sound inductive inferences regularly lead us to truths about the world, and it is a convention we take seriously on faith."[55] But if claims about the world and about the past were truly correspondent to reality, then faith would not be required to legitimize them as "true;" positivist truth and knowledge would be hegemonic as alternatives to them would be unthinkable; the fact that there are other possibilities logically proves that this is not the case. McCullagh further defends positivism on the grounds that it is culturally inherited and has served humans exceedingly well in the past and it would therefore be unwise to abandon such an approach, especially in the absence of a "better" alternative.

This last point is very weak insofar as positivist ontology holds that reality is as it is *regardless of whether or not humans can or do observe it*. If this is the case, then cultural inheritance is an irrelevant matter. The claim that we should maintain positivist practices because they "have served us well," regardless of evidence indicating their falsity, while certainly consistent with pragmatism, only weakens the claim that positivist rules of inference reveal truth.

McCullagh's call to maintain assumptions that are proved false unless and until they can be replaced by "better" ones is essentially an open appeal for the maintenance of certain narratives over others. It is thus impossible to reconcile this logic of justification with McCullagh's core positivist assumption that "the world exists . . . has existed independent of any beliefs about it" and that it is easily accessible to human observation.[56] Most significantly, however, is that McCullagh reveals a pragmatist line of thinking when he writes: "[i]n a philosophical context we may acknowledge that empiricist assumptions are inconsistent with the empirical facts of cognitive relativism. But for other practical purposes we should accept them as true just the same." Indeed, he justifies his faith in positivism on a practical basis because it enables humans to function in, predict, and control their environment. This position, while totally inconsistent with positivism, is perfectly in line with Deweyan pragmatism. The successful relation of humans to their environment is in any other terms a restatement of the pragmatist notion that humans form knowledge as a function of the need to resolve problematic situations.

Murphey's positivist theory of knowledge is certainly less polemically presented than is McCullagh's. But the basis of his argument, like that of McCullagh, ultimately collapses into pragmatism. We recall that Murphey asserts that "our best-confirmed present theory is our best estimate of what the truth is."[57] It is difficult, however, to reconcile this view with Murphey's assumption that "[t]here is a real world of which true knowledge is possible."[58] What is crucially lacking in Murphey's account is a human-independent verification mechanism that would explain how true knowledge is in point of fact the same as the "best estimate" that Murphey offers: these two conceptions—the true and the estimate—cannot logically be the same. In the absence of such a mechanism/procedure, Murphey's claims are inconsistent. In order to square them, he would need to adopt a position something like: "There is an ontologically real world; what its true characteristics are is anyone's guess; by using theories that are confirmed by experience—where 'confirmed' means the successful resolution of problematic situations—we can produce 'best-guess' estimates of what the real world might be like." But as was just suggested, such a position is more aptly a pragmatist than a positivist one.

Postmodern approaches toward history allude to a number of problems with the positivist project, two of which are most crucial. The first is the notion that the standards of inquiry and analysis, including the received method and practice of science, are merely a human constructed discourse and are thus not prior to language. This suggests that human understanding of the world can never be separated from the discourses of understanding. Second, insofar as "objective" ontological structures of knowledge have been posited by humans, whether of a religious, scientific, or other nature, such structures contain a power-laden dimension, which can and most certainly has been used for social separation, control, and subjugation. Positivism is ill equipped to account for either of these problems. Regarding the former, positivism contends that both the physical and historical worlds are human independent and therefore by definition prior to discourse, not placed within it. With regard to the latter, positivism clearly distinguishes "fact" from "value" and thus the structures of knowledge are always seen as totally apart from the question of power. In objecting to this position, postmodernists have revealingly demonstrated the problem of positing a realm of pure analytical inquiry that could be fully segregated from ethical and normative considerations. Thus, Derrida challenges us to contemplate the ethical implications not only of individual actions and deeds but also of the very analytical systems that are employed in social practice.[59] This is a profound contribution to the understanding of human social life.

The primary problem with postmodernism is, however, that it not only lacks but also is overtly hostile to the notion of arbitrating mechanisms or procedures. This is because in order to establish an arbitrating mechanism to distinguish "good" from "bad" or "true" from "false" there must be an "establisher;" an entity that by definition will have a privileged claim to authority by virtue of its position. In terms of politics, the postmodern rejection of establishing arbitrating mechanisms is quite liberating; after all, few who believe in democracy and emancipation are comfortable with having the notion of what is good *versus* bad arbitrated for them. With regard to historical inquiry, however, the postmodern position raises a major problem: if standards of arbitration are deemed undesirable, then how can good scholarship be distinguished from bad, biased from unbiased?

Turning to the problem of arbitration, one critic asserts that in the postmodern view, language "is itself 'duplicitous,' 'cryptic,' it has to be 'decoded' before it can convey any meaning. And since there is no single correct code, no reading of the text, no interpretation, has any more authority than any other. This interpretation is as 'indeterminate' as the text itself."[60] Another detractor argues that in postmodern historiography, "there are no events, people, reality, but only texts and their interpretation. Thus, every text is equal in value to every other, and each construct is equally legitimate."[61] This poses a significant problem insofar as having common understandings of certain historical events is a problematic situation for human social life.

Postmodernists offer little guidance as to how to approach this problem and to the extent that they do make positive claims, they typically parrot positivism by constructing arguments and marshaling evidence in support of them in a manner much the same as do positivists. Thus, for example, David Campbell argues that foreign policy practices are driven by a structural need to maintain a boundary between the systemic and domestic realms. "In so far as the logic of identity requires difference," writes Campbell, "the potential for the transformation of difference into otherness always exists." Thus "the logic of identity more readily succumbs to the politics of negation."[62] While Campbell's claim is clearly critical of American foreign policy and the Waltzian brand of self-help upon which it is premised, Campbell's point is in fact not very far removed from Waltz's, and his evidence for it is essentially the same. That is, when faced with the potentially destabilizing prospects of a more integrative collective identification, states will revert to basic assessment of their essential insecurity in anarchy and the subsequent need to adopt a protective posture that amounts to a form of self-help.

Postmodernism offers no solution to the need to make positive claims and to allow for standardized rules by which to support them. Positivism does, but it does so by "'craving' for an unattainable form of objectivity which is thought to reside in a description of the world 'as it is in itself, independent of perspective' and which can be provided by 'science and only science.'"[63] Pragmatism offers a resolution to this dilemma by suggesting that human knowledge, while admittedly formed *via* human experience, can be intersubjectively shared in ways that impute meaning to human existence. Thus, pragmatism privileges the "consensus of community rather than" either the relativism of postmodernism or the "relation to a nonhuman reality" of positivism with regard to matters of epistemology and ontology.[64] This position is in fact not very far removed from that articulated by Kuhn as his theory of paradigmatic science. "The status of a paradigm's argument," writes Kuhn, "cannot be made logically or even probabilistically compelling for those who refuse to step into the circle. . . . As in political revolutions, so in paradigm choice— there is no standard higher than the assent of the relevant community."[65] Compare the preceding with Dewey's argument that "the norms of particular practices, while empirically regulative, are human constructed and fallible: no cast-iron rules can be laid down."[66] Regarding the process of inquiry, Dewey asserts that "[i]n scientific inquiry, the criterion of what is taken to be settled, or to be knowledge, is being *so* settled that it is available as a resource in further inquiry; not being settled in such a way as not to be subject to revision in further inquiry."[67] This notion of "settled knowledge" is strikingly similar to Kuhn's conception of a "paradigm" in that both set the parameters of "normal inquiry" (Dewey's term) or "science" (Kuhn's term) while at the same time leaving enough problems unresolved so that further inquiry is necessary in order to round out and revise the current state of knowledge or paradigm.

This position also bears an important measure of congruity with Patomäki and Wight's critical realism, which suggests that ethical deliberation and "the world of real causal processes" are inherently interconnected. Patomäki and Wight agree with Dewey and Kuhn that "the manner in which we act in this world" emanates from "the knowledge we possess of that which we value and that which we can do."[68] In sum, pragmatism offers a consensus-based epistemology of inquiry into the present and past of human experience according to which intersubjectivity—not correspondence to an antecedent ontological reality—can provide arbitrating mechanisms for inquiry.

Against this position the postmodernist might object that intersubjectivity could conceivably be a façade for ideas and understandings that promote oppression and the maintenance of entrenched power interests. The pragmatist response is that in a democratic context, consensus may be difficult to achieve but it is *not inherently* a manifestation of oppression or abuse of power. Pragmatism, according to Rorty, allows "room for improved belief, since new evidence, or new hypotheses, or a whole new vocabulary, may come along. For pragmatists, the desire for objectivity is not the desire to escape the limitations of one's community, but simply the desire for as much intersubjective agreement as possible, the desire to extend the reference of 'us' as far as we can."[69] IR scholar Donald Puchala agrees: "The pragmatic value of any idea or interpretation is to be determined according to whether it is worthy of admission to the conversation among discourses about humankind. Its 'cash value' is its newness, differentness, imaginativeness, provocativeness—its 'abnormality' at the time it is articulated."[70] Of course, this presupposes an unproblematic, uncritical view of democracy that could be called into question. Admittedly, the detailed specifics of attaining consensus *via* democratic deliberation requires substantial theorization, a task that is certainly worthwhile, but beyond the scope of the discussion here.[71] In sum, the postmodern suspicion of an intersubjective approach toward grounding knowledge is a viable criticism but one that is potentially resolvable *via* democratic theorization. Further, the postmodern critique is not constructive insofar as it offers no coherent response to the problem of historical epistemology and ontology. As long as this is the case, pragmatist intersubjectivity represents a marked advance over both positivist foundationalism and postmodern relativism.

V. ETHICAL IMPLICATIONS OF DEWEY'S HISTORICAL INQUIRY

Dewey's theory of historical knowledge explodes the possibilities for normative inquiry into history. Whereas, for positivist history and social science, ethics is a subject that is divorced from scientific inquiry, this is not the case for Deweyan pragmatism. On the contrary, Dewey's pragmatist approach argues that it is functionally impossible within human practice to establish or even to theorize an apartheid of norms and analysis, nor would it be desirable to do so, even if it were possible. "The parrot-like repetition of the distinction between an empirical description of what is and a normative account of what should be," writes Dewey,

> merely neglects the most striking fact about thinking as it empirically is— namely, its flagrant exhibition of cases of failure and success—that is, of good and bad thinking. . . . The more study that is given to empirical records of actual thought, the more apparent becomes the connection between the specific

features of thinking which have produced failure and success. Out of this relationship as it is empirically ascertained grow the norms and regulations of an art of thinking.[72]

Dewey argued that the most pressing philosophical problem of his era was the divorce of applied, technical knowledge from the human and moral purposes that such knowledge served, whether consciously or not. Thus, "When physics, chemistry, biology, medicine, contribute to the detection of concrete human woes and to the development of plans for remedying them and relieving the human estate, they become moral; they become part of the apparatus of moral inquiry or science. . . . Natural science loses its divorce from humanity; it becomes itself humanistic in quality."[73] In other words, the notion that historical or scientific inquiry is a dispassionate quest for objective truth is inaccurate. Even if such a quest were possible, it would be unethical. But this begs the most basic question: how does pragmatism define and explain ethics?

Dewey responds to this question in his *Outlines of a Critical Theory of Ethics*, where he begins with the assertion that every human event and practice can be thought of in terms (1) of its occurrence, which can be explained scientifically; and (2) of its intended end, which only can be understood in terms of ethics.[74] Every human act, therefore, whether a declaration of war or a decision to write a book *about* war, has an ethical dimension. Furthermore, ethical matters, or morality, have two fundamental elements: (1) the feelings/inclinations of the character; and (2) the ideal consequences of the actions taken. Thus, one might: (1) have good intentions alone without action; or (2) no particular intentions but actions that inadvertently lead to good. Either in the absence of the other does not constitute an ethical action.[75] This theme resonated in Dewey's philosophy throughout his lifetime. Thus, some thirty years after the *Outlines*, Dewey would remark that "Education and morals will begin to find themselves on the same road of advance that say chemical industry and medicine have found for themselves when they too learn fully the lesson of wholehearted and unremitting attention to means and conditions—that is, to what mankind so long despised as material and mechanical. When we take means for ends we indeed fall into moral materialism. But when we take ends without regard to means we degenerate into sentimentalism."[76]

Dewey builds his case on a critique of the two most prolific prior ethical systems—hedonism/utilitarianism and Kantian ethics—for their failure to satisfy both components of his pragmatic ethics. On the one hand, hedonistic and utilitarian theories value the most good for the most people, but only in terms of results, not intentions. On the other, Kantian ethics posit that "Goodness belongs to the will and to that alone." Dewey says of the Kantian notion of goodness: "It is like a jewel which shines by its own light, having its whole value in itself." Kantian ethics could thus produce a world of good intentions but one that is utterly devoid of positive results.[77] Only via pragmatic ethics is good predicated on *both* the will of the individual and the end toward which will acts. In his later *Ethics*, co-written with James Tufts, Dewey clarifies this point:

> On the one side stand those who, like Kant, say that results actually attained are of no importance morally speaking, because they do not depend upon the will alone; that only the will can be good or bad in the moral sense. On the other side, are those who, like Bentham, say that morality consists in producing consequences which contribute to the general welfare, and that motives do not count at all save as they happen to influence the consequences one way or another. One theory puts sole emphasis on *attitude*, upon *how* the chosen act is conceived and inspired; the other theory lays stress solely upon *what* is actually done, upon the objective *content* of the deed in the way of its effect upon others. Our analysis shows that both views are one-sided.[78]

Individuals in society have a moral obligation to effect change according to their capacity to realize change, or what Dewey terms their "function." This moral obligation is regulated by the interrelationship between individuals and their environment. Just as individuals must adjust to their environment to fulfill their moral functions, so must they at times transform their environment as a matter of moral obligation. "It is evident," Dewey writes, "that *transformation* of existing circumstances is moral duty rather than mere reproduction of them. The environment must be plastic to the ends of the agent . . . the point is to see that 'adjustment,' to have a moral sense, means *making the environment a reality for one's self*."[79]

Dewey was especially concerned to apply this conception of ethics to the realm of scientific and political inquiry:

> [S]cience and art, up to a certain point, are social, and to draw a line where they cease to be so, is in reality to draw a line where we cease to *see* their social character. That we should cease to *see* it, is necessary in the case of almost every advance. Just because the new scientific movement is new, we can realize its social effects only afterwards. But it may be questioned whether the motive which actuates the man of science is not, when fully realized, a *faith* in the social bearing of what he is doing.[80]

Thus, it is ethical to engage in science so long as there is the expectation, however uncertain, that the product of the effort will be socially beneficial. Any effort toward inquiry, whether scientific, literary, or historical, that fails to attempt to further the common good is not only unethical, it is pointless: "[O]ne

of the pressing duties that every man of intelligence should do his part in
bringing out the public and common aspects of knowledge. *The* duty of the
present is the socializing of intelligence—the realizing of its bearing upon social practice."[81] With regard to the specific practice of historical inquiry,
Dewey would later write, "The past is recalled not because of itself but because of what it adds to the present."[82] This system of ethical science is quite
adaptable to the practice of historical and social inquiry.

> Social science without social philosophy was blind . . . [science] "can describe
> and record natural phenomena, but it cannot guide them or change them ac-
> cording to human ideals. . . . The relationship between the social sciences and
> social philosophy is thus one of interpenetration. . . . [The historical and social
> sciences must therefore] provide the material by means of which man can im-
> prove his lot and move towards the goal of peace and happiness."[83]

For Dewey, social science's sufficiency could be judged only on the basis of
its *practical* effects, where practical is defined according to normative criteria. Thus, he alludes to "an adequate social or political science—meaning by
science, not simply an abstract, technical thing but the continual application
of the daily social event of the highest principles of interpretation."[84] Dewey's
fusion of historical and social science and ethics would inherently further the
common good. "Instead of impersonal and purely speculative endeavors to
contemplate as remote beholders the nature of absolute things-in-themselves
[as per positivism] . . . we have a living picture of the choice of thoughtful
men about what they would have life to be, and to what ends they would have
men shape their intelligent activities."[85]

VI. DEWEYAN PRAGMATISM AND
HISTORICAL INQUIRY IN POLITICAL SCIENCE

The preceding discussion has shed light on the problem of grounding claims to
historical knowledge. While I have argued that the Deweyan approach holds
great promise, this does not change the fact that the problem of historical inquiry remains just that; a problem, and one with many different instantiations.
The following chapters of this book deal with one of the most widespread and
important of these, namely, the problem of historical revisionism, which I define as the process by which a new historical narrative emerges that takes issue
with or seeks to supplant an earlier narrative generally understood to pertain to
the same subject matter. The question posed by historical revisionism is quite
simple: namely, how can one undertake historical social scientific research under the assumption of precise knowledge of what happened when revisionism

will routinely contest the very basis of that knowledge? In chapters 3 through 6, I suggest that building arguments on the basis of a narrative no longer deemed historically valid by a large group of historians is a risky enterprise. Before jumping ahead to that problem, however, it is necessary to elaborate further on the nature of historical revisionism as it is understood here.

There are two precipitating factors that at first glance appear to trigger the emergence of revisionist projects. The first is the availability of an academically significant new source or sources of data. Typically, and especially in the field of diplomatic history, new data takes the form of archival records that in Western countries are commonly released in statutory increments. The second and more complex factor entails changes in political and ideological currents as they relate to given historical subjects. Such changes are manifest in a diverse array of forms and places. Whereas in some instances, social or political changes in overall national populations can influence the historical enterprise, in others, historical revisionism may derive from within a particular academic community situated in political/ideological insulation from the population at large.

However, if we think more carefully about the problem, the new ideas that often give rise to historical revisionism movements generally take root during times of crisis. After all, there are always countless new ideas floating about in the free market of intellectual discourse but only a very select few become theoretically or historically important. Those that do generally provide a better fit with troublesome aspects of reality than did the ideas that are revised or replaced. This is precisely how Dewey would see the matter: new histories arise in response to the need to resolve practical problems of understanding the past, or having the past "fit" with present common understandings. When the effort to square our understanding of the historical past with increasingly inconsistent features of current reality becomes sufficiently problematic, a crisis ensues, which provokes an interest in reinterpreting the past.

This contrasts sharply with the positivist understanding of historical revisionism, which sees revisionism as the effort to attain a better or truer picture of history as it really was. According to this positivist explanation, the revisionist scholar is empowered: (1) by the availability of new data; and (2) by the benefit of 20/20 hindsight to take a broad view of the literature on a given historical subject. With these advantages in hand, the revisionist scholar is better equipped to account for contradictions and problems within the literature as well as to address questions left unanswered by earlier scholars. The causal logic according this explanation thus proceeds along lines as follows: new data becomes available triggering an impulse to produce more accurate historical accounts. This in turn results in the production of a revisionist body of literature.

This positivist explanation for revisionism is exemplified quite nicely in the perspective and work of Benny Morris, the seminal figure among the Israeli critical historians. Morris, capitalizing on the release of previously classified British and Israeli archival records pertaining to the founding of Israel and the 1948–1949 Arab-Israeli war, became the first historian to employ the new data to construct historical accounts of that period.[86] In the process, however, he became the center of ongoing controversy among both historians and the Israeli general public for his claim that Israel was neither as innocent nor as unwitting in its conflict with the Arabs as the earlier historiography would have us think. Morris actively denies any political or ideological motivation behind his work, insisting upon a commitment to "positivist history" based upon the most thorough assessment of the evidentiary facts available. In Morris's view, then, his history provides a "truer" and more accurate portrayal than did previous accounts due to his use of the more thorough set of data analyzed and cited in his work.[87]

The Deweyan explanation for historical revisionism takes issue with this account. Rather, it suggests that historical revisionism is the reinterpretation of history in response to a crisis of the fit of historical evidence to new political or social realities. New data in itself is inconsequential absent a problem to which it can be applied. Historical revisionism is viewed as malicious or beneficial depending on the configuration of political positions among communities concerned with the revisionism in question. Thus, for instance, in the United States, historical revisionism that reevaluates (and criticizes) the relationship between white settlers and Native Americans in the context of American state expansion is widely viewed as a naturally progessive consequence of changes in both elite and popular American attitudes toward multiculturalism and American history.[88] On the other hand, historical revisionism that calls into question the factual basis for the Holocaust is generally deemed to be the work of malicious anti-Semites.[89] While Dewey could explain both types, only the former could be deemed ethical insofar as one is aimed at promoting a "common good" and the other is not. Of course, agreement over the common good is in itself an immense philosophical problem, albeit one that is beyond the scope of this book. The key conclusion here is to see that historical revisionism is not the effort to reach objective truth about the facts of the past. Rather, it is a constructed process of reassessing human *understandings* about the past with a mind toward realizing a different future.

NOTES

1. Leopold von Ranke, "On the Relations of History and Philosophy," in Leopold von Ranke, *The Theory and Practice of History*, eds. Georg G. Iggers and Konrad von

Moltke (New York: Irvington Publishers, 1973), 30. Incidentally, "the particular in and by itself" could also be read as an endorsement of historical relativism, though that is clearly not how most scholars read von Ranke.

2. E. H. Carr, *What is History* (New York: Vintage Books, 1961), 4.

3. Jenkins states: "this *Reader* presents extracts from works as engaged in a series of oppositional debates (and thus, I suppose, gives a further lease of life to 'binary oppositions')." *The Postmodern History Reader* (London: Routledge, 1997), 2. Jenkins further subdivides his two categories into five subcategories: (1) radical critics of metanarratives ("upper case History"); (2) radical critics of positivist archivalism ("lower case history"); (3) leftist traditionalists; (4) rightist traditionalists; and (5) "undecided" others. See Jenkins, *The Postmodern History Reader*, 21–24.

4. Georg G. Iggers, *Historiography in the Twentieth Century* (Hanover, NH: Wesleyan University Press, 1997), 3, 4.

5. Thomas W. Smith, *History and International Relations* (London: Routledge, 1999), 13–21.

6. Peter Novick, *That Noble Dream* (New York: Cambridge University Press, 1988). The four phrases are the titles, respectively, of parts I, II, III, and IV of the book. In Novick's words: "Part One . . . is concerned with various reasons for the establishment of objectivity as the central norm of the profession. Part Two . . . shows how a changed cultural, social, and political climate produced 'historical relativism.' . . . The theme of Part Three . . . is the attempt of the historical profession to establish a new, somewhat chastened, objectivist synthesis. . . . Part Four . . . is a story, necessarily lacking an ending, of the many factors which caused the collapse of the postwar synthesis, leading to the present period of confusion, polarization, and uncertainty, in which the idea of historical objectivity has become more problematic than ever before." Ibid., 16–17.

7. While it is the case that many positivists, such as those in the tradition of Hume, generally refrain from theorizing ontology, they nonetheless ground their claims on a foundation that assumes a real, human-independent ontological world.

8. Richard Rorty, *Philosophy and the Mirror of Nature* (Princeton, NJ: Princeton University Press, 1979), 12.

9. Hilary Putnam, cited in Richard Rorty, *Objectivity, Relativism, and Truth* (New York: Cambridge University Press, 1991), 6. Rorty attributes no citation to the quote.

10. On the importance of scientific discourse to positivist philosophy, Rorty asserts that "since the period of Descartes and Hobbes, the assumption that scientific discourse was normal discourse and that all other discourse need to be modelled upon it has been the standard motive for philosophizing." Rorty, *Philosophy and the Mirror of Nature*, 387.

11. Murray G. Murphey, *Our Knowledge of the Historical Past* (New York: Bobbs-Merill Company, 1973), 1.

12. William Stafford, review of McCullagh's *The Truth of History*, in *The English Historical Review* 114, issue 457 (June 1999): 807–8.

13. Martin Stuart-Fox, "Can History be True?: A Review Essay," *The Australian Journal of Politics and History* 44, issue 1, (March 1998): 113.

14. Norman R. Yetman introduces the symposium as "a tribute to Murray G. Murphey, an influential historian of American philosophy." *American Studies* 37, no. 2 (Fall 1996).

15. See Gertrude Himmelfarb, *New History and the Old* (Cambridge, MA: Harvard University Press, 1987).

16. C. Behan McCullagh, *Justifying Historical Descriptions* (Cambridge: Cambridge University Press, 1984), 1.

17. McCullagh, *Justifying Historical Descriptions*, 19.

18. C. Behan McCullagh, *The Truth of History* (London: Routledge, 1998), 16–18.

19. McCullagh, *The Truth of History*, 28, 33.

20. McCullagh, *Justifying Historical Descriptions,* 7.

21. McCullagh, *The Truth of History*, 302. See discussion of Lyotard in the following section.

22. McCullagh, *The Truth of History*, 19.

23. Murray G. Murphey, *Philosophical Foundations of Historical Knowledge* (Ithaca, NY: SUNY Press, 1994), x.

24. Murphey, *Philosophical Foundations of Historical Knowledge*, 287.

25. Murphey, *Philosophical Foundations of Historical Knowledge*, 254.

26. Roxanne Lynn Doty, "A Reply to Colin Wight," *European Journal of International Relations* 5, no. 3 (1999), 387–88. For recent dialogue on the subject of postmodernism in IR, see Doty, "Aporia: A Critical Exploration of the Agent-Structure Problematique in International Relations Theory," *European Journal of International Relations* 3, no. 3 (1997): 365–92; Colin Wight, "They Shoot Dead Horses Don't They? Locating Agency in the Agent-Structure Problematique," *European Journal of International Relations* 5, no. 1 (1999): 109–42; and Wight, "Interpretation All the Way Down? A Reply to Roxanne Lynn Doty," *European Journal of International Relations* 6, no. 3 (2000): 423–30.

27. Jean-Francois Lyotard, *The Postmodern Condition: A Report on Knowledge* (Minneapolis, MN: University of Minnesota Press, 1979), xxiv.

28. Lyotard, *The Postmodern Condition*, xxiv.

29. Lyotard, *The Postmodern Condition*, 27, 29.

30. A very creative positivist might hold out the possibility that all that separates us spatially from the past is our inability to travel in time. Regardless, the postmodern response is that we can never know the past separate from the subjective interpretation we each carry, and that representation of the past, even a past fantastically observed via time travel, would be "ruptured" from the past "as it really was."

31. Discussed in Keith Jenkins, *Why History?* (New York: Routledge, 1999), 158.

32. Hayden White, *Tropics of Discourse* (Baltimore: The Johns Hopkins University Press, 1978), 59. Emphasis in original.

33. White, *Tropics of Discourse,* 85.

34. Frank Ankersmit, "Reply to Professor Zagorin," *History and Theory* 29, no. 3 (1990): 277–82.

35. Jenkins, *Why History?*, 1.

36. Jenkins, *Why History?*, 28.

37. Jacques Derrida, "Remarks on Deconstruction and Pragmatism" in Simon Critchley, Jacques Derrida, Ernesto Laclau, and Richard Rorty, *Deconstruction and Pragmatism* (London: Routledge, 1996), 87.

38. Derrida, "Remarks on Deconstruction and Pragmatism," 85.

39. Willard Van Orman Quine, "Two Dogmas of Empiricism," in Willard Van Orman Quine, *From a Logical Point of View* (Cambridge, MA: Harvard University Press, 1980, [1953]), 44.

40. This notion is also quite similar and complementary to pragmatist scholarship in social psychology and in particular, the work of George Herbert Mead, who argued "that 'mind' and 'self' are formed within the social, communicative activity of the group." Ian Burkitt, *Social Selves* (London: Sage, 1991), 29. For an excellent example of contemporary pragmatist social psychology, see Shawn W. Rosenberg, *The Not So Common Sense* (New Haven, CT: Yale University Press, 2002), esp. 33–39.

41. Robert B. Westbrook, *John Dewey and American Democracy* (Ithaca, NY: Cornell University Press, 1991), 124, 126. Richard Rorty has more recently attempted to develop Dewey's pragmatist project to obliterate the realist/idealist debate further. In *Philosophy and the Mirror of Nature*, Rorty suggests that philosophy should abandon the project of epistemology altogether and replace it with a hermeneutics of understanding the contingency of incommensurable premises. See especially chapter 7, "From Epistemology to Hermeneutics."

42. John R. Shook, *Dewey's Empirical Theory of Knowledge and Reality* (Nashville, TN: Vanderbilt University Press, 2000), 4.

43. John Dewey, *The Public and Its Problems* (Denver, CO: Alan Swallow, 1954 [1927]), 154.

44. For the remaining fifteen principles, see Shook, *Dewey's Empirical Theory*, 267–69.

45. Westbrook, *John Dewey and American Democracy*, 130–31.

46. Michael Oakeshott, *Experience and Its Modes* (Cambridge: Cambridge University Press, 1933), 93.

47. John Dewey, *Logic: The Theory of Inquiry* (New York: Holt, Rinehart, and Winston, 1938), 19, 20.

48. Dewey, *Logic*, 7. Dewey's understanding of analytical inquiry is in many ways similar to that found in the contemporary sociology of science and in particular, the work of Thomas S. Kuhn in *The Structure of Scientific Revolutions* (The University of Chicago Press, 1962).

49. Dewey, *Logic*, 220–21.

50. Dewey, *Logic*, 222.

51. Dewey, *Logic*, 232.

52. Dewey, *Logic*, 233.

53. Dewey, *Logic*, 235. Emphasis original.

54. Dewey, *Logic*, 238–39.

55. McCullagh, *The Truth of History*, 28, 33.

56. Ibid., 1.

57. Murphey, *Philosophical Foundations*, 287.

58. Ibid, x.

59. For discussion of this point, see Derrida, "Remarks on Deconstruction and Pragmatism," esp. 85–88.

60. Gertrude Himmelfarb, "Some Reflections on the New History," *American Historical Review* 94, no. 3 (June 1989): 665.

61. Anita Shapira, "Politics and Collective Memory: The Debate over the 'New Historians' in Israel," *History and Memory* 7, no. 1 (1995): 25.

62. David Campbell, *Writing Security* (Minneapolis, MN: University of Minnesota Press, 1992), 70–71.

63. Hilary Putnam, *Renewing Philosophy* (Cambridge, MA: Harvard University Press, 1993), 18–19.

64. Richard Rorty, *Objectivity, Relativism, and Truth* (New York: Cambridge University Press, 1991), 23 n1.

65. Thomas S. Kuhn, *The Structure of Scientific Revolutions* (Chicago, IL: The University of Chicago Press, 1962), 94.

66. John Dewey, *How We Think*, in *The Middle Works, 1899–1924, Vol. VI*, ed. Jo Ann Boydston (Southern Carbondale, IL: Illinois University Press, 1976): 241.

67. Dewey, *Logic*, 8–9.

68. Heikki Patomäki and Colin Wight, "After Postpositivism? The Promises of Critical Realism," *International Studies Quarterly* 44, no. 2 (2000): 235.

69. Rorty, *Objectivity*, 23.

70. Puchala, "The Pragmatics of International History," 15.

71. Despite Dewey's strong interest in American democracy, he is strangely vague regarding the means by which the "rules of deliberation" for establishing discourse would be kept democratic. For Dewey on democracy, see *The Public and Its Problems* (Denver: Alan Swallow, 1954 (1927)) and Westbrook, *John Dewey and American Democracy* (Ithaca, NY: Cornell University Press, 1991).

72. Dewey, *Reconstruction in Philosophy* (Boston: Beacon Press, 1948 (1920)), 134.

73. John Dewey, *Reconstruction in Philosophy* (Boston: Beacon Press, 1948 [1920]), 173.

74. John Dewey, *Outlines of a Critical Theory of Ethics* (1891), in *The Early Works of John Dewey, 1882–1898*, vol. 3 (Carbondale: Southern Illinois University Press, 1969), 242.

75. Dewey, *Outlines*, 247.

76. Dewey, *Reconstruction*, 74.

77. Dewey, *Outlines*, 249–285, 290.

78. John Dewey and James H. Tufts, *Ethics*, revised edition (New York: Henry Holt and Company, 1932 (1908)), 184. Emphasis in original.

79. Dewey, *Outlines*, 313. Emphasis in original.

80. Dewey, *Outlines*, 317. Emphasis in original.

81. Dewey, *Outlines*, 320. Emphasis in original.

82. Dewey, *Reconstruction*, 2.

83. Dewey, *John Dewey: Lectures in China, 1919–1920*, Robert W. Clopton and Tsuin-chen Ou, eds. (Honolulu: University Press of Hawaii, 1973), 57, 59, cited in

Robert B. Westbrook, *John Dewey and American Democracy* (Ithaca, NY: Cornell University Press, 1991), 281.

84. John Dewey, "Lecture Notes: Political Philosophy" (1892), Dewey Papers, Special Collections, Morris Library, Southern Illinois University, Carbondale, IL, cited in Westbrook, *John Dewey and American Dem*ocracy, 54. Brackets added.

85. Dewey, *Reconstruction*, 26. Brackets added.

86. The result of that effort is the landmark Israeli critical historical work, *The Birth of the Palestinian Refugee Problem* (New York: Cambridge University Press, 1987). Morris has followed up on this first project with a several subsequent studies, including: *1948 and After: Israel and the Palestinians* (New York: Oxford University Press, 1990); *Israel's Border Wars 1949–1956* (New York: Oxford University Press, 1993); and, most recently, *Righteous Victims: A History of the Zionist-Arab Conflict, 1881–1999* (New York: Knopf, 1999), a 751-page synthesis of his various works.

87. Morris, "The New Historiography," Lecture given at the University of Pennsylvania, Philadelphia, PA, January 21, 1997. While Morris has not retracted any of his scholarship, he has become yet more politically controversial for revealing his sympathy with David Ben-Gurion, even stating that Ben-Gurion did not take harsh enough measures to create spatial separation of the Jewish and Palestinian communities. See, Morris, "Peace? No Chance," *Guardian* (February 22, 2002), <http://www.guardian.co.uk/israeli/comment/0,10551,653594,00.html> (June 2004).

88. For excellent discussion of this subject, see Thomas R. Hietala, *Manifest Design* (Ithaca: Cornell University Press, 1985), 35–36, 134–49.

89. The point here is certainly *not* to justify the politics of holocaust revisionism but, rather, to make perfectly clear that *there are in point of fact* politics behind holocaust revisionism.

Chapter Two

Writing the Arab-Israeli Conflict

I. INTRODUCTION

The untrained student of the Middle East is mystified when seeking to attain a sense of *the* history of the Arab-Israeli conflict. One reason for this rests in the striking contrast between the old versus the critical Israeli literature on the origins and trajectory of the dispute between Arabs and Jews in the Middle East. This chapter seeks to capture the incongruity between the old and the critical Israeli narratives of the conflict by examining the major themes of the two literatures, with a particular emphasis on the politics and conflicts of the 1950s.[1] One of the chapter's main conclusions is that the ostensibly straightforward matter of discerning "just the facts" of the Arab-Israeli conflict is no simple task. As the following sections well demonstrate, the answer to the question, "what caused the conflict?" depends upon whom you ask *as well as when you ask it*. As discussed in the introductory chapter of this book, if the basic understanding of what caused the Arab-Israeli conflict diverges radically from the old history to the critical, the implications for political science theoretic research conducted on the basis of a static view of the case are as unsettling as they are profound.

As a point of introduction, readers will note that the professional background of the authors who support each narrative is markedly different. Whereas the first generation of old historians predominantly consists of government officials who served and published during the period 1948–1967, the critical historians are almost exclusively academic historians, though some are historically-based social scientists as well. In other words, the older generation of historians were themselves "history-makers," while the newer, critical historians are "consumers" of history. While this may seem to create a quandary for symmetry, it does not insofar as each generation wrote texts that were then used to inform popular political beliefs as well as other, later scholarly accounts of the Arab-Israeli conflict. Put differently, one need not have an advanced degree in history to write influential historical texts.

What explains the striking difference in the professional background of the two generations of Israeli historians? The most important response is to consider the relatively short span of Israeli statehood and the typical progression of historical narrative in new nation-states: a first generation of national history is written by national founders and pioneers, which is later responded to and critiqued by academics specializing in the study of nation and state formation. This model is not universal, but it is common in advanced industrial democracies, Israel, Germany, and the United States being good examples.

As Avi Shlaim and Eugene Rogan point out, while under the influence of state-funding and supervision, "most Arab and Israeli historians have written in an uncritically nationalist vein" regarding the history of the Arab-Israeli conflict. With regard to the 1948 war, for example, "nationalist historians reflected the collective view of the Israeli public in depicting the Palestine War as a desperate fight for survival and an almost miraculous victory."[2] To a considerable extent, this nationalist narrative was until recently carried over to Israeli accounts of the Arab-Israeli conflict during the 1950s and beyond. Thus, "A balance of power which dominated the previous historiographical phase—Israelis were determining the agenda and orientations of the historiographical enterprise—demonstrated that they did not only colonize the land but also its history."[3]

During the 1990s, however, the Israeli critical historians sought to reconstruct the nationalist perspective and offered what they view to be a corrective to the distortions of the earlier Zionist narrative of state formation and the conflict with the Arabs. The critical historian Ilan Pappé suggests that within the critical Israeli historiography, "A more skeptical view towards national elites as well as towards the history of elites, is part of an effort . . . to rewrite into history the lives [of peoples and issues] excluded in the past by hegemonic groups of historians." The Israeli critical historians have thus expressed an important willingness "to reassess, with a critical eye, their country's past. . . . The self-criticism shown by [the critical historians] has, on the one hand, delegitimized some of the principal claims made by mainstream Israeli historians and on the other hand, legitimized some claims made in the past by Palestinian historians."[4] The following two sections of this chapter provide a sense of how these alternative narratives represent themselves within the context of the 1950s and in particular, of the events leading to the 1956 Arab-Israeli war.

II. THE OLD HISTORIOGRAPHY OF THE ARAB-ISRAELI CONFLICT

The old Israeli historiography of the Arab-Israeli conflict during the 1950s provides a number of interesting responses to basic questions that any researcher would ask in assessing the causes of the 1956 war as well as of the Arab-Israeli conflict, more generally speaking.[5] Those questions include: (1) Is Israel a unique case in political science?; (2) Who started the 1956 war?; (3) What were the causes of the war?; and (4) How was the war planned? In response to these questions, the early literature, especially the writings of Israel's most prominent first-generation historiographer, David Ben-Gurion, reveal a number of themes regarding Israel's role in the region, in history, and in the 1956 war. The first of these is the motif of Israeli strategic and historical uniqueness. The second is the motif according to which Israel is the indisputable victim of the Arab-Israeli conflict rather than a belligerent actor within it. The third is the hegemonic forgetting of the Palestinian question with regard to the Arab-Israeli conflict, which is cast instead as an interstate dispute between Israel and Egypt and to a lesser extent, Jordan. Finally, there is the motif of deception with regard to both the general preparations for and the Anglo-French-Israeli collusion preceding the 1956 war. The following pages discuss in more detail each of these motifs as they appear in the early historiographical literature.

1. Is Israel a Unique Unit in the International System?: Exceptionalism

David Ben-Gurion, Israel's founding prime minister, was for a generation also its most passionate and widely cited spokesperson with regard to explaining and justifying Israeli positions on matters of international politics and public opinion. In both his public addresses and published texts, Ben-Gurion provides a distinctive portrayal of Israel as historically and strategically unique in the international systemic context of his time. This notion of Israeli exceptionalism has two distinct components. The first, or security component, suggests that Israel's strategic position and general security requirements were in some sense fundamentally distinct from those of other states. This is due to the fact that, "The entire future of the Jewish people," as Ben-Gurion stated in his opening Knesset address in 1955, "now depends on the survival of the State of Israel. And just as our security problem is different from that of other countries, our means and needs for security are greater than those of any other country. We must view the crucial difference between ourselves and our enemies with brutal clarity."[6]

As Ben-Gurion would reiterate many times during his tenure, "The situation of the State of Israel is unique. It is doubtful whether there is another state in the world which, like Israel, is subject even in normal times to constant danger to its security."[7] Ben-Gurion linked this notion to Israeli geography: "[T]he State of Israel, by comparison with other countries, is sheer border area over much of its length and narrow breadth."[8] Thus, attacks along Israel's borders are in a unique sense attacks on the essence of Israel as a state.

After Ben-Gurion, perhaps Israel's most eloquent and influential spokesman was Abba Eban, the first Israeli Ambassador to the United Nations and later, Israel's Foreign Minister. Eban too believed that Israeli strategic position was unique among the states of the world. "The special theme of Israel's existence has been the implacable hostility of her neighbors. Being unable to mitigate against the Arab assault, Israel has, at least, contrived to resist it."[9] Closely associated with this position is the notion that unlike the case with other interstate rivalries, the Arabs' goal is not merely the military defeat of Israel but its utter and permanent annihilation. Former Foreign Minister Yigal Allon makes precisely this claim for the 1948–1949 war: "In many respects Israel's War of Independence was unique . . . in the war aims of each side — the Jews bent on securing their still non-existent state, the Arabs not merely on limiting the state-to-be or on changing its government-to-be but on obliterating it."[10] Even after 1948, according to Abba Eban, "Arab governments continued to regard Israel's emergence as a temporary disaster which would sooner or later be liquidated."[11]

The earlier historians characterize the scale of the Arab threat to Israel via comparisons with the Nazis and the Holocaust. In his 1955 opening Knesset address, Ben-Gurion remarked, "What Hitler did to six million helpless Jews in the ghettos of Europe will not be done by any foes of the House of Israel to a community of free Jews rooted in their own land."[12] In April of the following year, he reiterated: "The conscience of the great powers failed when Hitler sent 6 million of the Jews of Europe to the slaughter. Will that conscience fail again, now that the Egyptian dictator and his allies are planning to do the same thing to Israel in its own land?"[13] Abba Eban echoed Ben-Gurion on this point: "There is not a single image, phrase, or adjective in the Nazi vocabulary which Arab propaganda, directed from Cairo, has not adopted and diffused in the political warfare against Israel. . . . The murder of six million Jews by the Nazis was alternately denied and applauded. . . . Israeli's very existence was portrayed in Arab writings and politics as a crime for which the only expiation lay in Israel's disappearance."[14]

Ben-Gurion and the old historians also created the sense of impending holocaust by selectively referring to Arab power in terms of total populations of Israel vs. the Arab world and not in terms of actual battlefield distributions, where Israel typically fielded comparable troop distributions to those of the Arab states.[15] Regarding relative distributions of power, Ben-Gurion wrote that, "All the states that had raised their hands in favor of the creation of a Jewish State did not lift a finger to defend the young nation against attack by neighbors *forty times* the size of the Jewish community."[16] Alluding to the Czech arms deal of 1955, Ben-Gurion wrote: "Our adversary was making ready, as many Arab leaders publicly avowed, to hurl us into the sea."[17]

This theme is reiterated by nearly every state leader who spoke or wrote on the subject of Israeli security during the 1950s. Abba Eban presented the case for Israeli strategic exceptionalism to the UN General Assembly in 1956:

> Surrounded by hostile armies on all its land frontiers, subjected to savage and relentless hostility, exposed to penetration, raids and assaults by day and by night, suffering constant toll of life amongst its citizenry, bombarded by threats of neighbouring governments to accomplish its extinction by armed force, over-shadowed by a menace of irresponsible rearmament, embattled, blockaded, besieged—Israel alone amongst the nations faces a battle for its security anew with every approaching nightfall and every rising dawn.[18]

"The Arabs," wrote Foreign Ministry Director General Walter Eytan in 1958, "have never left room for doubt about their hostility to Israel. The nature of this hostility and the forms it takes are less familiar. It has become a chronic disease of the body politics. Arab spokesmen maintain it can be cured only by the excision of Israel, which they are fond of calling a 'cancer.'"[19]

Ben-Gurion maintained this theme even following and despite the impressive Israeli victory in the 1956 war. Just after the war, he noted, "In our own case we must remember that we are living in two different spheres—one is the Middle East. Within this sphere if we are not strong enough to stand up to the armies of our neighbors, we are liable to be wiped off the face of the earth."[20] While less dire in tone than his mentor, Moshe Dayan in his *Diary of the Sinai Campaign* reinforced Ben-Gurion's interpretation of Arab intentions: "For the Arabs, the question was not one of finding a solution to this or that problem; the question, for them, was the very existence of Israel. Their aim was to annihilate Israel, and this cannot be done at the conference table."[21] Similarly, Nadav Safran, though otherwise much more circumspect than Ben-Gurion and other early Israeli historiographers, says that with the rise to power of Gamal Abdel Nasser, "the destruction of Israel became an imperative for the realization of Egypt's national-Arab destiny."[22]

The second component of Israeli exceptionalism is embodied in a messianic teleology according to which the historical conception of Jews as the "chosen people" is revived and intertwined with the history of the modern state. This message was actively conveyed both at home and abroad. Thus did the New York-based Israel Office of Information write in its 1960 publication, *Israel's Struggle for Peace*, that:

> ISRAEL, AS STATE AND AS PEOPLE, is the living embodiment of the struggle, the aims and aspirations of the movement for the restoration of Jewish national autonomy. This movement has existed for nearly twenty centuries, ever since the SECOND JEWISH COMMONWEALTH was destroyed by the legions of Imperial Rome and deportation and slavery became the lot of many of its citizens. During the final quarter of the last century it assumed its modern form, and in 1948 achieved its purpose: Jewish independence and the reconstitution of the ancient Jewish sovereignty. The reborn State has been aptly termed THE THIRD JEWISH COMMWEALTH.[23]

Similarly, former Cabinet member Walter Eytan begins his account of Israel's first decade with: "Israel was born in circumstances which were truly unique. For two thousand years the revival of the Jewish state in Palestine had been a passion and dream of a scattered people."[24]

David Ben-Gurion makes an especially fascinating study as a spokesman for Jewish messianic teleology in that by most accounts he was a secular atheist. Despite his otherwise unreligious disposition, Ben-Gurion was a most effective articulator of the notion of Israeli exceptionalism in its messianic aspect. In his address to the twenty-fourth Zionist Congress in Jerusalem on May 22, 1956, Ben-Gurion remarked:

> [W]e shall struggle with God and men—and we shall surely gain the victory. But we cannot succeed by our own strength alone. Without the devoted assistance of world Jewry we shall not accomplish the great tasks that history has imposed upon us, or overcome the obstacles that have accumulated in our path. ... Though at various times it has been given different names and titles, the messianic ideal holds that we are the Eternal People by virtue of our heritage and our destiny. This country of ours is the Chosen Land, and the period of greatness and redemption is not in the past but in the future . . . and the redemption of Israel is bound up with the redemption of the world, the redemption of all the peoples, by the reign of mercy and truth, justice and peace in this world of ours, peopled by men of many nations.[25]

According to this motif, the process of Israeli state building is fundamentally different from that of any other state. "Unlike other states," Ben-Gurion writes, "ours was born of a great and glorious vision of the prophets of redemption for Israel and all mankind, proclaimed from the hills of Jerusalem and living on in Jewish hearts for thousands of years."[26]

The motif of teleological exceptionalism is proffered even by some of Israel's most cosmopolitan founding elites, such as Eban, who wrote that, "Nothing in history was comparable to the resurgence of a people in land from which so many centuries had kept it apart. . . . Israel's rebirth resembled neither of the conventional forms of national liberation. Here was neither an indigenous uprising against an occupying power nor a colonial migration to an unknown land, but a reunion between a people and a land which had been separated for nineteen hundred years."[27] As will be discussed in more detail later, the motif of Israel's strategic and historical exceptionalism is important insofar as it provided a political justification for Israel to adopt very specific and, in the eyes of some, unorthodox foreign and security policies.

2. Who Initiated the War?: Victimization

A second motif in the early Israeli historiography regards the characterization of Israel as the indisputable victim of Arab aggression and therefore not itself an aggressive or potentially aggressive actor in the Arab-Israeli conflict. This is important because while it is fairly clear to most contemporary political scientists that Israel "initiated" the second Arab-Israeli war in the most basic sense, the carefully stylized portrayal of Israel-as-victim casts a measure of doubt over the seemingly straightforward matter of who was attacking whom during the 1950s. In particular, the early Israeli historiography succeeds in portraying the 1956 conflict as a component of a war that had been ongoing for some time rather than as an Israeli-initiated war. Indeed, the common narrative of the old Israeli history makes precisely this point.

In Walter Eytan's words: *"This is the crux of the Arab-Israel conflict. The Arabs maintain that the war has never ended and that, so far from being under any obligation to end it, they are liberty to pursue it by any means they have at their disposal to choose to use."*[28] Yigal Allon wrote: "The infiltration of armed gangs from the Arab states into Israel began as early as 1949. . . . Before long, it became clear that this harassment . . . essentially constituted the first stage of a small and unrecognized war."[29] Similarly, The Israel Office of Information asserted that: "Since the signing of the Armistice Agreements in 1949, Israel has been the victim of constant Arab infiltration and rapine and has suffered heavy casualties. . . . It was not until 1953 that Israel took its first protective action. By that time there had been 7,896 cases of Arab infiltration, sabotage and murder, and 639 Israeli casualties. Nevertheless, Israel practices self-restraint."[30]

Regarding the notion of Israel as the victim of aggression, even Israeli moderates at the time, such as Abba Eban, were of the mind that "The Arab governments saw the armistice [of 1949] as a temporary phase in a continuing war which had never been renounced."[31] Ben-Gurion recounted that during the year prior to the war, he "was prepared to meet Nasser or any other Arab ruler, without prior conditions, at the earliest possible moment" in order to achieve a peace agreement or arrangement. Ben-Gurion "offered the Arabs the chance to show the world what they really wanted: war or peace."[32] In a speech on August 2, 1956, Ben-Gurion asserted, "There never was nor is there now any reason for political, economic, or territorial conflict between the two neighbors [Egypt and Israel]. . . . It never occurred to us to exploit Egypt's difficulty in order to attack her or take revenge upon her, as she did to us when our State was established."[33] Indeed, Ben-Gurion ridiculed an Egyptian radio report suggesting that Israel would launch a preemptive attack against Egypt—despite the fact that this is precisely what was to occur several months hence.[34]

Ben-Gurion asserted that during the years prior to 1956, "The Arab states still continued their war by blockade, boycott, and the organization of bands of terrorists who crossed our borders to commit murder and sabotage."[35] The more moderate Abba Eban put it similarly:

[T]he Egyptians were trying make the Negev uninhabitable; and the Syrians now attempted to drive Israeli fishing boats and patrol vessels out of the Sea of Galilee. . . . Raids by Arab armies and *fedayeen* were taking a heavy toll; it was becoming unsafe to live in an Israeli border settlement and insecure to go about one's business in the interior of the country; the blockade of Eilat by sea had been compounded by the promulgation in Cairo of regulations against flying over the Straits of Tiran to or from Israel.[36]

Even the balanced analyst Nadav Safran says, "The *fida'iyyun* raids were not the only reason prompting Israel to launch the Sinai campaign, but they were an important consideration since all other measures to deal with terrorists had proved ineffective."[37] Abba Eban agrees: "As one looks back, it seems that there was not a wide area of choice" regarding the Sinai Campaign. "In the absence of some sharp change of fortune, Israel's eruption from siege could at most have been postponed. By October 1956 the policies of Israel's foes and Israel's friends converged to destroy all other possibilities."[38]

The old Israeli history is quite careful to point out that the 1956 war was in fact not a new war initiated by Israel but rather, a constituent part of a war that had been ongoing for some time and in which Israel was indisputably the victim. Thus, the Israeli Office of Information would write that: "Israel's defensive action in Sinai and in the Gaza Strip at the end of 1956 eliminated Fedayin bases," which are assumed to be a primary cause of the Campaign.[39] Moshe Dayan provides a similar rationale for the Sinai Campaign in his *Diary*, suggesting that "If the Arab States, led by the ruler of Egypt, had not pursued a policy of increasing enmity towards her, Israel would not have resorted to arms, even when the Suez crisis between Egypt and Britain and France exploded into a military clash."[40] A decade later, he maintained this theme, with slight modification, in his autobiography: "The Egyptian blockade, her planning and direction of mounting Palestinian guerrilla activity against Israel, Nasser's own declarations, and now the Czech arms deal left no doubt in our minds that Egypt's purpose was to wipe us out, or at least win a decisive military victory which would leave us in helpless subjugation."[41]

3. What Were the Causes of the War?: Forgetting the Palestinians

A third motif in the writings of old Israeli history pertains to the portrayal of the recurring *fedayeen* military campaign against Israel as a strictly interstate dispute between Egypt, Jordan, and Israel. To the extent that Palestinians, who comprised large numbers among the *fedayeen* units, are mentioned at all, they are portrayed solely as agencyless automatons who blindly followed orders from Cairo and Amman. Absent from the early historiography is any mention of the hundreds of thousands of Palestinian refugees of the 1948–1949 War and the liquidation of 416 Palestinian towns and villages during that campaign. Thus, from the outset, the historiography of the causes and tensions of the Arab-Israeli conflict is a purposeful act of forgetting. The dispute is instead cast as one between states and their agents and therefore unrelated to the matter of refugees or their historical memories, including motives for violence against the new Israeli state.

As Nadav Safran writes, "Once the state of Israel was established in 1948, the conflict entered a new phase and became a dispute between sovereign states. This at once had significant implications for the course of the conflict within the region and the manner in which it was viewed."[42] Similarly, Dayan portrayed the Palestinians as agents of Egypt in his *Diary*: "In addition to their regular monthly wage of nine Egyptian pounds, fedayun troops received a cash bonus for every crossing into Israel and a further special payment for every 'successful' action—murder or sabotage."[43] As per Dayan's account, the Palestinians would have no motive at all to attack Israel other than the incitement and monetary reward provided by Egypt. Thus, it was only natural that "The Israeli Government could not, of course, remain indifferent to these actions and accept them with equanimity. It was clear that there would be no end to this terrorism as long as the Arab Governments, particularly the Egyptian, could harm Israel without endangering their countries and their armies."[44]

Ben-Gurion would reiterate this motif in a speech before the Knesset: "As far as I know, this is the only country in the world whose citizens are not sure of their lives owing to the dispatch of murderers against them by the rulers of neighboring countries. I cannot imagine that there is a single country in the world that would leave its people defenseless against murderers organized by neighboring governments."[45] The murderers—Palestinian *fedayeen* – possess no agency of their own; they exist solely to be "organized" by the interstate adversaries, Egypt and Jordan. The entire Palestinian-Israeli dispute and its origins in the refugee crisis and disenfranchisement of the Palestinians are thereby systematically forgotten and displaced with a revised theme of inter-state strategic interaction between the aggressors—the Arab states of Egypt and Jordan—and the victim—Israel.

4. How and When Was the War Planned?: Coincidence

The fourth prominent motif of the early Israeli historiography is that of the co-incidence of interest between Israel and France and Britain as they prepared for and planned in the 1956 war. The key aspect of this theme is the deliberate sup-pression of the Anglo-French-Israeli collusion that was carefully crafted in the weeks leading up to the war. In his public persona, Ben-Gurion actively denied that he had plans for war: "Just as I was convinced that, in the absence of other effective means, there was no alternative to using security forces [against the Arabs] . . . so was I convinced that war was not inevitable. Early in January, 1956, I expressed this view to the assembled Knesset in the name of every member of the Cabinet."[46] Neither Ben-Gurion's ninety-two-page chapter of his *Personal History*, "Suez Crisis, 1956–1957," nor the shorter chapter "Oper-ation Sinai" in *Years of Challenge* contain a single reference to the secret Franco-Israeli negotiations at Vermars in June 1956 or the Sevres conference of October, in which France, England, and Israel planned the Sinai Campaign.

Moshe Dayan reveals a little more regarding the Franco-Israeli collusion, noting in his *Diary* that:

> When I explained our relationship to the Anglo-French forces, I said that if our assessment is confirmed and they do indeed attack Egypt, we should behave like the cyclist who is riding uphill when a truck chances by and he grabs hold. We should get what help we can, hanging on to their vehicle and exploiting its movement as much as possible, and only when our routes fork should we break off and proceed along our separate way with our own force alone.[47]

The French and British are portrayed as parties—the "truck"—unrelated to the Israeli "cyclist" whose relationship is essentially unplanned and coinci-dental. Reference to Egypt's response to the Anglo-French ultimatum in the waning days before the war is presented as if the Anglo-French-Israeli strat-egy were not quite fully coordinated: "Egypt replied, as expected, that she was not prepared to accept the terms of the ultimatum. *If this is what the*

British and French had in mind, they got what they wanted, and they can now move against an Egypt that refuses to comply with their demands."[48] In his autobiography, published a decade later, Dayan is slightly more forthcoming about the extent of Anglo-French-Israeli cooperation, alluding to a jointly devised plan by which Israel would attack Egypt and provide a pretext for the Anglo-French seizure of the Suez Canal. However, the precise details and scope of the June negotiations in Vermars and the October Sevres Conference are still quite vague as compared with later accounts.[49]

5. Conclusion

The preceding discussion provides answers to very basic but important questions regarding the Arab-Israeli conflict during the 1950s. Firstly, the old Israeli history suggests that Israel is strategically and historically unique in the international system and thus by implication cannot be compared in any systematic way with other cases from the standpoint of international relations theoretic research. On the matter of who initiated the 1956 war, the early history clearly implicates Egypt and the Arab states. While the fact that there was a Sinai Campaign is never explicitly denied, the campaign is presented as merely a response to the violence of ongoing war rather than as the initiation of war itself. Regarding the causes of the war, as just suggested, the violent *fedayeen* raids into Israel along with the blockade of the Straight of Tiran and the Czech arms deal are cited by almost every author. However, the *fedayeen* raids are presented solely as the waging of *interstate war* by the Arab states and in particular, Egypt. The possibility that Arab "incursions" into Israel are explained as a function of the Palestinian refugee crisis is completely absent from the narrative. Finally, in depicting the Sinai Campaign as a responsive act in the context of interstate war, the old Israeli history decidedly does not view the conflict as a function of a long-planned "second round" war with the Arabs nor is the Israeli collusion to devise the campaign mentioned in the literature. Thus, an otherwise untrained inquirer investigating the Arab-Israeli conflict would attain from the early historiography a highly stylized view of the causes and character of that conflict. For a more thorough assessment of this conclusion, it is necessary to examine in some detail the Arab-Israeli conflict as portrayed by the Israeli critical historians.

III. CRITICAL ISRAELI HISTORY OF THE ARAB-ISRAELI CONFLICT

The Israeli critical historians view the causes and nature of the Arab-Israeli conflict quite differently than did the old historians. Thus, readers will note

that the prominent themes of the critical narratives do not correspond to those
of the old; the notion of Israeli exceptionalism, for instance, is not addressed
because for the Israeli critical historians, this is not an important question. It
is thus taken for granted in the critical historiography that Israel is not in any
fundamental sense distinct from other states in the international system.
Rather, the critical historians have concerned themselves to a much greater
extent with Israeli internal political competition and Israeli militarism in understanding Israel's relationship with the Arabs during the 1950s. The remainder of this section investigates the primary motifs of the Arab-Israeli
conflict of the 1950s as represented by the critical historians.

1. What Caused the War?:
Israeli Political Competition and Diverging Lines

Among the most prominent motifs of the Israeli critical history of the 1950s
is the rediscovered and profound political clash between two opposing camps
within the ruling Mapai party during that period. The first camp was headed
by Mapai Party Leader David Ben-Gurion (Prime Minister, 1948–1954
and 1955–1963), while the second was led by Ben-Gurion loyalist-turned-
adversary, Moshe Sharett (Prime Minister, 1954–1955). What is especially
significant about this struggle, according to the critical historians, is that this
was not merely a disagreement between individual adversaries but was rather
a broader existential/ideational conflict between strongly opposing world-
views of Israeli security and state-building. As Avi Shlaim asserts, "Israel's
behavior in the [Arab-Israeli] conflict was the product of an internal struggle
between two schools of thought: one hawkish, the other dovish; one activist,
the other moderate; one favoring retaliation. These two schools were epito-
mized by David Ben-Gurion and Moshe Sharett, who alternated as prime
minister during this eventful and critical period."[50] Benny Morris too believes
that the struggle over the Ben-Gurion vs. the Sharett lines, as the positions
were typically referred to at the time, "was a struggle between hardliners and
softliners, security-centredness and diplomacy, intractability and conciliation,
and the certainty of war and a chance for peace."[51] As Sharett's biographer
puts it: "In more than one sense the story" of Moshe Sharett's struggles with
David Ben-Gurion "is also a history of the moderate camp in the Yishuv and
Israel Labour movement, of the compromise reached between the moderates
and the activist hard-liners, and of their respective contributions to the establishment and well-being of the Jewish state."[52]

On the one hand, Ben-Gurion and his followers, most notably Pinhas
Lavon, Defense Minister (1954–1955), Moshe Dayan, IDF Chief of Staff
(1953–1958), and Shimon Peres, Director General of the Defense Ministry,

advocated a more militant and aggressive orientation, not only for Israel's foreign and military policies but also for the structuring of Israeli society in general. This included a hard line and escalatory approach toward retaliation
against Arab incursions, violent or otherwise, into Israel territory. As Dayan
asserted in 1955, the IDF "had the power to set a [high] price on our blood,
[a price] that no Arab village, army, or government would feel was worth pay-
ing."[53] According to the Ben-Gurion line, then, international legitimacy and
law were at best merely epiphenomenal and at worst serious impediments to
the ability of Israel to secure its existence territorially and economically. Foreign relations with the Arab world were most effectively communicated
through the language of force whereas diplomacy was perceived by the Arabs
to be indicative of Israeli weakness. As the British Minister in Amman, A. S.
Kirkbride, observed in a correspondence of June 1950: "The Jewish authorities . . . always preached the doctrine that the only way to control Arabs was
by the utterly ruthless exercise of force."[54]

On the other hand, Moshe Sharett and his supporters, including Ambassador to the UN, Abba Eban and at times, Levi Eshkol (Prime Minister,
1963–1969), were averse to military confrontation with the Arab states and
the Palestinians. Instead, the Sharett line promoted a commitment to diplomacy and negotiation as the means to address Israel's foreign and military
problems. According to the Sharett line, international legitimacy and diplomatic prestige were long-term means toward the end point of a secure existence and a just society. The Arabs, in Sharett's view, could understand
diplomacy as well as force as a means of resolving fundamental conflicts of
interest.

Sharett, who was "[p]rofoundly appalled by Ben-Gurion's strategic conclusions and recommendations," searched for "political solutions to the Arab-
Israeli conflict that would avert the possibility of another war." He felt an
overriding need to "consider dealing with this danger [of a new war] through
non-military means." This included a number of proposed initiatives for addressing the Palestinian refugee problem, providing for compensation to war
victims, improving relations with the great powers, and attaining peace with
Egypt. "In a nutshell this was the outline of the alternative political orientation that he would try to develop further and implement after his appointment
as Israel's second prime minister."[55]

Sharett himself similarly defined the two lines, his and Ben-Gurion's, and
the sharp distinctions between them. "The activists believe that the Arabs understand only the language of force," asserted Sharett in a November 1957
speech, "The State of Israel must," he continued, "from time to time, prove
clearly that it is strong, and able and willing to use force, in a devastating and
highly effective way. If it does not prove this, it will be swallowed up, and

perhaps wiped off the face of the earth. As to peace—this approach states—
it is in any case doubtful; in any case, very remote.... If [retaliatory] operations . . . rekindle the fires of hatred, that is no cause for fear for the fires will
be fuelled in any event." But according to Sharett, the activist approach was
not the only alternative. Thus, a more moderate line called for the pursuit of
peace under all circumstances. "This is not only a political calculation," wrote
Sharett, "in the long run, this is a decisive security consideration [as well]....
We must restrain our responses [to Arab attacks]. And there is always the
question: is it really proven that retaliatory actions solve the security problem?[56] Thus at this early phase of the Arab-Israeli conflict, we find two alternative and conflicting notions of how Israel could attain long-term security.
Whereas Ben-Gurion's militarist line called for the use of force in order to
push through the incontrovertible reality of Israel's permanence and strength,
Sharett believed that political accommodation would best preserve the stability of Israeli existence in the long term.

The clash of these two perspectives was especially significant toward understanding the motivations for and planning of the 1956 war. "The three years
preceding the Suez War of October 1956 were an important and formative period in the evolution of Israel's policy toward the Arab world. Israel's leaders
were deeply divided among themselves on the nature of the threat facing them
and on the best way of safeguarding the country's security."[57] Thus, the fundamental divide between the two lines in Israeli politics manifested itself across
the entire range of policy issues in Israel during the 1950s: the problems of Israeli Palestinians, Palestinian refugees, water concerns, international diplomacy, and military spending. But in no sector was the clash between Sharett and
Ben-Gurion more prominent than in the activist Israeli reprisal campaign
against Arab incursions, both violent and nonviolent, into Israeli territory.
Sharett "had never been enthusiastic about retaliation, doubting its political and
military efficacy either as a punishment or deterrence."[58] This is evidenced
clearly in numerous diary entries in which he sharply criticized a growing Israeli lust for revenge under the guise of security-based reprisal. In March 1954,
Sharett wrote, "I said to [Teddy Kollek]: here we are, back at the point of
departure—are we headed for war or do we want to prevent war? According to
Teddy the army leadership is imbued with war appetites.... Completely blind to
economic problems and to the complexities of international relations."[59]

In response to calls for retaliation against an Arab raid during January
1955, Sharett writes: "The [Israeli public's and army's] rage must be defused.
That alone is the logic, none other [in launching retaliatory strikes]. I do not
believe that the reprisal will help in any way in terms of [improving] security.
On the contrary." Two months later following a major raid into Gaza (later
known as "the Gaza Raid"), Sharett laments:

We have taken off the psychological and ethical brakes on this [revenge] instinct [*yetzer*], which is embedded, for ill, in human nature, and have thus permitted and enabled the Paratroop Battalion to turn the matter of revenge into a moral principle. . . . [The principle of revenge] has been sanctified in this battalion, which has become the State's collective tool of revenge.[60]

Following an incident in which Israeli troops killed five Bedouin boys in the aftermath of the Gaza Raid, Sharett wrote:

I meditated on the substance and destiny of this People who is capable of subtle delicacy, of such deep love for people and of such honest aspiration for the beauty and nobility, and at the same time cultivates among its best youth youngsters capable of calculated, cold-blooded murder, by knifing the bodies of young defenseless Beduin. Which of these two biblical souls will win over the other in this People?[61]

These themes were repeated time and again throughout the pages of Sharett's *Personal Diary*. The Bedouin incident in particular resonated with Sharett so much so that he would revisit the matter six years later:

The phenomenon that has prevailed among us for years and years is that of insensitivity to acts of wrong . . . to moral corruption. . . . For us, an act of wrong is in itself nothing serious; we wake up to it only if threat of a crisis or a grave result—the loss of a position, the loss of power or influence—is involved. . . . Once, Israeli soldiers murdered a number of Arabs for reasons of blind revenge . . . and no conclusion was drawn from that, no one was demoted, no one was removed from office. Then there was Kafr Kassem . . . those responsible have not drawn any conclusions. This, however, does not mean that public opinion, the army, the police, have drawn no conclusion, their conclusion was that Arab blood can be freely shed. . . . All this must bring about revulsion in the sense of justice and honesty in public opinion; it must make the State appear in the eyes of the world as a savage state that does not recognize the principles of justice as they have been established and accepted by contemporary society.[62]

Sharett's views were thwarted by an institutionalized interest in military solutions to the Arab-Israeli conflict; an interest that was strongly reinforced by Ben-Gurion's long-standing dual capacity as Defense in addition to Prime Minister. Even while out of government for most of 1954, Ben-Gurion's position on Israeli military activism was advanced through his loyal disciple, Moshe Dayan. "Dayan's ideas on the paramount role of force in regulating relations between Israel and the Arabs were intimately connected to his conception of the nature of the conflict. He perceived the Arab-Israel conflict as a struggle for survival between two communities whose interests were irreconcilable. . . . Israel's only hope lay in vigilance, strength, and determination."[63]

Moshe Sharett portrays Dayan in precisely this light in his *Personal Diary*. He recalls Dayan's rejection of the possibility of a joint security pact with the United States:

> We do not need (Dayan said) a security pact with the US: such a pact will only constitute an obstacle for us. We face no danger at all of an Arab advantage of force for the next 8–10 years. Even if they receive massive military aid from the West, we shall maintain our military superiority thanks to our infinitely greater capacity to assimilate new armaments. The security pact will only handcuff us and deny us a freedom of action, and this is what we need in the coming years. Reprisal actions which we couldn't carry out if we were tied to a security pact are our vital lymph. First, they make it imperative for the Arab governments to take strong measures to protect their borders. Second, and that's the main thing, they make it possible for us to maintain a high level of tension among our population and in the army. Without these actions we would have ceased to be a combative people and without the discipline of a combative people we are lost.[64]

As a result of militarist institutional preferences and Dayan's effectiveness in advancing them, "Sharett was constantly under pressure to authorize reprisals in order to avoid being discredited inside Mapai, in the Knesset, in the press, and in the country at large. Reports reached Sharett that the army leaders were growing restive and more militant and that they were heading for war."[65] Despite Sharett's efforts during his stint as prime minister to effect change, Israeli militarism had profound policy outcomes, the most notable of which were large scale reprisal raids against Arab targets, many of which resulted in substantial loss of life. As the frequency and scale of the raids increased during the years 1953–1956, so too did the divide between the two political camps widen. The dispute over the logic and appropriateness of reprisal raids reached its first major crisis with the Qibya operation in October 1953, which resulted in the death of more than seventy Palestinians, including a number of women and children. "There is no doubt that the Qibya affair profoundly exacerbated relations between Sharett and Ben-Gurion. In turn, these recurrent clashes influenced Ben-Gurion's attitude towards the succession question: these tensions pushed him to an even more determined support of Eshkol" over Sharett to succeed him as prime minister.[66]

Sharett won out in this first round of political competition, gaining the crucial support within Mapai's inner circle to be appointed prime minister in 1954. No sooner had Sharett assumed office, however, then did Ben-Gurion, through his proxies in the government, most importantly Defense Minister Pinhas Lavon and IDF Chief Moshe Dayan, begin to criticize and undermine the prime minister's authority. Sharett fought back, proposing cuts in military spending to the 1954–1955 budget and immediately incurring the wrath of Dayan and Lavon.[67] By 1955, relations between Sharett and Ben-Gurion further deteriorated and it soon became clear that the Sharett line in Israeli politics was gradually losing support among both elites and the public. Cognizant of the realities surrounding him, Sharett wrote in his diary in April 1955:

> Ben-Gurion was heading towards war and any barrier that would be erected on his way should be removed . . . his belief in reprisals remained strong as ever, and he justified it by saying that the masses of citizens in this country as well as military leaders, like Moshe Dayan and Yigal Allon, would not tolerate murderous actions without punishment . . . a strange justification for the doctrine of revenge.[68]

Ben-Gurion's response was straightforward: "Contrary to Moshe [Sharett]'s opinion . . . reprisals are imperative. There is no relying for our security on UN observers and foreign states. If we do not put an end to these murders now—the situation will get worse."[69] Upon his return to the defense ministry in February 1955, Ben-Gurion tellingly remarked to an aide that Sharett "is raising a generation of cowards. Infiltrators are coming in and we are hiding behind fences again. I will not let him. This will be a fighting generation."[70] "Relations between Ben-Gurion and Sharett became progressively more strained, tense, and envenomed, causing the latter endless frustration and mental anguish. There were recurrent clashes over the respective jurisdictions of the Foreign Ministry and the defense establishment . . . and above all, over the question of reprisals."[71] By the November of 1955, the Ben-Gurion line finally won out over Sharett's more moderate worldview and Ben-Gurion himself replaced Sharett as prime minister.

2. Who Initiated the War?: Israeli Militarism

That Ben-Gurion ultimately won out in his personal competition with Moshe Sharett is clear regardless of the historiographical position, critical, old, or otherwise, one adopts. What is less clear but perhaps more interesting are some of the broader underlying causes and implications of the victory of the Ben-Gurion line. Critical historian Uri Ben-Eliezer argues that the course of the Arab-Israeli conflict can be understood in large measure as an outcome of entrenched and institutionalized militarism within Israeli society and culture. Thus, "during the two decades beginning in 1936 the idea of a military solution to the Arab-Israeli conflict was gradually legitimated first within the Yishuv, the Jewish community in Palestine, then within the new state and crystallized into a value, a formula, and an ideology."[72] Israeli militarism is

most vividly seen in the growth and prominence of the Ben-Gurion line during the 1950s. Accordingly, an

> institutional trade-off was undertaken between central forces in society, by
> which the inculcation of the idea that it is possible and desirable to solve "the
> Arab problem" by military means was counterbalanced by the clarification and
> concomitant order of relations of authority . . . the military solution was univer-
> sally accepted as the legitimate and desirable way to end the Israeli-Arab con-
> flict. *It became part of the natural order and was preferred over possible polit-
> ical solutions involving diplomacy and compromise.*[73]

According to this interpretation, then, Israeli security decisions, such as large-
scale reprisal raids and the Sinai Campaign itself, are better viewed as choices
that were to an extent predetermined by cultural and institutional norms and
ideology rather than strategic calculations based on rational assessments of
systemic variables.

This perspective is supported by the findings of Yagil Levy, who suggests
that Israeli militarism can be explained by the relationship between super-
ordinate and subordinate groups within Israeli society. More specifically, the
selection of military solutions to the Arab-Israeli conflict over other potentially viable alternatives coupled with the promotion of military prominence
within Israeli society served the ability of the Ashkenazi elite to solidify and
enhance their dominant role within society. The Arab-Israeli conflict thus provided a basis for the Ashkenazim to attain a "legitimation of inequality owing to the war-driven internal empowerment of the state."[74] Increased milita-
rization and bellicosity helped the Ashkenazim to assert their dominance over
other ethnic groups in the hierarchy of the military. The more violent and aggressive the operations planned by the military leadership, the more admiration and prestige were given the military from the Ashkenazi political leadership, especially Dayan and Ben-Gurion. The more admiration and prestige
was given from the top down, the more the elite units of the military responsible for implementing the most bellicose operations became magnets for
Ashkenazi youth. Thus, "the military had taken part in aggravating the external threat and concomitantly acquired prestige by repulsing this very threat.
Self-creation of symbolic resource was at work."[75]

> Satisfied with the newly created war-based reality, social groups' openness to re-
> ceiving force-oriented signals transmitted by the military command was greater
> than their openness to hearing moderate calls voiced even half-heartedly in Arab
> countries. . . . Satisfaction by nature, dictates low demand for information. A
> public discourse that allowed for two or more alternative avenues to deal with
> the regional threat . . . was averted. Nor was the Ben-Gurion-Sharett debate
> voiced publicly.[76]

Key to the logic of this argument is that strategic decisions were not taken in response to systemic stimuli *per se*. On the contrary, "agents did not rationally calculate several alternatives in terms of losses and gains; at least in the long term they possibly could have partly satisfied their interests even had the state selected a more pacifist policy. Rather, agents reconciled their interests to the newly created reality that satisfied them *relative* to a past reality, not necessarily to a tentative one."[77] In other words, militarism empowered already dominant groups in society, inspiring them to press for further militarism regardless of future losses in terms of war with the Arabs. "The immediate results were pronounced in the Sinai Campaign. It was managed as an "elite war. Conceived and planned in complete secrecy by Prime Minister Ben-Gurion and a few advisors, it was not brought to the cabinet for approval until almost the eleventh hour."[78]

3. How and When Was the War Planned?: Deception and Israel's Search for War

The critical historians clearly support the idea that Israeli militarism would lead Israel into war with the Arabs. Motti Golani, who was the first to review the most recently released archival material in London and Israel on the Sinai Campaign, argues that "My research led me to conclude that Israel had been 'in search of a war' before the onset of the Suez Crisis and without any connection to it."[79] Thus, during 1954–1955, Israel's retaliation policies underwent a subtle but crucial shift away from punishment and deterrence toward provocation and escalation in the effort to explore the possibility of a war of choice. Benny Morris too argues that "Paradoxically, during the years 1955–1956 (and perhaps as early as 1954), retaliatory strikes were also launched by the IDF in order to draw the Arab states into a premature war."[80]

While this is a stylized interpretation, it is not very far removed from the perspective of a number of firsthand participants in the events of the 1950s. Thus did David Ben-Gurion privately reveal plans as early as October-November 1953 for reorganizing the IDF "based on the assumption that the 'second round' would occur in 1956 when, according to his evaluation, the Arab armies would be ready to launch a new war against Israel. This assessment dictated Ben-Gurion's future political and military actions and moves and would contribute to the decision to launch a 'war of choice' in 1956."[81] No Israeli leader was intent on war more than Moshe Dayan: "Dayan wanted war, and, periodically, he hoped that a given retaliatory strike would embarrass or provoke the Arab state attacked into itself retaliating, giving Israel cause to escalate the shooting until war resulted."[82] Avi Shlaim concurs in full with Golani and Morris: "In short, Dayan wanted war, he wanted it soon, and he used reprisals both to goad the Egyptians into war and to prepare his army for that war."[83] Moshe Sharett provides a tellingly similar portrayal of Dayan in a summary of a conversation relayed to the Prime Minister through intermediaries:

> The conclusions from Dayan's words are clear: This State has no international worries, no economic problems, the question of peace is nonexistent. . . . It must calculate its steps narrow-mindedly and live on its sword. It must see the sword as the main, if not the only, instrument with which to keep its morale high and to retain its moral tension. Toward this end it may, no—it *must*—invent dangers, and to do this it must adopt the method of provocation-and-revenge. . . . And above all—let us hope for a new war with the Arab countries, so that we may finally get rid of our troubles and acquire our space.[84]

Dayan's desire for war is a constant theme, which Sharett recalled at least as far back as a ministerial meeting of January 1954:

> Moshe Dayan unfolded one plan after another for "direct action." The first—what should be done to force open the blockade of the Gulf of Eilat. A ship flying the Israeli flag should be sent, and if the Egyptians bomb it, we should bomb the Egyptian base from the air, or conquer Ras al-Naqb, or open our way south of the Gaza Strip to the coast. There was a general uproar. I asked Moshe, "Do you realize that this would mean war with Egypt?" He said, "Of course."[85]

Eventually Dayan's persistence prevailed upon his mentor: "Ben-Gurion forced Sharett's resignation in order to give himself the option of launching a war against Egypt. In October 1956 he exercised that option."[86]

The key turning point in the Israeli retaliation policy discussed above was the massive Gaza Raid of February 28–March 1, 1955, code-named "Operation Black Arrow," which led to the death of thirty-eight Egyptians and Palestinians, with several dozen more wounded. "Far from curbing infiltrator attacks, the Gaza Raid proved a great catalyst of Israeli-Egyptian violence. Before February 28, 1955, attacks across the Gaza frontier into Israel had been local and sporadic, not state policy; thereafter, they were promoted and directed by Cairo. . . . The Gaza Raid proved to be a turning point in Israeli-Egyptian relations and in the history of the Middle East. . . . Gaza had not only led to Egyptian counter-raiding. It had also set in motion a massive arms race, bound to end in war." President Nasser justified the stepping up of Egyptian sponsored *fedayeen* training and operations as well as the Czech arms deals in just these terms, suggesting that "Egypt was not acting but reacting to Israeli aggression and that it was therefore Israel, not Egypt, that bore responsibility for the subsequent escalation."[87]

Of course, Nasser's position could be easily dismissed were it not the case that "Records of Egyptian and Jordanian military intelligence captured by the Israeli army in the course of the 1956 and 1967 wars conclusively" dispute the early Israeli position on the causes of conflict in 1955–1956 "and substantiate Nasser's version. These records show that until the Gaza raid, the Egyptian military authorities had a consistent and firm policy of curbing infiltration by Palestinians from the Gaza Strip into Israel and that it was only following the raid that a new policy was put in place, that of organizing the *fedayeen* units and turning them into an official instrument of warfare against Israel."[88] It is not surprising, then, that both "Sharett and Dayan showed far greater concern over possible escalation due to border incidents, the former viewing it as a danger, the latter as a prospect."[89] Sharett would write in his diary:

> I am shocked. The number [of Egyptian victims (39 dead and 30 wounded, including a 7-year-old boy)], changes not only the dimensions of the operation but its very substance; it turns it into an event liable to cause grave political and military complications and dangers. . . . The army spokesman, on instructions from the Minister of Defense, delivered a false version to the press: a unit of ours, after having been attacked supposedly inside our territory, returned the fire and engaged a battle which later developed as it did. Who will believe us? . . . I am tormented by thoughts as to whether this is not my greatest failure as Prime Minister. Who knows what will be the political and security consequence?[90]

Even one contemporary Israeli historian who disagrees with the overall revisionist interpretation of the Arab-Israeli acknowledges that "It was Israeli reaction that overlaid the infiltrations with a political dimension, as Israel did not treat them for what they were but linked them to the broad Arab-Israeli context and to the country's political and security problems."[91]

Yet other participants in the events at the time support the view of the critical historians that Israel's reprisal policy had motives beyond mere defense and deterrence. At a meeting of Israeli intelligence executives during February 1953, Yair Elgom, head of the Jordan desk in the Foreign Ministry asserted, "most of Jordan's violations [of the armistice agreement]—were a reaction to our own violations. Jordan's secondary violations do not justify our sharp reprisals. . . . Justice . . . was not on our side. This in itself may not be important, but it is so obvious that it will be difficult to hide it for long from the West. . . . It is time that we reviewed our actions."[92] Similarly, the IDF Intelligence Department in early 1953 reported that, "During the past few months all our reprisal raids have ended in failure, lowering Israel's prestige in Arab eyes and causing other damage. . . . The existing retaliatory strikes against border villages must cease, as it does more harm than good."[93]

The notion of Israel's search for war during the 1950s suggests a substantially different interpretation of the role of the Czech arms deal than that provided in the preceding section by the old historians. We recall that the dominant opinion of the old historians discussed above is that the unfavorable shift in the regional balance of power caused by the arms deal led Israel to seek a preventive war. According to the critical historians, rather than instigate war due to the imbalance it created, the Czech arms deal actually caused Ben-Gurion to *postpone* plans for war until Israel could attain arms to match the gains of the Egyptians in 1955.[94] According to Golani, then:

> Ben-Gurion reasoned that even if Israel were to start and win a war, it would then face a "third round." Only this time it would have to deal with a well-equipped Egypt, whereas no one would sell arms to an "aggressor" Israel. Thus, the Egyptian-Czech deal did not push Israel into war: on the contrary, it put an end, for the time being, to Israel's efforts to bring about war. The course of events which started with the intensification of terrorism in March 1955 seemed to have been halted.[95]

Also important toward understanding Israel's search for war is the precise nature and extent of the Israeli-French collusion to prepare for and execute the Sinai Campaign. The critical history indicates that the Israeli-French collusion was significantly more elaborate and premeditated than was indicated in the earlier accounts.[96] Thus, at the secret Franco-Israeli meeting in Vermars on June 26, 1956, Moshe Dayan proposed joint military cooperation toward the goal of toppling Gamal Abdel Nasser. While the French opposed the overthrow of Nasser, they did agree to "Joint action to foil Nasser's initiatives."[97] The Vermars conference was thus a watershed in a number of ways. Not only did it provide for Israeli acquisition of French military hardware but it also contained a substantial "intelligence aspect, according to which the respective intelligence services started exchanging information on topics of mutual interest."

> Even more important was the issue of operational collaboration and the creation of a liaison apparatus for joint military planning. Within this framework, procedures were developed to obtain mutual approval, from the lowest planning echelon to the highest political level. The joint planning, which began well before the Suez Crisis, showed that France wanted Israel to pull its chestnuts out of the fire, at least as far as covert operations against Egypt were concerned.[98]

This laid the foundation for the later and more well-known conference at Sevres in October when Israel, France, and Britain planned the exact operations of the Sinai Campaign/Suez war in detail, including the logistics of a war initiated by Israel to provide cover for the French and British plan to retake the Suez Canal. Says Avi Shlaim:

The documentary evidence does not leave any room for doubt that at Sevres during those three days in late October 1956, an elaborate war plot was hatched against Egypt by the representatives of France, Britain and Israel. The Protocol of Sevres . . . lays out in precise detail, and with a precise timetable, how the joint war against Egypt was intended to proceed and shows foreknowledge of each other's intentions.[99]

In conclusion, then, the Franco-Israeli (and to a lesser extent British) collusion instantiated at Vermars and Sevres and depicted in the critical historiography hardly resembles Dayan's portrayal of "truck" and "cyclist" passing on the highway.

4. Conclusion

The preceding discussion yields a markedly different picture of the Arab-Israeli conflict than that provided by the old history. The depiction presented in the old narrative of Israel as a weak, victimized state struggling at the margins of existence diverges radically from the strong, aggressive state represented in the more recent literature. According to the critical historians, Israel had in fact been searching for a war with Egypt for at least several years prior to 1956, possibly as early the end of the 1948–1949 war. This search is evidenced by the repeated statements of Israeli leaders regarding the inevitability of a second round war with the Arab states and the increasing proliferation of retaliatory raids into Arab areas. However, unlike the earlier interpretation of the evidence, this inevitability was *not* predicated on either Arab belligerence or rational systemic considerations but was instead grounded in a fundamentally militaristic Israeli doctrine regarding the Arab-Israeli conflict. According to this doctrine, military solutions to the Arab-Israeli conflict were preferred over potentially viable alternatives without regard to rational strategic calculation. As a result, more moderate policies were not seriously considered. This turns the interpretation of the old history on its head: the very *fedayeen* raids cited by Ben-Gurion and the early historiographers as constituting a war eliciting an Israeli reaction are depicted by the critical history as themselves instigated and provoked by Israeli militarism.

NOTES

1. For overviews of the Israeli critical historians and their impact on the study of the Arab-Israeli conflict, see Steven Heydemann, "Revisionism and the Reconstruction of Israeli History," in Ian S. Lustick and Barry Rubin, eds., *Critical Essays on Israeli Society, Politics, and Culture* (Albany, NY: SUNY Press, 1991); Jerome Slater,

"The Significance of Israeli Historical Revisionism," in Walter P. Zenner and Russell A. Stone, eds., *Critical Essays on Israeli Social Issues and Scholarship* (Albany, NY: SUNY Press, 1994); Avi Shlaim, "The Debate about 1948," *International Journal of Middle East Studies* 27, no. 3 (1995); contributions to the special issue, "Israeli Historiography Revisited," *History and Memory* 7, no. 1 (Spring/Summer 1995); Israel Studies, Ian S. Lustick, "Israeli History: Who is Fabricating What?" *Survival* (Autumn 1997): 157–62; Daniel Levy, "The Future of the Past: Historiographical Disputes and Competing Memories in Germany and Israel," *History and Theory* 38, no. 1 (February 1999); and Ilan Pappé, ed., *The Israel/Palestine Question* (London: Routledge, 1999). See also "History Textbooks Replace Myths with Facts," *New York Times*, August 14, 1999, A1; and "Israel: The Revised Edition," *New York Times*, November 14, 1999, Section 7, 6.

The three seminal works of the Israeli critical history are Benny Morris's, *The Birth of the Palestinian Refugee Problem* (New York: Cambridge University Press, 1987); Avi Shlaim's *Collusion across the Jordan* (Oxford: Clarendon, 1988); and Ilan Pappé's *Britain and the Arab-Israeli Conflict, 1948–1951* (London: MacMillan, 1988). Important subsequent works include Morris's *1948 and After: Israel and the Palestinians* (New York: Oxford University Press, 1990); *Israel's Border Wars 1949–1956* (New York: Oxford University Press, 1993); *Righteous Victims: A History of the Zionist-Arab Conflict, 1881–1999* (New York: Knopf, 1999); Shlaim's *The Iron Wall* (New York: W.W. Norton, 2000); and Avi Shlaim and Eugene Rogan, eds., *The War for Palestine* (Cambridge: Cambridge University Press, 2001).

2. Shlaim and Rogan, "Introduction," in Shlaim and Rogan, eds., *The War for Palestine*, 2.

3. Pappé, ed.. *The Israel/Palestine Question*, 2.

4. Pappé, ed., *The Israel/Palestine Question*, 2, 4, brackets added. It is also worth noting that the tradition of old history is still maintained by a number of contemporary scholars who have taken serious issue with the general narratives and perspectives of the critical historians. For a prominent example, see Anita Shapira, *Land and Power: The Zionist Resort to Force, 1881–1948* (New York: Oxford University Press, 1992). For more polemical contemporary works written in the vein of the old history, see Efraim Karsh, *Fabricating Israeli History: The "Critical Historians"* (London: Frank Cass, 1997); Yoram Hazony, *The Struggle for Israel's Soul* (New York: Basic Books, 2000); and Benyamin Netanyahu, *A Durable Peace* (New York: Time Warner, 2000). See also the journal *Azure: Ideas for the Jewish Nation*, published simultaneously in English and Hebrew by the Shalem Center, a think tank headed by Hazony and dedicated to a reinvigoration of Zionist ideology and thought. A promotional letter from *Azure's* editor, Daniel Polisar, promotes the journal as "the only publication that was established to explore" the "deeply disturbing trends in Israeli and world Jewish culture" brought about by the "critical history" and "to forge a coherent alternative, and to develop a common language that can unite Jews and their friends everywhere."

5. As this chapter necessarily deals with Israeli historiography, a number of early works on the Suez Crisis/Sinai Campaign as seen from non-Israeli perspectives are intentionally not discussed but are worth mentioning. Any discussion of traditional Is-

raeli historiography should mention Howard M. Sachar's *A History of Israel* (New York: Alfred A. Knopf, 1993 (1979)), which is among the most widely-cited overviews of Israeli history, narrated from a decidedly pro-Israeli perspective, although Sachar himself is American. Kennet Love's *Suez: The Twice-Fought War* (New York: McGraw-Hill, 1969) is perhaps the most meticulously researched and ideologically balanced early account of the war. Another balanced but substantially less detailed account with a main emphasis on Israeli foreign policy is Ernest Stock's *Israel on the Road to Sinai* (Ithaca, NY: Cornell, 1967). Former British Minister Anthony Nutting's *No End of a Lesson* (New York: Clarkson N. Potter, 1967) and Hugh Thomas's *Suez* (New York: Harper and Row, 1966) discuss the war from a distinctively British perspective and thus focus primarily on the Suez Crisis engendered by Egypt's nationalization of the Canal Company. Terrence Robertson's *Crisis* (London: Hutchinson, 1964) similarly narrates the Suez Crisis/Sinai Campaign from an Anglo-European orientation and one that is decidedly unsympathetic to the early Israeli position on the war. Andre Beaufre's *The Suez Expedition 1956* (London: Faber & Faber, 1964) discusses the war from the French perspective. S. L. A. Marshall, a career American military officer and historian, provides in his *Sinai Victory* (New York: William Morrow, 1958) a military-strategic analysis of the war that is surprising in its flowery praise for Israel and in particular, Moshe Dayan.

6. Text of first Knesset address on November 2, 1955, reproduced in David Ben-Gurion, *Israel: A Personal History* (New York: Funk and Wagnalls, 1971), 447.

7. Speech given on August 2, 1956, Ben-Gurion, *Personal History*, 462.

8. David Ben-Gurion, *Israel: Years of Challenge* (New York: Holt, Rinehart, and Winston, 1963), 81.

9. Abba Eban, *My People* (New York: Random House, 1968), 488. Eban's general agreement with Ben-Gurion on matters of security in his early writings is especially significant in that Eban was a one-time supporter of Moshe Sharett, Ben-Gurion's chief rival for power within the ruling Mapai party.

10. Yigal Allon, *Shield of David* (London: Weidenfeld and Nicolson, 1970), 185.

11. Eban, *My People,* 500.

12. Ben-Gurion, *Personal History*, 448, and also *Years of Challenge*, 69–70.

13. Ben-Gurion, *Personal History*, 476.

14. Eban, *My People,* 500.

15. Importantly, Benyamin Netanyahu in his book, *A Durable Peace*, resurrects the misleading practice of comparing Israeli geography and demographics to the entire Arab world and not to any particular rival or enemy. For estimates of military distributions during the period 1948–1967, see Jon and David Kimche, *A Clash of Destinies* (New York: Praeger, 1960); Edgar O'Ballance, *The Arab-Israeli War 1948* (New York: Praeger, 1957); Gunther E. Rothenberg, *The Anatomy of the Israeli Army* (London: B. T. Batsford, 1979).

16. Ben-Gurion, *Personal History*, 454. Emphasis in original.

17. Ben-Gurion, *Years of Challenge*, 69.

18. Cited in Abba Eban, *My Country* (Random House, 1973), 139.

19. Walter Eytan, *The First Ten Years* (London: Weidengeld and Nicolson, 1958), 82

20. Ben-Gurion, *Personal History*, 515.

21. Moshe Dayan, *Diary of the Sinai Campaign* (Jerusalem: Steimatzky's Agency, 1965), 15. Dayan's historiography of the Arab-Israeli conflict is interesting in that it is generally less polemical and more forthcoming than that of his mentor, David Ben-Gurion. Furthermore, there is somewhat of a progression toward moderation and openness in Dayan's attitude toward the conflict from his *Diary*, published in 1965, to his autobiography, *Story of My Life* (New York: William Morrow and Company, Inc.), published in 1976. Apparently, this progression was even more dramatic than was at first known based on an interview Dayan gave to *Yediot Ahronot* reporter Rami Tal in 1976, which was not published until May 1997. While the interview did not discuss the 1956 War in any depth, Dayan's revelation of his deep regret over Israeli occupation of the Golan Heights and his decision to authorize Israeli settlement in Hebron represents an incredible transformation of his general approach toward the Arab-Israeli conflict. See "Dayan Reveals Regrets over Golan, Hebron in Newly Disclosed Interview," *The Associated Press*, May 11, 1997.

22. Nadav Safran, *From War to War* (Indianapolis: Pegasus, 1969), 22.

23. Israel Office of Information, *Israel's Struggle for Peace* (New York: Israel Office of Information, 1960), xv.

24. Eytan, *The First Ten Years*, 1.

25. Ben-Gurion, *Personal History*, 488.

26. Ben-Gurion, *Years of Challenge*, 93.

27. Eban, *My Country*, 21.

28. Eytan, *The First Ten Years*, 96. Emphasis in original.

29. Allon, *Shield of David*, 230.

30. Israel Office of Information, *Israel's Struggle,* 62.

31. Eban, *My Country*, 124. Brackets added.

32. Ben-Gurion, *Years of Challenge*, 72–73.

33. Ben-Gurion, *Personal History*, 461.

34. Ben-Gurion, *Personal History*, 464.

35. Ben-Gurion, *Years of Challenge*, 76.

36. Eban, *My Country,* 124, 138.

37. Safran, *From War to War,* 46.

38. Eban, *My Country,* 141.

39. Israel Office of Information, *Israel's Struggle,* 64.

40. Dayan, *Diary,* 3.

41. Dayan, *Story of My Life*, 180.

42. Safran, *From War to War*, 22.

43. Dayan, *Diary,* 5.

44. Dayan, *Diary,* 8.

45. October 15, 1956, reprinted in Ben-Gurion, *Personal History*, 498.

46. Ben-Gurion, *Years of Challenge*, 89. Brackets added.

47. Dayan, *Diary,* 64.

48. Dayan, *Diary,* 99. Emphasis added.

49. Dayan, *Story of My Life*, 211–34. Later accounts of Vermars and Sevres are discussed in section II of this chapter.

50. Shlaim, *The Iron Wall*, 95. Brackets added.

51. Morris, *Israel's Border Wars*, 227.

52. Gabriel Sheffer, *Moshe Sharett* (New York: Oxford University Press, 1996), 2.

53. Cited in Morris, *Israel's Border Wars*, 176.

54. Cited in Morris, *Israel's Border Wars*, 175, n6.

55. Sheffer, *Moshe Sharett*, 690.

56. Cited in Morris, *Righteous Victims*. Brackets in original.

57. Shlaim, *The Iron Wall*, 95.

58. Sheffer, *Moshe Sharett*, 684.

59. Moshe Sharett, *Personal Diary*, March 31, 1954, 426, reprinted in Livia Rokach, *Israel's Sacred Terrorism: A Study Based on Moshe Sharett's Personal Diary* (Belmont, MA: Association of Arab-American University Graduates, Inc., 1980), 32–33. Teddy Kollek was an aide in the Prime Minister's Office at the time.

60. Morris, *Israel's Border Wars*, 173–74. Brackets in original.

61. Sharett, *Personal Diary*, March 8, 1955, 823, reprinted in Rokach, *Israel's Sacred Terrorism*, 35.

62. Sharett, *Personal Diary*, January 11, 1961, 769, reprinted in Rokach, *Israel's Sacred Terrorism*, 36.

63. Shlaim, *The Iron Wall*, 101.

64. Sharett, *Personal Diary*, May 26, 1955, 1021, reprinted in Rokach, *Israel's Sacred Terrorism*, 44.

65. Shlaim, *The Iron Wall*, 107.

66. Sheffer, *Moshe Sharett*, 690.

67. Sheffer, *Moshe Sharett*, 714.

68. Sheffer, *Moshe Sharett*, 798.

69. Cited in Morris, *Righteous Victims*, 280, and *Israel's Border Wars*, 233.

70. David Tal, "Israel's Road to the 1956 War," *International Journal of Middle East Studies*, No. 28 (1996), 67. Also in Shlaim, *The Iron Wall*, 124.

71. Shlaim, *The Iron Wall*, 131.

72. Uri Ben-Eliezer, *The Making of Israeli Militarism* (Bloomington: Indiana University Press, 1998), x.

73. Ben-Eliezer, *The Making of Israeli Militarism*, 13–14. Emphasis added.

74. Yagil Levy, *Trial and Error* (Albany, NY: SUNY, 1997), 23. There is an ambiguity to Levy's logic here; namely that Moshe Sharett and most of his supporters too were members of the same Ashkenazi elite. This is a question in the literature that is unresolved and, though outside of the scope of this book, merits further research.

75. Levy, *Trial and Error*, 85–86.

76. Levy, *Trial and Error*, 91.

77. Levy, *Trial and Error*, 92.

78. Levy, *Trial and Error*, 93.

79. Motti Golani, *Israel in Search of a War* (Portland, OR: Sussex, 1998), viii.

80. Morris, *Righteous Victims*, 276.

81. Sheffer, *Moshe Sharett*, 690.

82. Morris, *Israel's Border Wars*, 178–79.

83. Shlaim, *The Iron Wall*, 144.

84. Sharett, *Personal Diary*, May 26, 1955, 1021, reprinted in Rokach, *Israel's Sacred Terrorism*, 44.

85. Cited in Shlaim, *The Iron Wall*, 105.

86. Shlaim, *The Iron Wall*, 185.

87. Morris, *Israel's Border Wars*, 334; Shlaim, *The Iron Wall*, 128–29.

88. Shlaim, *The Iron Wall*, 128–29.

89. Golani, *Israel in Search of a War*, 8.

90. Sharett, *Personal Diary*, March 1, 1955, 804–805, reprinted in Rokach, *Israel's Sacred Terrorism*, 42.

91. Tal, "Israel's Road to the 1956 War," 61.

92. Cited in Morris, *Israel's Border Wars*, 216–17.

93. Cited in Morris, *Israel's Border Wars*, 217.

94. Golani, *Israel in Search of a War*, 20.

95. Golani, *Israel in Search of a War*, 183.

96. For a related discussion of American knowledge regarding the Franco-Israeli collusion, see Charles G. Cogan, "From the Politics of Lying to the Farce at Suez: What the US Knew," *Intelligence and National Security* 13, no. 2 (Summer 1998).

97. Shlaim, *The Iron Wall*, 165.

98. Golani, *Israel in Search of a War*, 185.

99. Shlaim, "The Protocol of Sevres, 1956: Anatomy of a War Plot," *International Affairs* 73, no. 3 (1997), 528. "Written in French and typed in three copies, this *Protocol* was signed by Patrick Dean, an Assistant Under Secretary at the Foreign Office for Britain, by foreign minister Christian Pineau for France, and by prime minister David Ben-Gurion for Israel." Shlaim, "The Protocol of Sevres, 1956: Anatomy of a War Plot," 509.

Chapter Three

History as Case Study: Qualitative Political Science Scholarship

I. INTRODUCTION

This chapter examines the way that qualitative political science scholarship constructs and employs historical case studies to test theories of war and peace.[1] In section I, I argue that the vast majority of political science scholarship on the second Arab-Israeli war is based primarily, if not exclusively, on the old historiography of the case. Thus, the emergence of a sharply divergent critical historiography problematizes the political science treatment of the case, empirically speaking. This, I argue, also has implications for the theoretical conclusions made in some political science studies on the basis of the case. It is crucial here to note that the purpose of this chapter is not to claim that the narrative of the Israeli critical historians has in some sense achieved a monopoly of objective truth regarding what happened in 1956. Hypothetically, the old history is as good as the critical history, although it will be argued later in the book that in practice, there are definitive reasons to prefer the critical narrative over its older counterpart. For now, the main purpose is to demonstrate that political science literature is generally selective in its use of sources and that had other sources been consulted, a vastly different picture could have been drawn.[2]

II. POLITICAL SCIENCE, THE 1956 ARAB-ISRAELI WAR, AND HISTORICAL REVISIONISM

The 1956 Suez-Sinai war has been the subject of numerous books, articles, chapters, and case studies in the qualitative political science literature on war and conflict. The appeal of the case is obvious: it pertains to a broad range of important topics, including: deterrence, state building, ethnic conflict, and of course, causes of war, generally speaking. Indeed, the 1956 war is actually an instance of two historical cases in one: on the one hand, there is the Suez Crisis engendered by Gamal Abdel Nasser's nationalization of the Suez Canal Company. The Crisis led Great Britain and France to plot secretly to regain the Canal and in so doing, triggered one of the most significant East-West confrontations during the Cold War as well as arguably the deepest rift among the NATO allies during that period. This episode had been discussed at length within literature from the political science subfield of international relations (IR) from a diverse number of perspectives.

The case has inspired classics, such as Herman Finer's *Dulles over Suez*. Finer discusses the episode's important ramifications for the development of the Cold War, arguing that despite the United States's successful coercion of Great Britain and France, the American Secretary of State John Foster Dulles nonetheless failed to stand up to Egypt and the Soviet Union as forcefully as he might have.[3] Henry Kissinger portrays the American role in the 1956 crisis more favorably, suggesting that the Suez Crisis "marked America's ascension into world leadership." The year 1956 was a wakeup call to Great Britain and France that their lingering imperial aspirations in the Middle East were based more on past glory than on present reality. Thus, "vacuums always get filled . . . the principal issue is not whether, but by whom. Having evicted Great Britain and France from their historic roles in the Middle East, America found that responsibility for the balance of power in that region had fallen squarely on its own shoulders."[4]

In one of several more recent examinations, Jonathan Kirshner examines the strain in relations among the United States, Great Britain, and France during the war. Kirshner sets out to address the question of why Britain and France called an abrupt halt to the war without having attained their ultimate objective, namely, the reacquisition of the Suez Canal. In response, Kirshner argues that the coercive monetary pressure applied by the United States is the most persuasive among alternative explanations.[5] Thomas Risse-Kappen also discusses the implications of the intra-NATO rift caused by the Suez Crisis. In contrast to Kirshner, whose focus is on the coercive aspect of intra-ally relations, Risse-Kappen argues that 1956 was anomalous in the context of Western relations during the Cold War in being a rare instance of American coercion on its allies for "violation of consultation norms and the temporary breakdown of collective identity."[6] So rather than exemplifying an erosion of liberal norms, the Suez Crisis was instead the exception that proved the rule of those norms. Rose McDermott perceives the Suez Crisis as a telling example of why different actors take different risks as per the expectations of prospect theory. According to prospect theory, states that are faced with sudden losses and are thrust into the "domain of loss" are more likely to take risks with higher stakes attached to them. States in the "domain of gain" are likely to be more risk-averse. Thus, faced with the sudden loss posed by Nasser's nationalization of the Canal Company, Britain and France took a relatively large risk in plotting secretly with Israel without American approval to retake the Canal by force. The United States, on the other hand, took a small and certain gain in prestige at the expense of the deteriorating colonial powers and in so doing chose to forego the much larger risk of using military force itself against Egypt.[7]

In contrast to the previous authors, who look at the crisis from a predominantly interstate perspective, David Auerswald argues that the Suez Crisis demonstrates that domestic institutional arrangements are the key factor influencing decision making on the use of force in democratic states. Thus, the United States was most reluctant to use force against Egypt in 1956 due to the difficulty President Eisenhower would have encountered in attaining Congressional approval, especially during an election year. France was slightly less cautious but was willing to agree to use force "only after receiving British-Israeli commitments that greatly increased" the chances of success. In all three cases, the alignment of domestic forces in democratic political systems determined the response of each state to the Crisis triggered by Egypt.[8] Finally, Charles G. Cogan suggests that despite U.S. intelligence information that a military confrontation might be in the offing during October 1956, Britain and France were nonetheless able to successfully deceive the United States on the plans for war, at least in the short term. Thus, American officials, including Secretary of State John Foster Dulles, "could not quite believe in the perfidy of [their] Anglo-Saxon cousins. However, the Anglo-French-Israeli collusion could only remain secret for so long, and when its extent began to be revealed, the U.S. was forced to pressure its allies to halt the conflict." The Suez Crisis is thus an example of interstate collusion gone awry.[9]

While each of the preceding accounts focuses on the nationalization of the Suez Canal by Gamal Abdel Nasser and the implications of that act on Britain, France, and the Cold War superpowers, the 1956 War is also a second case study. More specifically, the Suez/Sinai Crisis/War also contains an Arab-Israeli dimension that is to some extent unrelated to and apart from of the post-colonial and Cold War balance of power episode described above. This second 1956 case includes the planning and execution of the Sinai Campaign, which was devised by Israel in order to wage a second Arab-Israeli war and in the process greatly weaken Egypt's military capacity to threaten the Jewish state. I emphasize that it is solely this second aspect of the case—the Arab-Israeli dimension—with which this chapter is henceforth concerned. The reason for this is that it is solely with this second case of 1956 that the Israeli critical history is concerned and thus it is only in this area that a major shift in the historical narrative can be examined and assessed. The primary question of this chapter is a simple one: to what extent has the qualitative political science literature gotten it right with regard to the case of the 1956 Arab-Israeli war? By this, I mean to evaluate the degree to which the basic historical contours of political science case studies of the 1956 war are consistent, logically and empirically, with the historical record, or records as the case may be.

In the pages that follow, I assess the qualitative political science literature on the second Arab-Israeli war in light of both new data and new ideas about 1956. The discussion focuses on two interrelated questions that have been most influential to the political science-IR studies that examine the case: (1) What were the causes of the 1956 war?; and (2) What are the implications of problematic historical revisionism for theoretical claims arrived at in light of this case?[10] In assessing these questions, I arrive at two overall conclusions. The first is the weaker claim that the qualitative political science literature has indeed empirically misconstrued the case of the 1956 Arab-Israeli war in a number of important ways, at least so far as the critical Israeli history is concerned. The second, stronger argument is that this problem not only is an empirical one but also has profound implications for the validity of theoretical arguments made by the political scientists who have examined the case. The following section of the chapter evaluates the preceding two arguments by critically analyzing the political science literature in light of the critically revised history of the 1956 war discussed in the preceding chapter. I conclude that both of the chapter's arguments stand up fairly well. That is, I find that the political science literature is sufficiently problematized empirically by the critical literature on the 1956 Arab-Israeli war and that this matters because this empirical-historiographical problem creates significant difficulties for political science theory building.

The political science-IR literature is remarkably consistent on the established causes of war in the 1956 Arab-Israeli war. The most oft-cited factors leading to the militarized dispute are: (1) the campaign of *fedayeen* raids into Israel orchestrated by Egypt and Jordan; (2) the Egyptian blockade of Israeli shipping in the Straights of Tiran; and (3) the Soviet orchestrated Czech arms deal that provided a vast supply of modern weaponry to Egypt in September 1955. These themes are to a greater or lesser extent woven into the characterizations of authors representing a wide range of reputation and theoretical persuasion in the field.

We begin by looking at one of the most influential political science studies of Middle East politics in recent decades. In the *Origins of Alliances*, Stephen Walt argues that the Egyptian leader Gamal Abdel Nasser's nationalization of Suez

Canal Company in 1956 "brought his principal adversaries together against him." Israel joined the Anglo-French coalition in light of the events of the two years prior to 1956: "Britain's withdrawal from Suez, the expanded Arab blockade, the rising level of *fedayeen* activity, the Soviet-Egyptian arms deal, and the tripartite alliance of Egypt, Syria, and Saudi Arabia," which "had already led the Israelis to begin planning for offensive action on their own."[11] It was for purely systemic reasons, then, that Israeli initiated the 1956 Arab-Israeli war. Accordingly, Israel, a rational unitary state-actor, grew fearful of the strategic consequences of the growth and consolidation of Egyptian and Arab power. The British withdrawal from the Sinai removed an important buffer against Egyptian adventurism, while the tripartite alliance of Egypt, Syria, and Saudi Arabia indicated a dangerous growth in Arab strategic solidarity.

Whereas the Czech arms deal altered the "strategic balance" propelling Israeli fears about the balance of power, the increased Egyptian orchestration of *fedayeen* raids into Israel provoked Israeli concerns over the "balance of threat," or the degree to which Egypt represented an adversary intent on belligerent action versus Israel. Importantly, Walt cites the 1956 war as an instance of France, Great Britain, and Israel forming an "alliance" to "balance" against the threat and power of Egypt. The case is thus an important one that enables Walt to support his influential claim that balancing is in fact more prevalent than bandwagoning in modern Middle Eastern history, one of the key conclusions of his book.

In order to see how the critical history problematizes the way Walt has described and employed the 1956 war, it is necessary to examine in more detail the manner in which Walt devises his argument. Walt asserts, "Failure to understand the origins of alliances can be fatal." Alliances typically form in order to engage in balancing, "which is defined as allying with others *against the prevailing threat.*"[12] Walt, in order to bolster his claim regarding the prevalence of balancing, proceeds to list all of the alliances in the Middle East between 1955 and 1979. Included in this list is what Walt lists as the "Suez War Coalition," in which Israel, France, and Great Britain formed an alliance to *balance against the prevailing threat* of Egypt.[13] In light of the critical history on 1956, this is a bit problematic. We recall that our concern here is with Israel's, as opposed to France's or Britain's, decision for war. According to the critical historians, the notion that Israel was responding to a "prevailing threat" in 1956 is simply incorrect. On the contrary, Israeli political and military decision makers, socialized by and reinforcing a long-term strategy of military force as the preferred means to cope with the Arab-Israeli conflict, had apparently decided on a war of choice some years prior to 1956. In fact, archival evidence indicates that David Ben-Gurion had preestablished the year 1956 as a target for such a war of choice as early as 1953, long prior to the Czech arms deal and the Suez Canal Company nationalization.[14]

If this evidence is taken into account, then it is difficult to view the "Suez War Coalition" as "balancing against a prevailing threat" so much as a measure of convenience in a long-term state-building strategy entrenched and institutionalized within the Ben-Gurion wing of the Mapai party. More importantly, it is quite possible that the events in Israel leading to the 1956 war might be similar to those that have preceded war in other countries. To be more specific, the Israeli case suggests the possibility that many new and potentially insecure states may opt for the language of force as their mode of choice for relating to unfriendly neighbors. If this is true, then it is possible that other cases that have been coded as "balancing" by Walt may have instead been instances of alliances formed for the purpose of state-building rather than for balancing against threat. Alternatively and not mutually exclusively, one could make the case that the 1956 war represents an instance of Israel bandwagoning with France and Britain in an encouraging and aggressive endeavor versus Egypt. This calls into question the very premise of Walt's argument by suggesting that the predominance or lack thereof of balancing in international politics might have more to do with the way "balancing" is defined and operationalized than one might readily admit.

In another oft-cited study, in this instance regarding the relationship between democracy and preventive war, Randall Schweller suggests, "The Suez Campaign of 1956 came in the wake of a terrorist campaign by the *fedayeen*, accompanied by the blockade of Israeli shipping in the Gulf of Aqaba and the Suez Canal."[15] Schweller cites causes for the war in common with other authors but arrives at a different conclusion regarding the overall character of the war. Whereas most authors argue that the various events pertaining to the shifting balances of power and threat led Israel to launch a preventive war, Schweller views the 1956 Arab-Israeli war as a response to *fedayeen* terrorism and the Arab blockade of Israeli shipping. Schweller asserts, "Israeli military doctrine, which is based on preemption and reprisal, offers strong support for the realist proposition that the anarchic structure of the international system overrides variations in domestic structure." In addition, "Israel faces extreme systemic constraints: it is a small state, geographically isolated from other democracies, that is continuously fighting to survive."[16] Schweller elaborates that:

> Israel is the only state in history to be surrounded by hostile countries that do not recognize its legitimacy as a sovereign state and that possess far greater demographic and material resources. Moreover, Israel does not belong to any formal military alliance. . . . Moreover, encircled by four hostile Arab states and

threatened by naval blockade during war, "Israel's geographic position until 1967 was," in the words of Michael Brecher, "a strategist's nightmare." From the military perspective, Israeli is a state under siege.[17]

Thus, Israel paradoxically responds to systemic threats within the self-help systemic context in a fashion similar to that of other states despite the fact that its position within the international system is said to be strategically and geopolitically unique. As a result of the uniquely intense pressures that faced it, Israel launched the 1956 war as a "responsive" rather than a preventive war. While Schweller concedes that Israel's "unique" strategic and geopolitical position make it a likely candidate to initiate a preventive war in the future, he asserts that with the exception of the preventive strike against the Osiraq nuclear facility in 1981, "Israel has not launched a preventive war."[18]

There are a number of significant problems with this interpretation of the Arab-Israeli conflict. First, the Israeli critical history of the 1950s reveals that the 1956 Arab-Israeli war was anything but a reaction to terrorism or the tightening of the shipping blockade against Israel. To the contrary, an increasing number of Israeli historians argue that Israel intentionally provoked *fedayeen* activity along its borders in several key ways: (1) refusal to alleviate the fundamental problem of the Palestinian refugees of the 1948–1949 war; (2) settlement in strategically prone border areas; and (3) a policy of intentionally belligerent and escalating reprisal raids aimed at provoking a war. This notion of a cycle of provocation is highlighted most clearly by Yagil Levy, who describes the cycle of border violence as follows:

> Once a new settlement was built on the site of an abandoned Palestinian village, it became a magnet for infiltration regardless of its distance from the border. . . . By establishing border settlements as a means of coping with infiltration and fixing the state borders, the state exposed the settlers to existential danger. Yet it concurrently took measures to repulse that danger, mainly in the form of reprisal raids in which Israel escalated the military frictions by its reactions to the infiltrations; those reactions made the infiltrators and the neighboring states more hostile and willing to translate their hostility into active violence, aggravating the potential danger to Israel.[19]

Second, and more important, however, the critical history, as argued above, suggests that more than anything else, the 1956 war was a war of choice long in the planning and not a response to any particular short-term event or sequence of events. Third, Schweller's account falls prey to a number of myths about Israel's strategic position in the Middle East. Since Israel fielded comparable or superior battlefield forces, quantitatively and qualitatively, in each of the first three Arab-Israeli wars, the hypothetical demographic and material resources of the Arab states are totally irrelevant to the strategic balance, which is made clear by careful readings of Israel's military planners during the period.[20] In addition, the claim that Israel is the "only state in history" surrounded by steadfast enemies that refuse to acknowledge its legitimacy is not empirically supportable, which is important inasmuch as Schweller wishes to make the case for Israeli exceptionalism within the international system.[21]

Finally, and perhaps most importantly, the "validation" Schweller seeks for realist claims that anarchic pressures guide strategic decisions is seriously undermined. According to the Israeli critical history, the principal motivation for Israeli military engagement with the Arab world was the victory of the Ben-Gurion line over the more moderate Sharett line and the accompanying entrenchment and institutionalization of Israeli militarism, which had in turn been ongoing since the 1930s. If the 1956 war is viewed in this light, then it is not in anyway a self-help response under severely constrained systemic pressures produced by anarchy. Rather, the war was the product of a conscious or semiconscious choice of strategy among potentially viable but not seriously-considered alternatives resulting from the fact that militarism and the use of force addressed a number of problems for Israeli state-builders and helped the Ashkenazi elite to consolidate their hold on the political and military institutions of the state.[22]

Schweller's principal detractors, Jack Levy and Joseph Grochal, in a recent and thorough examination of the 1956 Arab-Israeli war argue in favor of the proposition that the strategic imbalance caused by the Czech arms deal with Egypt was crucial in motivating the Israeli leadership to plan for a preventive war. Thus,

> Israeli leaders were driven by the fear that the 1955 Soviet arms sales to Egypt, once fully integrated into the Egyptian arsenal, would constitute a significant shift in the balance of military power between Israel and Egypt. They feared that the new arms would provide Egypt with superiority in both quantitative and qualitative terms and negate the qualitative advantages upon which Israeli security had rested since its independence. This shift in the balance of power would be particularly dangerous in the context of ongoing border incidents and reprisals, the Egyptian blockade of Israeli shipping, Israeli perceptions that Egyptian bellicosity toward Israel under the Nasser regime would continue and that a second round of war was inevitable within a few years.[23]

Levy and Grochal cogently critique the analytical utility of "preventive war" as a concept. They suggest that rather than label this or that war as "preventive," it is more useful and accurate to assess the degree to which "the preventive motivation arising out of the perception of an unfavorable power shift and the fear of its consequences" is either a necessary or sufficient condition leading to war.[24] In the case of 1956, they argue that it was a necessary but not a sufficient condition. But Levy and Grochal nonetheless stress that the unfavorable shift in the balance of power caused by the Czech arms deal triggered a strong preventive motivation among the Israeli political and military leadership, which, along with other factors, formed the necessary conditions for the initiation of war. Thus, they cite the standard systemic causes for the war: fear inspired by changes in the balances of power and threat brought on by the Czech arms deal and Egyptian belligerency.

The primary difficulty with this interpretation is fairly clear in light of Israeli critical history of the conflict. If Israel had been in search of a war for at least several years prior to 1955–1956, then the Czech arms deal is essentially a trivial factor with regard to the causes of the war. Indeed, we recall that Motti Golani specifically argues based on the use of new archival evidence that the Czech arms deal caused Ben-Gurion to postpone, not develop or accelerate plans for war with Egypt.[25] Levy and Grochal counter that "Golani's argument significantly underestimates the extent that the Czech arms sales gave Egypt a qualitative advantage in tanks and aircraft over the Israelis and overestimates the extent to which subsequent Israeli acquisitions from the French compensated for these disadvantages."[26] This is a curious line of reasoning because it essentially disregards the evidence of what the Israeli leaders actually said, thought, and did—as expressed in the archival record—and substitutes instead an iron logic of strategic imperative in place of that evidence. Put differently, Levy and Grochal argue that the Czech arms deal triggered a preventive motivation based on the notion that certain balances or imbalances of military capability *will automatically do so*. By measuring the extent of these balances or imbalances, independent observers can explain observed outcomes.

However, the available evidence is seriously at odds with this reasoning. Golani suggests that IDF Chief of Staff Moshe Dayan's desire to initiate a war remained consistent prior to the Czech arms deal, during the interim between the deal of the Sevres collusion, and up to the actual Sinai Campaign.[27] This is supported by the historical research even of historians who otherwise disagree with the Israeli critical history, such as David Tal, who argues that "In the wake of the arms deal, Israel briefly considered the possibility of going to war against Egypt. Dayan was eager to strike and tried repeatedly to convince Ben-Gurion, whether by raising tensions through reprisal raids or by initiating a military operation to capture the Gulf of Eilat."[28] Tal's point agrees with Dayan's claim in his *Diary*, which is that the IDF Chief was supremely confident of Israel's ability to defeat Egypt militarily—with or without the Czech arms deal. So as a counterclaim to that of Levy and Grochal, it was Moshe Dayan, not Motti Golani, who significantly underestimated, or to be more accurate, was unconcerned with the military imbalance caused by the Czech arms deal. If this is accurate, then the causal weight of the military balance for explaining the 1956 Arab-Israeli war is serious diminished.

While neither the Czech arms deal nor the Suez Crisis instigated by Gamal Abdel Nasser seem to have concerned Dayan, the latter did concern Ben-Gurion. That is to say, Ben-Gurion appears to have "wanted" a war with Egypt, whether or not such a war was inevitable or even necessary from a purely strategic perspective. However, Ben-Gurion was certainly not unconcerned with the question of the timing of such a "war of choice." Thus, Ben-Gurion wrote in his diary in 1953 of a possible war in 1956. But he began to fine-tune the matter of timing by exploiting the opportunity for European assistance afforded by the Suez Crisis. One factor—that Ben-Gurion jumped at the opportunity to get Anglo-French assistance in fighting Egypt—does not lessen the salience of the other—that Ben-Gurion had been contemplating a "war of choice" with Egypt for at least three years, perhaps more, but it may have had an effect on the precise timing of the war, at least in Ben-Gurion's mind.

David Rodman sets out to explain the causes of war initiation in each of the Arab-Israeli wars. His overall framework hinges on four independent variables:

> (1) Perceived threat, based on the assumption that "decision makers base their judgments on the intentions and capabilities of a potential adversary. . . . Decision makers who believe that their state is threatened, it is reasonable to conclude, are more likely to initiate war than decision makers who think otherwise."
> (2) Patron attitude, alluding to the likelihood or lack thereof that a patron state's initiation of war corresponds to its patron's attitude toward such action.
> (3) Military options, which assumes that "A state's decision makers . . . are more likely to initiate war if their state possesses a blitzkrieg option," that being less costly than a "limited aims" or an attrition strategy.
> (4) Foreign policy orientation, which suggests that a state with an anti-status quo foreign policy orientation is more likely to initiate war than a state that is satisfied with the status quo.[29]

According to Rodman, Israel opted for war because of a perceived threat from Egypt, it possessed the firm support of a patron as well as a "blitzkrieg option," and because of its antistatus quo foreign policy.[30] Further, the causes of the 1956 war "can be traced back to the Czech-Egyptian arms deal of autumn 1955. . . . Decision makers in Jerusalem assumed that Egypt would act on its frequently stated intention to destroy Israel once it had the military capabilities to do so." Additionally, as a result of Egyptian sponsored terrorist attacks from Gaza and the blockade of the Straits of Tiran, "Egypt was already infringing upon Israel's right to a secure and prosperous existence."

Rodman adds that France's support as a patron and the fact that Israel was an "anti-status-quo" state affected the Israeli decision to go to war.[31] Thus, Rodman too cites the standard set of systemic causes for the war in 1956: Israel, as a rational unitary state-actor in a self-help system responded accordingly to the need to enhance its security against power and threat, although he adds the importance of great power assistance and Israel's opposition to the status quo as important variables.

In light of the Israeli critical history, it seems that Rodman has his emphases in explaining the 1956 war reversed. It was precisely Israel's opposition to the status quo—as evidenced by its militaristic strategy and search for a war of choice—that led to the war. However, this is not what Rodman means by opposing the status quo. Rather, Rodman specifically defines the "status quo" as "the current resolution of international issues (e.g., territorial, security, and trade) of concern to" a given state.[32] He argues that what Israel wished to revise was short-term terrorism and the shipping blockade; rather, it seems Israel had a more ambitious understanding of revision embodied in David Ben-Gurion's vision of consolidating the security institutions of the state and transforming Israel's demographic and territorial position through expansion and Judaization of the land. Furthermore, the historiographical record seriously disputes the notion that Egypt represented an existential threat to Israel. While the attainment of France as a patron was important, this was itself a function of a predetermined militaristic Israeli strategy, not itself a causal factor leading the war. In sum, then, Rodman's explanation of the cause of the 1956 war does not fare particularly well in light of new historiographical evidence on the conflict.

In contrast to the views on the causes of the 1956 war discussed thus far, Jonathan Shimshoni offers a somewhat different explanation for the Israeli decision to initiate the 1956 war. According to Shimshoni, "The Sinai Campaign can be seen as a declaration of the failure of deterrence, a recognition that the threat of continued reprisal was not deterring and that the threat of escalation to general war was either not credible or not worrisome to the challenger."[33] Thus, in this instance, Israel's inability to deter Arab aggression led to an acknowledgment of the need for a new policy and culminated in the Sinai Campaign of 1956. This explanation, however, is not wholly inconsistent with the previous ones in that the object of Israel's failed deterrence—namely Egyptian sponsored *fedayeen* raids—is by definition a necessary cause in order that deterrence could fail thereby leading to war. Likewise, Shimshoni's focus is exclusively on systemic rather than domestic factors with regard to his understanding of the causes of the war. In order to assess deterrence—defined as "the dissuasion of one's opponent from either initiated or expanding (in time or extent) violence against oneself by threat of

negative sanctions"—Shimshoni looks at six factors to evaluate the success
or failure of deterrence in the events of 1956. It is worth examining each of
these factors in more detail.

The first factor is the balance of interests, by which Shimshoni assesses the
nature and strength of Egyptian and Israeli interest in initiating violence and
deterring that violence, respectively, toward one another. According to
Shimshoni, "Egypt's interest in harassing Israel was incomparable with Israel's interest in survival," yet in spite of this imbalance of interests, deterrence failed. Shimshoni attributes this counterintuitive finding to the relative
weakness of balance of interests as an explanatory variable.[34] The second factor is political asymmetries, by which Shimshoni means the degree to which
Egypt and Israel were constrained internationally and domestically with regard to initiating violence against one another. According to Shimshoni,
Egypt was relatively unconstrained while Israel was greatly restrained, both
internationally and domestically, in its ability to initiate hostility.[35] The third
factor is power asymmetries, or in traditional parlance, the balance of military
capabilities. Shimshoni raises an interesting point by asking, "Had the Egyptians really understood the sources and details of Israeli superiority, had they
known what and how Israel was planning, would they have been deterred? Or
would they have therefore known how to prepare and hence been undeterred?
. . . These are the contradictory and unresolvable knowledge requirements of
victory and deterrence."[36] Fourth is the issue of escalation and brinkmanship
according to which Israel's escalatory reprisal actions were intended to im-
press upon Nasser the unpleasantness that outright war would spell for Egypt.
According to Shimshoni, this effort failed because it did not convince Nasser
of the superiority of Israel as a foe.[37] The fifth factor is "spiraling" and "de-
escalation," whereby either Egypt or Israel or both may have had an interest
in creating a spiraling dynamic to the conflict, although Shimshoni asserts
that no such dynamic was present in 1956. Finally, Shimshoni cites reputation
and knowledge, according to which the "Israeli failure to deter Egyptian harassment demonstrates why reputation is so necessary yet so difficult to create and apply." For Egypt, 1956 was a key part of Nasser's appeal to leadership of the causes of Pan-Arabism and the liberation of Palestine. According
to Shimshoni, "Nasser's pan-Arab legitimacy was to rest on proven Egyptian
power." Shimshoni cites as further evidence of this factor Nasser's discussion
in his autobiography of the importance of the Palestine question for the Arab
people.[38]

There are a number of significant problems with this interpretation of 1956
in light of the historiographical record as discussed in this chapter. First, with
regard to the balance of interests among Israel and Egypt, Shimshoni defeats
his own argument: if Israel had a much greater interest than Egypt in ongoing

hostility, then Egypt should have been easily deterred by the substantially forceful Israeli reprisals. Clearly, this was not the case. However, the real reason this argument doesn't work is because Israel was not attempting to deter Egyptian belligerence but was in fact provoking it through an escalatory strategy devised by Moshe Dayan and in large measure endorsed by David Ben-Gurion. Second, contrary to Shimshoni's analysis, the historiographical record indicates that Israel was relatively unconstrained—either domestically or internationally—in its decisions and ability to use force. The substantial efforts of Moshe Sharett and his supporters to moderate Israeli policies were ultimately overcome by entrenched Israeli militarism of the Ben-Gurion line. Third, Shimshoni again defeats his own argument by pointing out that Egypt's inability to truly comprehend Israeli military strength points up the "contradictory and unresolvable knowledge requirements of victory and deterrence." On the one hand, if the Egyptians had *really* known what Israel was up to, would they have adjusted their strategy in order to match Israel's challenge, or, on the other hand, would they have been successfully deterred? Shimshoni himself admits that this question is unanswerable.

This raises a broader question about the utility of deterrence theory and its research program, generally speaking. If two different states (or the same state at two different points in time) would respond differently to an adversary attempting to deter them, then this suggests that there may not be an objective "logic" of deterrence. That is to say, one hypothetical Egypt might have been successfully deterred by Israel had Egypt "really known" Israel's decision making. But another hypothetical Egypt might not have been. Relatedly, even if a state were to behave "as if" it had been deterred, it is extremely difficult to ascertain empirically that the observed behavior was in fact a product of successful deterrence and not of an unrelated factor. While the logic of deterrence theory—that when *a priori* requirements for deterrence are met, deterrence will be achieved—is internally consistent, it seems to produce a regressive research program insofar as it entails asking unresearchable questions. Thus, for instance, if Egypt appeared to be deterred by Israeli retaliation, how could it be determined that Egyptian behavior was in point of fact a function of Israel's deterrence strategy? The question is essentially unresearchable and all the more so if Shimshoni fully accedes that it is as likely as not that Egypt would be deterred had it possessed perfect information of Israeli capabilities and intentions. Finally, with regard to the matter of reputation, it is difficult to believe Shimshoni's claim that "Nasser's pan-Arab legitimacy was to rest on proven Egyptian power." If this were the case, then how can the tremendous boost in Nasser's appeal throughout the Arab world following the utter failure of Egyptian power in both 1956 and 1967 be explained?

A second deterrence theorist, Avner Yaniv, takes a more broad-ranging view of the 1956 Arab-Israeli war than that adopted by Shimshoni. Yaniv implicitly suggests that the 1956 war was in large measure a function of Israel's overall deterrent strategy during the period 1949 to 1956. According to Yaniv, "Deterrence is the be all and end all of Israeli strategy."[39] Israeli grand strategy, in turn, is predicated on five issue areas: capabilities and force structure; alliances; threats; force-employment predispositions; and the relevant domestic political backdrop.[40] In light of this typology, Yaniv suggests that the 1956 war can be explained as a result of the decline in prevalence of an infantry-based standing army, the absence of a secure great power ally, and a perceived threat of attack from Egypt. Unlike Shimshoni, Yaniv additionally points out that an increased Israeli propensity to escalate its use of force as well as the political disputes within Mapai leadership were also influential in a consensus leading to war in 1956.[41]

Avner Yaniv's deterrence analysis of the second Arab-Israeli war encounters almost precisely the opposite difficulty as that of Shimshoni. Yaniv in many respects "gets the case right" but still "gets the theory wrong." Yaniv spends considerable space discussing the importance of the Mapai split between the Ben-Gurion line and the Sharett line as well as the importance of Moshe Dayan as a consistent advocate for Israeli belligerence. This accounting is very much in line with the subsequent investigation of key archival materials on the period undertaken after Yaniv's study. However, we recall that Yaniv concludes that "Deterrence is the be all and end all of Israeli strategy."[42] He then proceeds to assess the years prior to 1956 through the lens of a perceived Israeli obsession with deterrence and thus fails to appreciate the dominant elements of Israeli thinking that bore no relation to the matter of deterrence, namely, the evolution of Israeli militarism manifested in the victory of the Ben-Gurion line and the search for war. It is difficult to see how this reading of history affirms deterrence theory in any of its forms. As alluded to earlier, the problem here seems to be not one of historical interpretation but rather of the deterrence theory's more general failure to ask questions that can be reasonably answered through empirical testing. In sum, then, by casting his discussion in the language of deterrence, Yaniv confuses the case more than he explains it.

In an earlier and somewhat different angle onto the second Arab-Israeli war, Osgood and Tucker discuss in their classic *Force, Order, and Justice* the legal and normative motivations and consequences of the 1956 Arab-Israeli war within the broader context of the problem of proportionality. Osgood and Tucker note that there is a lack of consensus on whether proportionality pertains to a state's right to repel immediate danger as opposed to its right to eliminate altogether the source of the danger. They point out that Israel was condemned internationally during 1956 according to the "repelling standard" because the 1956 war was deemed to be a disproportionate response to its provocations, namely *fedayeen* attacks and "what was alleged to be an impending attack on Israel by Egyptian forces." However, Osgood and Tucker proceed to add that "In defense of the Israeli position . . . it may be contended that the action was without purpose or reason unless directed to removing the source of danger." Thus, if the "elimination standard" is employed, the 1956 war can be normatively justified.[43] In either case, they agree with the preceding accounts and authors that Egyptian belligerence was behind the Israeli decision to initiate war.

Osgood's and Tucker's analysis of Sinai falls prey to the theme common to much of the preceding discussion. They suggest that if the standard for proportionality defined as the elimination of danger to a state is applied, then Israeli action in 1956 can be deemed as morally just because Israel merely sought to take action to eliminate the source of its danger, namely the Egyptian orchestrated *fedayeen* network. As has by now been discussed at length, the Israeli critical history calls seriously into question the extent to which the *fedayeen* were a danger to Israel's existential stateness at all. To the contrary, *fedayeen* activity was often instigated by provocative Israeli settlement policy coupled with a purposefully aggressive military campaign along its borders. Put differently, the critical history provides a state-expansion narrative rather than a state-defending narrative with regard to Israel and the Palestinians. More damaging to Osgood and Tucker, however, is the evidence for Israel's search for a war independent of external stimuli. In light of that argument, the 1956 war, while it certainly did both repel and eliminate the *fedayeen* as a danger, was neither caused nor justified by this factor.

In addition to Avner Yaniv, as discussed above, two additional authors cite domestic factors as well as systemic ones in their analyses of the 1956 Arab-Israeli war. Michael Brecher's explanation for the causes of the 1956 war suggests that there were a number of necessary conditions, none of which was in itself a sufficient one, leading to the Israeli decision for war. These include: the withdrawal of British troops from Egypt in 1954; increased *fedayeen* raids; tightening of closure of Straits of Tiran; the Czech arms deal; and the removal of Moshe Sharett from the Israeli government in 1956. According to Brecher, however, the most decisive condition for the war was what he labels the "French factor," referring to the decision of France to supply Israel with arms and provide air cover during the campaign.[44] Thus, Brecher agrees with the standard explanation with an added emphasis on the role of French military assistance to Israel immediately prior to the war, although, as suggested above, he is in a relative minority among political scientists who have studied 1956 in that he explicitly mentions the role of a domestic factor—namely the ouster of Moshe Sharett from the inner circle of Mapai—as a contributing cause. Despite this important distinction, Brecher's overall argument nonetheless emphasizes international-systemic over the domestic factors leading in accounting for the second Arab-Israeli war.

The problem with Brecher's account is not so much that he has gotten the causes of the 1956 war wrong but rather that he cites so many possible factors as leading to the war that at least one or two are bound to be correct by default.[45] In this sense, Brecher's account devolves from an explanation into more of a "thick description."

While Brecher's historical interpretation is reasonable in some degree, there are nonetheless some serious methodological difficulties in his analysis. In order to measure Israeli decision makers' "images of the global system," Brecher employs a content-analysis methodology in which he tabulates the number of references Israeli leaders made to the superpowers and the UN during the months of March through October 1956. By observing that "The Cold War dimension of global politics is virtually absent from the content-analyzed speeches delivered before" the 1956 war, Brecher concludes that the "Soviet-American competition for Middle East or world hegemony did not find expression in Israeli elite images relevant to the Sinai issue."[46] Brecher makes this claim, however, without providing an explanation of how this methodology more accurately reveals decision makers' choices than do other approaches, such as examining private documents (diaries, etc.) and comparing the accounts of different actors who participated in the same events (private meetings, etc.). It may or it may not, but Brecher assumes, rather than explains how and why his version of content-analysis is useful.

Employing the content-analyzed data, Brecher, like other political science scholars influenced by the IR subfield, concludes that the military balance between Egypt and Israel was foremost on the minds of Israeli decision makers between March and October 1956.[47] However, as discussed above, this factor has causal weight only to the extent that it led Israeli leaders to make decisions that they otherwise would not have made. The critical history makes a compelling argument that Israeli decision making with regard to war was more a function of internal domestic factors than a response to the distribution of military capabilities in the region.

In a more recent study of the relationship among domestic institutions, democracy, and war, David Rousseau cites the Czech Arms Deal and the French collusion with Israel combined with an Israeli domestic consensus for war as the primary causes of the 1956 war. Rousseau argues that prior to 1956, David Ben-Gurion "believed that war with Egypt was inevitable; a preventative strike before Egypt absorbed the weapons would increase the odds of success."[48] Rousseau also indicates that Israel's strategic position as a "small country with hostile neighbors who openly advocated" its destruction as well as the fact that the Egyptian leader "Nasser had always indicated a willingness to invade Israel" are important for understanding the Israeli motivations for the campaign. But these factors are not themselves viewed as more important than the domestic consensus among the Israeli political and military leadership in favor of war. Thus, Rousseau, alone among political scientists who have written on the 1956 Arab-Israeli war, gives considerable weight to the importance of domestic political factors in explaining the causes of the 1956 Arab-Israeli war.

Unlike the scholars discussed above, Rousseau examines the 1956 war in light of broader debates over "Democratic Peace," assessing the extent to which the monadic hypothesis of the democratic peace theory holds in light of the Suez-Sinai war. According to this hypothesis, democratic states—as a result of their being democratic—are less likely to initiate war against other states, regardless of whether the latter are democratic or not. According to Rousseau, the 1956 war fails to support the monadic hypothesis of the democratic peace research program because "opposition to the use of force failed to emerge within the potentially constraining institutions (i.e., coalition cabinets and legislatures)."[49] This explanation is certainly consistent with the historiographical record, although it does discount somewhat the existence and intensity of the struggle between Sharett and Ben-Gurion and their respective lines during the years preceding 1956. So while Rousseau may not have gotten the case of the 1956 war fully right as per the critical historical narrative, this partial failure does not greatly affect the overall salience of his broader theoretical argument. In an important sense, then, the critical history supports Rousseau insofar as it demonstrates that there were in fact democratic opponents to Israeli militarism and the war option in 1956, although history has shown that they were ultimately outnumbered and defeated within the Mapai party.

III. CONCLUSION

Several conclusions can be drawn from the preceding discussion of the qualitative political science literature on the 1956 Arab-Israeli war. First, international or systemic factors are much more significant in the literature than are domestic ones for understanding how and why Israel chose to initiate war in 1956. Second, the various specific factors mentioned generally fall into two categories: (1) shifts in the regional balance of power pertaining to the Czech arms deal and the fear this provoked in Israel; and (2) shifts in the balance of threat pertaining to a perceived rise in Egyptian belligerence toward Israel in the form of increased sponsorship of *fedayeen* raids and an intensification of the blockade of Israeli shipping in the region. It is explicitly not the purpose of this chapter to question the historical validity of these factors per se: they occurred and they were not wholly insignificant. However, if we are to take the critical Israeli history seriously, the two arguments presented in the introduction to the chapter appear to command considerable support.[50]

That is, first, the political science literature generally speaking has gotten the case of the 1956 Arab-Israeli war wrong in light of the revised narrative of the case. Second, there appears to be substantial support for the claim that the political science case studies on 1956 are sufficiently flawed empirically to suggest serious inconsistencies in the theoretical claims made by a number of authors who examined the case. According to critical historical scholarship based on both new archival material and new political understandings about Israel, it is more important and accurate to characterize the 1956 Arab-Israeli war as the result of a political struggle between two sharply divergent political strategies toward Israeli state-building; a competition that had been ongoing for at least a decade prior to the war. That factor, bolstered by the steady institutionalization of militarism within the Israeli state-society nexus, appears to have been significantly more salient than the balance of power or threat in explaining why Israeli leaders decided to plan and launch the Sinai Campaign. Again, this is not to say that power and threat are causally inconsequential; it would be foolish to say that Israel would have undertaken a war if its border with Egypt were akin to the American border with Canada. But there is nonetheless compelling evidence indicating that the dominant elites in power within Israel *preferred* war over other potentially viable alternatives, all else being equal.

Second, in terms of traditional IR theory, the preceding analysis sheds some light on the unresolved dispute between adherents to Waltzian third-image structural realism and their various critics, most notably second-image neoliberal institutionalists.[51] As presently conceived, the preceding evidence and arguments appear, at least superficially, to score a victory for the second-image; a triumph of the importance of domestic politics over systemic and strategic factors in understanding causes of conflict and decisions to go to war. Despite the attractiveness of this position, I strongly caution against rushing to such a conclusion because to do so obscures the more profound point of this chapter, which is that the problem of historical epistemology as manifested in historical revisionism is a major issue in political science research. The chapter argues that domestic politics matter not because they inherently do so but because in this particular case the most recent historical narrative indicates that they do. Had the narrative been different—and in other cases, it is likely to be so—a different IR paradigm might have emerged victorious, so to speak. Thus, this analysis should not be seen as a simple validation of neoliberal international relations theory. Indeed, if any theoretical research program is ultimately "validated" by the Israeli critical history, it is neither IR realism nor IR liberalism, but the macrohistorical sociological literature on state building in the tradition of Charles Tilly. Thus, the dual purpose of domestic institution building and political posturing while simultaneously coping with the Arab threat should sound a strong note of familiarity to those acquainted with Tilly's work on war making and state making.[52]

A third conclusion one might draw from this chapter is that the preconceived balance-of-power proclivity of IR led to a generally distorted process of case construction in the instance of the second Arab-Israeli war. That is to say, it was assumed that the balance of power and threat matters *prior to* creating the case study. This in turn seems to have led many authors to construct cases in which Israel was found to be solely or predominantly concerned with—lo and behold—the balance of power and threat. A more interesting and fruitful way to proceed would have been to ask: what does the historiographical record—seen as a multilayered and often problematic set of literatures—reveal in a given case? The preceding discussion indicates that this is a critical question, and one that requires a good deal of time and research to respond to.

Finally, this chapter is not intended as a wholesale critique of deductive theorizing in political science. However, it does suggest that political scientists should not assume historians to be atheoretical, since they clearly are not. Given this to be the case, the real problem here is political scientists' proclivity to treat the narratives of historians as a cumulative sum of unproblematic data, analogous to the elements and compounds of the chemist's lab. This project takes issue with that view and suggests that the "give and take" of theory and historiography needs to be more of a two-way dynamic between political science and history. In terms of theory development, I would suggest that political scientists have been engaged in too much deductive "giving" and not enough "taking," in the sense of ascertaining the preexisting theories already embedded in the historical narrative necessary for empirical political science research. This matter is discussed in more depth in chapter 7.

NOTES

1. I specify that the literature surveyed in this chapter is qualitative. The quantitative IR literature is discussed in detail separately in chapter 4.

2. This chapter is *not* aimed at critiquing secondary-source research for its reliance on secondary historical texts. To the contrary, it is assumed that many, if not most political scientists work with secondary sources—that is, texts written by historians,

broadly defined—and that genuinely insightful, first-rate scholarship can be produced on that basis. My aim, then, is to help political scientists produce more discriminating and sophisticated scholarship when using secondary sources.

3. Herman Finer, *Dulles over Suez* (Chicago: Quadrangle, 1964), see esp., 491–512.

4. Henry Kissinger, *Diplomacy* (New York: Random House, Simon and Schuster, 1994), 548; see discussion, 522–49.

5. Jonathan Kirshner, *Currency and Coercion* (Princeton, NJ: Princeton University Press, 1995), 63–82. Kirshner concludes that "The Suez case is not the story of one isolated attempt at the practice of monetary diplomacy, but rather is a part of a complete cycle of currency manipulation involving the United States and Britain." Ibid., 81.

6. Thomas Risse-Kappen, *Cooperation among Democracies*, (Princeton: Princeton University Press, 1995), 84; see discussion, 83–104.

7. Rose McDermott, *Risk-Taking in International Politics* (Ann Arbor: The University of Michigan Press, 1998), 135–64.

8. David P. Auerswald, "Inward Bound: Domestic Institutions and Military Conflicts," *International Organization*, vol. 53, no. 3 (Summer 1999), 489; see discussion, 481–89.

9. Charles G. Cogan, "From the Politics of Lying to the Farce at Suez: What the US Knew," *Intelligence and National Security* 13, no. 2 (Summer 1998): 119. Brackets added.

10. One study not discussed at length here is worthy of mention: Richard K. Betts refers to the 1956 Sinai Campaign as an example of when states "skip" steps of escalation, as Israel apparently did in 1956. Betts's point is well taken, but the reference is too brief to merit substantial discussion in the present study. Betts, "Surprise Despite Warning: Why Sudden Attacks Succeed," *Political Science Quarterly* 95, no. 4 (Winter 1980–1981): 562.

11. Stephen M. Walt, *The Origins of Alliances* (Ithaca: Cornell University Press, 1987), 63.

12. Walt, *The Origins of Alliances*, 2, 17. Emphasis added.

13. Walt, *The Origins of Alliances*, 159.

14. Sheffer, *Moshe Sharett*, 690.

15. Randall L. Schweller, "Domestic Structure and Preventive War," *World Politics* 44, no. 2 (1992): 264.

16. Schweller, "Domestic Structure and Preventive War," 265.

17. Schweller, "Domestic Structure and Preventive War," 265–66.

18. Schweller, "Domestic Structure and Preventive War," 264.

19. Y. Levy, *Trial and Error*, 64.

20. See, for instance, Moshe Dayan, *Diary of the Sinai Campaign* (Jerusalem: Steimatzky's Agency, 1965). For statistical measures of battlefield capabilities, see Edgar O'Ballance, *The Arab-Israeli War 1948* (New York: Praeger, 1957); Gunther E. Rothenberg, *The Anatomy of the Israeli Army* (London: B. T. Batsford, 1979); and Nadav Safran, *From War to War* (New York: Pegasus, 1969).

21. Schweller's claim is especially weakened by the presence of a robust tradition in the historical sociology of Europe describing how proto-states failed to survive the

predatory behavior of their neighbors. See Charles Tilly, "War Making and State Making as Organized Crime," in Peter Evans et al., *Bringing the State Back In* (Cambridge: Cambridge University Press, 1985) and Tilly, *Coercion, Capital, and European States* (Cambridge, MA: Blackwell, 1992). Similarly, a number of aspirant states in the contemporary world suffer from the hostility of their neighbors, including East Timor, Kurdistan, Nagorno-Karabagh, Western Sahara, Tibet, Kosovo, Chechnya, and Somaliland.

22. It is admittedly problematic to consider that Moshe Sharett and most of his supporters too were members of the same Ashkenazi elite. This is a question in the literature that is unresolved but which likely merits further attention.

23. Jack S. Levy and Joseph R. Grochal, "Democracy and Preventive War: Israel and the 1956 Sinai Campaign," Paper presented at the Annual Meeting of the American Political Science Association (APSA), September 2–5, 1999, 9; see more detailed discussion of the Czech arms deal on 12–19.

24. Levy and Grochal, "Democracy and Preventive War," 3–6.

25. Golani, *Israel in Search of a War,* 20.

26. Levy and Grochal, "Democracy and Preventive War," 17.

27. Golani, *Israel in Search of a War,* 13–20.

28. Tal, "Israel's Road to the 1956 War," 72.

29. David Rodman, "War Initiation: The Case of Israel," *The Journal of Strategic Studies* 20, no. 4 (December 1997): 3–4.

30. Rodman, "War Initiation," 6.

31. Rodman, "War Initiation," 5–6.

32. Rodman, "War Initiation," 4.

33. Jonathan Shimshoni, *Israel and Conventional Deterrence* (Ithaca, NY: Cornell University Press, 1988), 120.

34. Shimshoni, *Israel and Conventional Deterrence,* 95.

35. Shimshoni, *Israel and Conventional Deterrence,* 96–103.

36. Shimshoni, *Israel and Conventional Deterrence,* 108.

37. Shimshoni, *Israel and Conventional Deterrence,* 109.

38. Shimshoni, *Israel and Conventional Deterrence,* 95, 114, 117.

39. Yaniv, *Deterrence without the Bomb,* 1.

40. Yaniv, *Deterrence without the Bomb,* 24–25.

41. Yaniv, *Deterrence without the Bomb,* 55–71.

42. Yaniv, *Deterrence without the Bomb,* 1.

43. Robert E. Osgood and Robert W. Tucker, *Force, Order, and Justice* (Baltimore: The Johns Hopkins Press, 1967), 300, n65.

44. Brecher, *Decisions in Israeli Foreign Policy,* 262.

45. The density of Brecher's study is explained by the fact that he, along with Avner Yaniv, alone among the IR scholars cited in this chapter is also an Israel Studies specialist.

46. Brecher, *Decision's in Israel's Foreign Policy,* 238–39.

47. Brecher, *Decision's in Israel's Foreign Policy,* 246.

48. Rousseau, "Domestic Political Institutions," 75.

49. Rousseau, "Domestic Political Institutions," 77.

50. To reiterate: the purpose of this chapter is only to take the Israeli critical historiography seriously, not to claim that it has attained a monopoly of historical truth over and above any other interpretation.

51. For the seminal volumes encapsulating that debate, see Robert O. Keohane, ed., *Neorealism and Its Critics* (New York: Columbia University Press, 1986); and David A. Baldwin, ed., *Neorealism and Neoliberalism* (New York: Columbia University Press, 1993). For a more recent discussion of the debate from the realist perspective, see Gideon Rose, "Neoclassical Realism and Theories of Foreign Policy," *World Politics* 51 (October 1998): 144–72.

52. See "War Making and State Making as Organized Crime," in Peter Evans et al., *Bringing the State Back In* (Cambridge: Cambridge University Press, 1985); and Charles Tilly, *Coercion, Capital, and European States* (Cambridge, MA: Blackwell, 1992).

Chapter Four

History as Data Point:
The 1956 Arab-Israeli War
and Quantitative IR

I. INTRODUCTION

The previous chapter examined the problem of historical revisionism in the context of qualitative political science literature on the 1956 Arab-Israeli war. In contrast, this chapter seeks to assess the way in which scholars approach historical inquiry in the construction of large sample data sets. As discussed in the introduction to this book, it is assumed that all political science inquiry—whether qualitative or quantitative—is historical in character. If this is the case, then the questions and problems discussed in the previous chapters should be equally pertinent to an analysis of quantitative political science scholarship. This chapter thus seeks to assess the cogency of that claim. In order to do so, the chapter begins by discussing very briefly the aims of quantitative political science scholarship and the process by which historical material is made into data in the construction of large sample data sets, such as the various Correlates of War (COW) project data sets, widely cited and employed in the subfield of international relations (IR).

It is important to note for readers unfamiliar with the COW that it is not itself a single data set, but rather a collection of data sets and offshoot projects that have accumulated over time. Since its establishment by J. David Singer at the University of Michigan in 1963, the COW project has helped to spur a generation of increasingly larger and more sophisticated data sets. This was even more so the case during the past two decades following the widespread use and availability of personal computers. Well-known data sets affiliated with the COW include, among others, the COW International and Civil War data set, Behavioral Correlates of War (BCOW) data sets, and the various Militarized Interstate Disputes (MID) data sets, which were first reported by

Gochman and Maoz in 1984. The most recent MID, Version 2.1 (1996), is discussed in section II of this chapter.[1]

Sections III, IV, and V below examine the coding of both the 1956 War and the specific Israeli involvement in the war as per the data in the Militarized Interstate Dispute (MID) Version 2.1 data set, the Correlates of War (COW) International and Civil War data set, and the Interstate Crisis Behavior (ICB) Project data set, respectively. The chapter concludes that despite the best efforts of the Correlates of War project and its adherents and disciples to standardize and streamline the process of quantitative historical analysis, their project is riddled with problems, especially in light of the complexity of historical inquiry alluded to in the previous three chapters.

II. CREATING DATA FROM HISTORIOGRAPHY: CODING AND ITS CRITICS

The relationship between quantitative political science and history during the past thirty or so years has not been especially smooth. The principal lines of disagreement among adherents to and detractors from the quantitative methods are twofold. First, historians and quantitative political science scholars have a basic disagreement about what each actually does and what is possible to be achieved in terms of historical analysis. Thus, of the divide between the quantitative movement and its detractors, Bruce Russett alludes to "substantial criticism of outsiders who, partly because of the practitioners' failures to communicate adequately, do not entirely understand what they are criticizing."[2]

J. David Singer, founder of the Correlates of War (COW) project at the University of Michigan, asserts that in the absence of rigorous quantitative analysis, "our understanding of the past will remain in the hands of the literati, responding to one revisionist or counter-revisionist interpretation after another, as the consensus ebbs and flows."[3] Singer further criticizes historians writ large: "undue preoccupation, yea obsession, with the unique, the discrete, the non-comparable, is what has largely kept history from developing into a cumulative discipline."[4] "True, the historian can continue to pile up facts and do his case studies, but only as he borrows from the social sciences can he produce hard evidence or compelling interpretations of the past."[5] Diplomatic historian Paul Schroeder responds that "judging present actions and intentions solely on the basis of the pattern of past actions, the behavioral science approach, cannot work, or must work badly. . . . Surely a sounder way is the normal historian's method: to consider what lay behind an action, including the pattern of past actions, to consider its purpose, looking for evidence both in the action itself and in the testimony of participants and observers; to see how it developed and what it led to; and to weigh these elements together and against each other."[6]

A second line of disagreement in the debate over quantitative political science regards the theory-rich vs. data-rich distinction among political scientists. More specifically, Singer and like-minded quantitative scholars are critical of qualitative political science for being long on theorization ("theory-rich") but impoverished in terms of substantive data with which to test theoretical claims. Singer thus asserts, "The discipline can only prosper to the extent that each of us is both a producer and a consumer of operational evidence."[7] Employing history quantitatively, Singer argues, is clearly the best alternative to "armchair analysis and polemics."[8] "We either rediscover the wheel via cyclical repetition of fashionable arguments or we pull up our socks and commit ourselves to a cumulative search for regularities and patterns—as well as deviations there from—in the dynamics of world politics."[9]

This, in turn, will produce far-reaching benefits not only for political science, but for policy making and governance as well. "As our knowledge base expands and is increasingly integrated in the theoretical sense, the better our predictions will be. . . . That is, more and more value conflicts will be translatable into the more tractable form of predictive conflicts thus bridging the gap between fact and value, and liberating our predictions from our preferences."[10] In order to overcome inherent human bias in the effort to eliminate or at least reduce the incidence of war, quantitative methods are most essential: "The inertia of collective beliefs and institutionalized folklore is a wondrous force indeed, and it" is evident to Singer and his colleagues "that some combination of an epistemological revolution and a cascade of hard evidence would be essential ingredients in the ultimate abolition of war and its related disasters."[11] "Put another way, many of humanity's tragedies might have been avoided, had the social sciences been further along and had the relevant knowledge been available to (and credible to) those whose acts contributed to such tragedies."[12]

Michael Brecher, co-founder with Jonathan Wilkenfeld of the ICB data set discussed in section V below, has a similar view: "the aim of the project is to shed light on a pervasive phenomenon of twentieth-century world politics through the accumulation and dissemination of knowledge about all international and foreign-policy crises. . . . In terms of policy relevance to the future of world politics, the aim is to use this knowledge to enhance the quality and effectiveness of crisis management . . . and, at the macrolevel, to reduce the likelihood of escalation of crises to full-scale war."[13] The quantitative approach is further superior to qualitative in that the former's "central goal is to put its entire argument in the public domain so that others may judge, accept, or reject, and build upon the research." Quantitative scholars thus emphasize in particular the "exact specification of assumptions . . . and the use of standard forms of logic and mathematics to draw conclusions for the assumptions, a precise statement of measurement rules . . . a careful attention to possible biases . . . and an explicit selection of decision rules used in assessing hypotheses."[14] But it is the evidence generating function that is the heart of the quantitative movement. "In the absence of a formal theory," says Singer, the "search for regularity and covariation may seem pointless to some, but I would argue that it is the most useful and creative work we can do now."[15] Insofar as producing evidence—that is, historical evidence—in the form of data is crucial to the quantitative research program, it is worthwhile to discuss in some additional detail the manner in which this is done.

In their recent explanation of the Militarized Interstate Dispute (MID) database of the COW project, Singer, Jones, and Bremer articulate two goals of the project. The first is to "attempt to develop a full understanding of what conceptually constitutes a militarized interstate dispute by providing an operational definition and a detailed description of the process used to collect historical information within the data set." The second is to "seek to add to existential and correlational knowledge about the distribution and characteristics of militarized interstate disputes since 1816."[16] The data collection process is predicated "On the assumptions that the intelligent student, regardless of major field, could learn to prepare and adhere to highly operational coding rules and that knowledge of the sources was needed more than conceptual or theoretical sophistication." Accordingly, the COW project originally turned to historians as coders for the data set. Singer notes that "much of our data is literally *made* by converting the buzzing welter of historical traces into analytically useful indicators."[17] "'Unrefined' pieces of information must be combined or manipulated to produce empirical indicators of complex concepts, such as severity of war or the degree of bipolarity in the international system."[18] In order to collect and process the data for the more recent MID 2.1 project:

> A wide variety of source material was used . . . including government documents, historical monographs, case studies, diplomatic histories, and newspapers. Whenever possible, coder were assigned to collect chronological data in their regional or language area of expertise. Sources in several languages were consulted, including Russian, Polish, German, Italian, French, Spanish, Portuguese, Turkish, Greek, Arabic, Hebrew, Chinese, Japanese, Korean, and English. To help ensure that the militarized interstate dispute data is as historically accurate as possible, several chronologies of militarized events were independently constructed for each dispute. Upon completion, these overlapping chronologies were checked for intercoder convergence and then combined to

form one chronology after all discrepancies were reconciled. Each MID was formed by aggregating incidents into the rules laid out above. Before a militarized dispute was officially accepted, all spatial and temporal characteristics of the dispute were independently verified by two senior coders not involved with the original framing of the militarized dispute. When discrepancies in case formation or characteristics surrounding the dispute appeared, each problem was resolved through further consultation of experts and diplomatic historians.[19]

While this to some extent clarifies the process by which history becomes data, certain significant questions remain. First, certain historical events provoke vociferous and unresolved debate as to their basic narratives. How, specifically, were discrete, unified narratives derived by Singer and company from the disparate literatures on problematic cases? The focus of this book provides an ideal example: which narrative—the old or the Israeli critical history, or both—was consulted to code the Arab-Israeli cases? How were distinctions in interpretation of the facts accounted for by the coders? A response to these questions is far from apparent in the description of the coding procedure cited above. Defenders of the quantitative data-creating project claim that the coding process "is not biased by interpretive differences among historians since it seeks only to isolate the atomic event, the interaction among states."[20]

But this is not satisfying to historians, such as Paul Schroeder, who responds that "An historian might question this claim on general grounds. Given the great difficulty of selecting the most important events out of the extremely complex web of international history, how confident can one be that any seven general diplomatic histories are reliable in their selection."[21] All we can say for certain from the information provided in respect to the MID coding is that problems and irregularities were hashed out among the coders. What we are left with is a streamlined account of the coding process that is conspicuously purged of the messy details. According to project cofounder, Jonathan Wilkenfeld, the ICB coding process seems to have been admittedly more complicated. For ICB cases, two coders were assigned to log twenty hours compiling each case. Upon completion of the code sheets, the coders would attend a debriefing session with one or more of the project founders. In instances of disagreement, coders were called upon to justify their initial coding and in some instances, a third coder was assigned. Debriefing sessions over problematic cases in some instances took "many hours."[22]

Commenting on an earlier data set, Schroeder says: "Obviously, I cannot explain the high intercoder reliability achieved, at least not without knowing what exact instructions the coding teams were given. The original criteria of what constituted a separate event or action . . . and what constituted evidence of cooperation or conflict in these actions, would seem to be all-important.

Clear definitions and instructions on these points would seem to account for high intercoder reliability. But the basic question of whether these definitions and criteria were intrinsically sound would remain."[23]

It seems, then, that while quantitative methodologists have taken stringent measures to standardize the way in which they go about the business of coding, those standards are inherently limited in three crucial ways. First, there is no procedure that could conceivably eliminate basic human disagreement. Though humans can attempt to emulate computers, we cannot in effect become them. Second and perhaps more important, the process by which the coding of history takes place is not itself reproducible. Thus, "Even with the coding manual in hand, it is impossible to know exactly how statistical indices were tabulated in the first place. We cannot re-create the individual and group decisions regarding historical selection, interpretation, and reconciliation taken by COW investigators."[24] This is a crucial point. While the general methodology for the coding of history is in the light of day, the actual coding that occurs in practice is itself a past event that cannot be replicated.

This alludes to a third problem, which is that "The COW bibliography lists, with a handful of exceptions, only those sources finally adopted, not all the materials consulted. If a particular historian's estimates or interpretations are ultimately discarded, the book does not appear. This practice gives a smoother gloss to data-making and to the data themselves than was perhaps the case."[25] The ease with which COW, MID, and ICB coders attain agreement on what happened in a given case is inversely proportional to the amount of literature processed by the coders on the case. While two coders might come to easy agreement on a case on the basis of three or four texts, it is much less likely that three or four historians on the case would attain the same consensus and even less so if the historians are themselves partial to different theoretic persuasions. While the COW, MID, and ICB projects have attempted to alleviate this problem, it seems more that they have simply swept it under the carpet. Put differently, if historians themselves cannot agree over the basic historical narrative of a much-studied case, then the fact that data set coders seem to overcome this difficulty should raise questions.

For example, while the correlation-analyses undertaken by Singer and his disciples undoubtedly are scientific in their methodology, *the process of data making required to generate the data for the studies is not in itself scientific.* "'Guesstimates' snowball into conjecture as imprecisions and biases in selection, interpretation, and coding are reproduced throughout the data. However candid COW researches are about the agonies of data-making, the project nevertheless proceeds on the basis of a clean set of data points which effectively conceals, but does not eliminate, the problem of historical epistemology."[26] In order to assess the extent to which this might make a significant difference in the persuasiveness of the quantitative approach, the following sections analyze the quantitative coding of the 1956 Arab-Israeli war in three oft-cited data sets.[27]

III. THE MILITARIZED INTERSTATE DISPUTE (MID) DATA SET AND THE 1956 ARAB-ISRAELI WAR

The preceding section alludes to a number of epistemological problems regarding the rendering of historiography into quantitative data. The question remains, however, as to whether these problems really matter. That is to say, even if the practices of quantitative methodologists are problematic on epistemological grounds, so too are those of professional historians and qualitative political scientists. What would really matter is the revelation of seriously questionable history as revealed through the numbers of the data sets. In order to answer this question, this section looks at the way in which a recent and oft-cited data set, the Militarized Interstate Dispute (MID) Version 2.1 data set codes the 1956 Arab-Israeli war as well as the specific Israeli involvement in that war. Tables 4.1 and 4.2 below provide a summary of the basic data of the case decoded from the actual data set.

Beginning with the seemingly straightforward matter of the start date of the war, we encounter some puzzling questions. What is the rationale for a start date of September 1, 1955? In short, this start date appears purely arbitrary. Two of the most-cited Israeli critical historians discussed in chapter 2, Avi Shlaim and Motti Golani, provide basic chronologies of the Arab-Israeli conflict during the 1950s in their recent studies. Neither indicates September 1,

Table 4.1. Coding of the "Sinai War" in the Militarized Interstate Dispute (MID) Data Set Version 2.1

Start Date	September 1, 1955
End Date	November 5, 1956
Outcome	Victory for Side B
Settlement	Imposed
Fatality Level	>999 Deaths
Duration	433 Days
Highest Act	Interstate War
Hostility Level	War
Reciprocated Dispute	Yes
States on Side A	Egypt, Soviet Union (2)
States on Side B	Egypt, France, Israel, U.S. (4)

SOURCE: Militarized Interstate Dispute (MID) Data, available online at http://pss.la.psu.edu/MID_DATA.HTM.

**Table 4.2. Coding of Israeli Participation in the
"Sinai War" in the Militarized Interstate Dispute
(MID) Data Set Version 2.1**

Start Date	September 1, 1955
End Date	November 5, 1956
Side of Conflict	Side B
Revisionist State	No
Fatality Level	>999 Deaths
Highest Act	Interstate War
Hostility Level	War
Originator of Dispute	No

SOURCE: Militarized Interstate Dispute (MID) Data, available
online at http://pss.la.psu.edu/MID_DATA.HTM.

1955 as a significant date.[28] It would seem that there are two more logical choices for a start date, which are July 26, 1956, the day that Gamal Abdel Nasser nationalized the Suez Canal Company, and/or October 29, 1956, the date of initiation of the 1956 war. Alternatively, perhaps an earlier date was selected to indicate the importance of border incidents in precipitating the war. If this is the case, then again, why September 1, 1955? A more logical choice here would be February 28, 1955, the date of the major Gaza Raid, which is cited in the literature, both old and critical, as a major turning point in the events leading up to the war.

The end date of the conflict is more clear in its significance, but still questionable. While November 5, 1956 is indeed the day that Israeli consolidated its occupation of the Sinai and hostilities ceased, the conflict could not be said to be fully concluded until the completion of the Israeli withdrawal from the Sinai on March 7, 1957. Clearly the coders made choices in respect to these basic issues, *but the rationale for these choices is conspicuously missing from the data*. This points up a related problem with the data as revealed through the coding. Does the case titled "Sinai War" in the data set refer to the Suez Crisis brought about by the nationalization of the Canal Company, or the 1956 war, which was primarily an Arab-Israel war, or both? While the two events are clearly related, to classify them as a single "case" requires an explanation, and it is precisely that which is missing from the data.

A second problematic issue pertains to the matter of who attacked whom in the conflict. According to the data, the war ended in a victory for "Side B," where Side A is the initiator and Side B the respondent. Further, Side B in the conflict is listed as consisting of Israel, Great Britain, France, and the United States. Side A consists of Egypt and the Soviet Union. Thus, *the MID 2.1 data clearly states that in the "Sinai War," Egypt and the Soviet Union initiated a militarized dispute against Israel, Great Britain, France, and the United States.*

This conclusion is extremely problematic. Only by the greatest stretch of imagination could one say that Egypt attacked Israel in the 1956 war. What might be said is that Egypt initiated a crisis by nationalizing the Canal Company, which—through a serious of complex and contingent events—led to the 1956 war several months later. But this is a different claim from the one that Egypt is the initiator of war. Since the data-making enterprise is opaque, we can't say for certain what the coders intend to convey. What precisely is meant by "initiator" in the conflict cannot be ascertained because it is unclear at the outset as to what was "initiated"—the Suez Crisis or the 1956 war. The matter of the United States and the Soviet Union adds further confusion to the matter. Based on the coding of the data, one could easily be led to believe that the United States and the Soviet Union were *actual participants* in the military conflict. Not only is this clearly not the case, but the 1956 war itself engendered one of the most significant Cold War rifts between the United States and its allies, Great Britain and France. So while the United States wasn't on Side A (the initiator); it is nonetheless extremely misleading to say that the United States was part of "Side B" and thus deemed to be in support of the Anglo-French-Israeli war.[29]

The coding of the overall case, represented in table 4.1 above, is for the most part replicated in the coding for Israel specifically, represented in table 4.2. Thus, the same problematic start and end dates are reiterated. The data adds two additional categories. The first specifies a "no" with regard to Israel as initiator of the conflict, which is especially problematic for the reasons discussed above. The second category regards the coding of "revisionist states," for which Israel is coded "no" (i.e., not a revisionist state). In their explanation of the coding, Jones, Bremer, and Singer assert that, "Within the data, the revisionist variable attempts to indicate which states are dissatisfied with the existing status quo prior to the onset of a militarized interstate dispute."[30] Taking this definition for granted, is it really accurate to say Israel was "satisfied with the existing status quo" prior to the 1956 war? Contrast this assertion with the following views of three Israeli historians:

Motti Golani: "My research led me to conclude that Israel had been 'in search of a war' before the onset of the Suez Crisis and without any connection to it."[31]

Benny Morris: "Paradoxically, during the years 1955–56 (and perhaps as early as 1954), retaliatory strikes were also launched by the IDF in order to draw the Arab states into a premature war."[32] "Dayan wanted war, and, periodically, he hoped that a given retaliatory strike would embarrass or provoke the Arab state attacked into itself retaliating, giving Israel cause to escalate the shooting until war resulted."[33]

Avi Shlaim: "In short, Dayan wanted war, he wanted it soon, and he used reprisals both to goad the Egyptians into war and to prepare his army for that war."[34] "In October 1956 Ben-Gurion forced Sharett's resignation in order to give himself the option of launching a war against Egypt. In October 1956 he exercised that option."[35]

While the notion of what it means to be "satisfied with the status quo" could certainly be interpreted in numerous ways, it stretches the bounds of credulity to suggest, as per the MID 2.1 data, that Israel was a "status quo" state at the outset of the Suez Crisis/1956 war. The MID 2.1 data on Israel contain one additional curiosity, which pertains to the number of battlefield deaths. The data indicate that Israeli suffered in excess of 999 battlefield deaths in the "Sinai War." But this flies in the face of most research, both old and critical, on the war. In *Israel in Search of War*, Motti Golani, a critical historian, puts the total figure at 176.[36] David Ben-Gurion, whose narrative of the war is in every other context divergent from that of Golani, offers a comparable figure of 171.[37] It is difficult, then, to comprehend how and/or where the MID coders arrived at their figure of greater than 999. In light of the preceding discussion, the MID 2.1 data on the "Sinai War" are vague at best and erroneous at worst.

IV. CORRELATES OF WAR (COW) INTERNATIONAL AND CIVIL WAR DATA ON THE 1956 WAR

In comparison to the MID 2.1 data discussed in the previous section, the Correlates of War (COW) International and Civil War data set seems to fare better when compared with the historiography of the case (see table 4.3 below).

The COW data, unlike the MID 2.1 data, codes only for each country participant and does not have a separate listing for the overall case. According to the COW data, Israel initiated the 1956 war on October 29, 1956 and "left" the war on November 5. These dates are sensible inasmuch as they reflect the duration of combat, although they fail to reveal that Israel did not withdraw from the Sinai until March 12, 1957. Unlike the MID data set, the COW does not include the United States and the Soviet Union as actors in the conflict. While this helps to avoid confusion as to identity of the actual combatants in the war, it glosses over the important secondary roles played by the superpowers in the conflict. A problematic issue in the data is the indication that no "central sub-system member" participated in the war, but at least one "major power" did, although not on each side of the war. The problem here is that neither the designation "central sub-system member" nor "major power" is defined in the codebook for the data.[38] We can only assume that Britain and

Table 4.3. Coding of Israeli Participation in the 1956 Arab-Israeli War in the Correlates of War (COW) International and Civil War Data Set

Crisis Actors	Egypt, France, UK, Israel
Date Israel Entered War	October 29, 1956
Date Israel Left War	November 5, 1956
War Type	Interstate
At Least One Major Power in War	Yes
At Least One Major Power on Each Side	No
At Least One Central Sub-System Member in War	No
Israeli Population at Start of War	1.827 Million
Pre-War Size of Israeli Armed Forces	75,000
Outcome	Israel on Winning Side
Number of Months Israel Fought in War	.3
Israeli Battlefield Deaths	200
Did Participant Initiate War	Yes
Date Version Case Added to Data Set	1972

SOURCE: Singer, J. David, and Melvin Small. Correlates of War Project: International and Civil War Data, 1816–1992 [Computer file], (Ann Arbor, MI, 1993) J. David Singer and Melvin Small [producers], Inter-university Consortium for Political and Social Research (ICPSR) [distributor], 1994.

France are the "major powers" involved in the war, but are these countries to be coded the same as the United States and the Soviet Union? Or is there a distinction between "major power" and "superpower?" The answer is not revealed in the either the codebook or data.

Another problematic issue in the data is the listing of Israel's armed forces at 75,000 at the start of the war. The number is problematic firstly because it is at odds with figures offered by Israel specialists such as Nadav Safran, who put the standing armed force figure for 1956 at 50,000.[39] The figure is also misleading because while Israel's standing armed forces may have been 50,000, any observer familiar with Israel is aware that Israel's defense structure rests on an enormous rapidly mobilizable military reserve, which would bring the 1956 figure up to 200,000 in a matter of days. In light of this, Safran lists both figures. Perhaps most troubling is the data entry indicated in the version update for the case. The Correlates of War (COW) International and Civil War data set was originated in 1972 and has gone through three updates since that time (1980, 1990, and 1992). But the data for the 1956 war remains that which was originally input in 1972. If this is the case, then the vast changes in the understanding of the conflict that were brought about in the Israeli critical history during the 1990s are not acknowledged by the data and will not be, unless the case were to be recoded. Unfortunately, the procedures and methods for updating of the COW data are not explained in the project summary.

V. INTERNATIONAL CRISIS BEHAVIOR (ICB) PROJECT
AND THE 1956 ARAB-ISRAELI WAR

In contrast to the MID and COW data sets just discussed, the ICB Project data is contained in a series of published volumes, beginning with the two-volume, *Crises in the Twentieth Century* (1988) and more recently, *A Study of Crisis* (2000), which contains an expanded and substantially revised set of cases and data. Unlike the MID and COW data, the ICB founders had an original intent to produce a data set that would contain not only numeric codes (horizontal data) but also a smaller set of more in-depth case studies that would provide important qualitative information (vertical data) about critical representative cases.[40] Also in contrast to the MID and COW data, the ICB data contain a significant change in the fundamental coding of the 1956 war resulting from revision of the dataset during the past fifteen years. It is thus especially worthwhile to look in more detail at the way in which the ICB project portrays the 1956 war. In the 1988 version of the data, the 1956 war is coded as a distinct crisis independent from the Suez Canal Company nationalization. Volume I of *Crises in the Twentieth Century* provides the following background synopsis of the war:

> Israel had been subjected to increased terrorist infiltrations from Egypt-controlled Gaza and the Sinai Peninsula and was concerned about the flow of arms to Egypt from Czechoslovakia in 1955–56. . . . Britain and France perceived a threat from Egypt's declaration to nationalize the Suez Canal. . . . A decision was made by the three countries on October 1956 to invade Sinai.[41]

The crisis synopsis proceeds to specify the dates of the Israeli invasion and British and French bombing campaign along with the dates of cease-fire and eventual Israeli withdrawal from the Sinai.[42] While the dates and basic chronology of the war provided in the ICB qualitative synopsis are generally unproblematic, the background to the crisis cited above is not. In particular, the background synopsis cites only the threat to Israel from "terrorist infiltrations" and the Czech arms deal. The important rift between the dominant militaristic activists and their opponents within Israel is unmentioned. Nor is the role of Moshe Dayan in attempting to instigate war by provoking *fedayeen* raids alluded to in the ICB background. In short, the entire ICB understanding of the causes of the 1956 war adopts a purely system-strategic interstate perspective toward the conflict and thus disregards the core of the interpretation provided by the Israeli critical historiography. At the more specific level, the 1988 version of the ICB data codes the case as follows (see table 4.4). In the updated and revised version of ICB contained in *A Study of Crisis*, the 1956 war and Suez Nationalization crises have been merged into a single,

**Table 4.4.   Coding of 1956 Arab-Israeli War in the International Crisis
Behavior (ICB) Data Set (1988)**

Crisis Actors	USSR, Egypt, France, UK, USA, Israel
Start Date Overall Crisis	October 29, 1956
Start Date for Israel	November 5, 1956
End Date Overall Crisis	March 12, 1957
End Date for Israel	March 12, 1957
Triggering Entity	Israel
Triggering Act	Violent
Highest Value Threat	Grave Damage
Intensity of Violence	War
Superpower Activity-US	Political
Superpower Activity-USSR	Semimilitary
Global Organization Involvement	Emergency Military Force
Form of Outcome	Agreement

SOURCE: Michael Brecher, Jonathan Wilkenfeld, Sheila Moser, *Crises in the Twentieth Century*, vol.
1, "Handbook of International Crises," (Oxford: Pergamon Press, 1988), 45.

comprehensive case study titled, "Suez Nationalization War." The background for the case with regard to Israel's role reads almost precisely as it did in the 1988 data:

> Israel had been subjected to a steady increase of cross-border infiltrations from Egypt-controlled Gaza and the Sinai Peninsula since 1953. It was even more acutely concerned about the flow of arms to Egypt from Czechoslovakia in 1955–56.[43]

However, in a substantial revision upon the earlier data, the 2000 data provide a more detailed qualitative discussion of the 1956 war within the context of a decades-long "protracted conflict," namely the Arab-Israeli conflict. The revised data also explain the 1956 Arab-Israeli war as a component of the sequence of events triggered by Gamal Abdel Nasser's July nationalization of the Suez Canal Company. The more formal coding of the case in the 2000 data includes several changes from the earlier version as follows (see table 4.5).[44]

In contrast to the MID and COW data, the ICB data have two unique characteristics. First, the ICB alone provides a fully updated and revised effort to improve and clarify the data in light of new information and new understandings of international conflict generally speaking. Second, the ICB data provides a very substantial qualitative prose description of its cases that is absent from the MID and COW data. In this sense, the ICB data fares somewhat better than the previous two data sets in terms of understanding the case of the 1956 war. That said, one could make the case the ICB data has in a sense "regressed" by merging the 1956 war and the Suez Nationalization into a single integrated case. From the data codes alone, one would not be able to identify

Table 4.5.   Coding of "Suez Nationalization War" in the International Crisis Behavior (ICB) Data Set (2000)

Crisis Actors	USSR, Egypt, France, UK, USA, Israel
Start Date Overall Crisis	July 26, 1956
Start Date for Israel	November 5, 1956
End Date Overall Crisis	March 12, 1957
End Date for Israel	March 12, 1957
Triggering Entity	Egypt
Trigger	Economic
Gravity of Threat	Grave Damage
Overall Violence	Full-Scale War
Global Organization Involvement	Emergency Military Forces
Form of Outcome	Unilateral Act

SOURCE: Michael Brecher and Jonathan Wilkenfeld, *A Study of Crisis* (Ann Arbor: University of Michigan Press, 2000), CD-ROM, Case #152.

much less comprehend the unique and important characteristics of the Israeli decision to participate in the crisis, especially if taking into account the critical historiography on the case. However, this problem is somewhat, though not completely addressed in the qualitative prose background to the case provided in the 2000 ICB CD-ROM, which helps to explain how the 1956 war fits into the sequence of events begun with the July 1956 nationalization. Thus, it is necessary to supplement the quantitative aspect of the data with the qualitative in order to make the data comprehensible and historically meaningful. The ICB founders allude precisely to this point in the preface to the 2000 volume, where they assert: "we were convinced that no single path to knowledge is flawless or even adequate."[45]

VI. CONCLUSION

From the preceding overviews of the coding of the second Arab-Israeli war in three major political science data sets we can make several conclusions. The first is that in many instances, especially with regard to the MID 2.1 data set, the data is simply inexplicable. It is difficult to contemplate how a balanced rendering of the 1956 war would portray Egypt as initiating the conflict. Further, while the Soviet Union was certainly Egypt's patron, the data reads as if the Soviet Union were in fact a combatant in the war. The figure of greater than 999 Israeli battlefield deaths is also inexplicable. In short, it is difficult to reconcile the MID 2.1 data with a balanced, informed understanding of the historiography of the case. On this point, the COW (1992) and ICB data sets fare better, although each contains several inconsistencies and problematic points as discussed above. However, even to the extent that the data is acceptable, one is still struck by the incomplete character of the cases as they appear in coded form. Thus, a second conclusion is that even if the dates, numbers of deaths, and superpower alignments of the case were presented in an unproblematic fashion in each data set, the data don't reveal very much about the case that a researcher would want and/or need to know. Missing from the data is practically every important factor cited in the historiography of the case, both old and critical. Thus, there is no allusion to the Czech arms deal, the *fedayeen* campaign and Israeli countercampaign, the blockade of the Straights of Tiran, or the triumph of military activism within the context of Israeli internal state-building. In short, there is a general paucity of information in the data that anyone interested in the case of the 1956 war would or could use.

It might be rebutted that this is not the purpose of the data. That is, large sample data research is designed to test patterns across large swaths of time and space, not to reveal significant characteristics about individual cases. While this is a valid point, the streamlining of the messy historical details that occurs in producing the data remains problematic in two important senses. First, there is the strong possibility that historians expert in the cases would not accept many of the data points in the sets. Second, even if the former were not as serious a problem as it could be, many historians would simply reject the streamlined description of the case as fundamentally incompatible with the extremely complex character of historical events. That is, the data points do not represent what they claim to and to the extent that they represent anything, they are so hypersimplified and decontextualized that any lessons the history might reveal are ultimately lost. This would imply that the patterns that quantitative researchers see across large samples of data are not more than precisely that: patterns that exist in the numbers generated by scholars. However, this is a different claim from the one that the patterns are in actuality existent in the history that the numbers purport to represent. On this latter point, which is the only one that matters, many historians would vehemently disagree with the claims of quantitative political science scholars.

A third conclusion regards the incomparability of the data sets themselves. Insofar as the quantitative project in international relations has sought to systematize the process of inquiry, it is interesting to assess the extent to which the various data sets do or do not agree with one another on certain basic facts of the cases. In order to do so, table 4.6 below highlights the key differences among the three data sets assessed in this chapter with regard to the 1956 Arab-Israeli war. The low level of interdata set reliability raises a point that is most significant with regard both to the quantitative project in political science as well as to this book. Each of the three data sets cited in this chapter is generally respected in the field, yet they fail to generate like data. If the data derived from different data sets and the coders that produced them cannot agree, who or what is to distinguish the good data from the bad? This is a question to which there does not appear to be an answer at present.

This leads to a fourth and final conclusion, which is that every epistemological-methodological approach entails tradeoffs. The quantitative data-generating project in international relations seeks to trade historiographical complexity for scientific generalizability and methodological replicability. But in the process, the fact that *there really are* massive disagreements within the historiography over questions of what happened is completely ignored. As Singer puts it, we must be sensitive "to the crucial distinction between subjective belief and verifiable knowledge."[46] But the nature of historical inquiry and historical revisionism discussed in chapter 1 of this study makes a strong case that the line between belief and knowledge is in fact less well delineated than scientific methodologists would have us think. By design, then, the quantitative project requires that historical meaning in the cases remains static. That is, there must be a unified understanding of who did what to whom, when, and for what reason.

Unfortunately, this is simply not the way historiography works. Historiography is not predicated on the assumption that answers to historical questions will remain static. Basic understandings of historical events change over time from generation to generation and across space from culture to culture. Historical revisionism signifies the guarantee that intersubjective meaning in historiography is anything but static. One way in which quantitative methodologists could seek to address this matter would be to introduce frequent and comprehensive updating procedures into the maintenance of data sets.[47] On this point, the ICB project seems to have an advantage vis-à-vis the other data sets examined in this chapter in that the ICB founders "periodically reopen cases for re-coding," although this is not done systematically. The criticism

Table 4.6.   Inter-Data Set Reliability for the 1956 war

Data set	MID 2.1	COW (1992)	ICB (1988)	ICB (2000)
Start Date of 1956 war-Israel	September 1, 1955	October 29, 1956	November 5, 1956	July 26, 1956
End Date of 1956 war-Israel	November 5, 1956	November 5, 1956	March 12, 1957	March 12, 1957
Crisis Initiator(s)	Egypt and Soviet Union	Israel	Israel	Egypt
Israeli Battlefield Deaths	Greater than 999	200	N/A	N/A

here is also well-taken by ICB cofounder Jonathan Wilkenfeld, who acknowledges that when major data sets such as the COW and ICB are completed, there is a "tendency . . . to sit back and admire it for a while and before you realize it, it's outdated." Thus, there is an obligation to keep the data set updated.

Consistent and careful updating would acknowledge that the data are in effect living and dynamic. Accordingly, data sets would have to be understood as works in progress that could never be made complete (unless there truly were an "end" of history). Such an approach would, however, involve a massive allocation of time and labor. But even then, it is difficult to imagine the extent to which the scientific aspect of the data generation project could ever be fully reconciled with the historiographical aspect. That is to say, it is unlikely that a project whose goal is to treat events as fixed data points could ever truly present them as the contested, constructed, understandings based on intersubjective consensus that they really are.

NOTES

1. Thomas W. Smith, *History and International Relations* (London: Routledge, 1999), 119; and Daniel M. Jones, Stuart A. Bremer, and J. David Singer, "Militarized Interstate Disputes, 1816–1992: Rationale, Coding Rules, and Empirical Patterns," *Conflict Management and Peace Science* 15, no. 2 (1996): 165.

2. Bruce Russett, "Foreword," in Francis W. Hoole and Dina Z. Zinnes, eds., *Quantitative International Politics* (New York: Praeger, 1976), v.

3. J. David Singer, "The Incompleat Theorist: Insights without Evidence," in K. Knorr and J. N. Rosenau, eds., *Contending Approaches to International Politics* (Princeton University Press, 1969), 82, cited in Smith, *History and International Relations*, 119.

4. Singer, "The Incompleat Theorist," 77.

5. Singer, "The Incompleat Theorist," 82.

6. Paul W. Schroeder, "A Final Rejoinder," *Journal of Conflict Resolution* 21, no. 1 (March 1977): 66–67.

7. Jones, Bremer, and Singer, "Militarized Interstate Disputes," 166.

8. Singer, "The Correlates of War Project: Continuity, Diversity, and Convergence," in Hoole and Zinnes, eds., *Quantitative International Politics*, 21.

9. Singer, "The Making of a Peace Researcher," in Joseph Kruzel and James N. Rosenau, eds., *Journeys through World Politics* (Lexington, MA: Lexington Books, 1988), 225.

10. Singer, "The Incompleat Theorist," 66–67.

11. Singer, "Introduction," in J. David Singer, ed., *Correlates of War, Volume I* (New York: The Free Press, 1979), xiv.

12. Singer, "Individual Values, National Interests, and Political Development," in J. David Singer, ed., *Correlates of War, Volume I*, 5.

13. Michael Brecher, "Turning Points: Reflections on Many Paths to Knowledge," in Joseph Kruzel and James N. Rosenau, eds., *Journeys through World Politics* (Lexington, MA: Lexington Books, 1988), 128.

14. Francis W. Hoole and Dina Z. Zinnes, "Introduction," in Hoole and Zinnes, eds., *Quantitative International Politics*, 5–6.

15. Singer, "The Correlates of War Project," 24.

16. Jones, Bremer, and Singer, "Militarized Interstate Disputes," 165. Thomas Smith distinguishes existential knowledge from correlational knowledge as follows: the former entails transforming historical narrative and other artifacts into data sets on war, whereas the latter measurement of the association between two or more variables to produce the goal of a "correlational coefficient." Smith, *History*, 125–26. Job and Ostrom define three types of knowledge as follows: "Existential knowledge, the 'bedrock' of all other knowledge, is composed of propositions that describe regularities and patterns in a data set generated by a sequence of observations. Correlational knowledge, is knowledge of the similarity or covariation between two or more sets of observations. Explanatory knowledge provides a theory or 'causal' sequence." Brian L. Job and Charles W. Ostrom, "An Appraisal of the Research Design and Philosophy of Science of the Correlates of War Project," in Hoole and Zinnes, eds., *Quantitative International Politics*, 44.

17. Singer, "The Correlates of War Project," 27. Emphasis in original.

18. Job and Ostrom, "An Appraisal," 55.

19. Jones, Bremer, and Singer, "Militarized Interstate Disputes," 180–82.

20. B. Healy and A. Stein, "The Balance of Power in International History: Theory and Reality," *Journal of Conflict Resolution* 17 (1973), cited in Paul W. Schroeder, "Quantitative Studies in the Balance of Power," *Journal of Conflict Resolution* 21, no. 1 (March 1977), 5.

21. Schroeder, "Quantitative Studies," 5.

22. Wilkenfeld, interview with author, University of Maryland, June 15, 2001.

23. Schroeder, "Quantitative Studies," 16. Schroeder is referring to the Situational Analysis Project at Cornell University.

24. Smith, *History*, 128–29

25. Smith, *History*, 128–29.

26. Smith, *History*, 139.

27. The three data sets examined here were selected on the basis of their general influence on and widespread use within the IR literature. However, several European data sets are worth mentioning insofar as they were used to produce a study focusing specifically on the Arab-Israeli conflict. David Kinsella employs event data from the Conflict and Peace Data Bank (COPDAB) and the World Event/Interaction Survey (WEIS) and Arms transfer data from the Stockholm International Peace Research Institute (SIPRI) to asses the impact of superpower arms transfers to the Middle East with regard to war in the region from 1948 to 1988. Kinsella conducts a time-series analysis to test the hypothesis that Soviet transfers to Egypt and Syria provoked conflict in the region while U.S. assistance to Israel has had no similar effect. Kinsella concludes that his hypothesis "is supported by even the most conservative reading of

the evidence: *Soviet arms transfers to Egypt and Syria have both exacerbated conflict in the Middle East and provoked U.S. arms transfers to Israel."* Kinsella, "Conflict in Context: Arms Transfers and Third World Rivalries during the Cold War," *American Journal of Political Science* 38, no. 3 (August 1994). Emphasis in original.

28. Motti Golani, *Israel in Search of War* (Portland, OR: Sussex, 1998), 200–203; Avi Shlaim, *The Iron Wall* (New York: Norton, 2000), xxi-xxxi.

29. For discussion of the rift among the United States and France and Britain, see Charles G. Cogan, "From the Politics of Lying to the Farce at Suez: What the US Knew," *Intelligence and National Security* 13, no. 2 (Summer 1998); Herman Finer, *Dulles over Suez* (Chicago: Quadrangle, 1964); and Thomas Risse-Kappen, *Cooperation among Democracies*, (Princeton: Princeton University Press, 1995), chapter 4, "Unworthy and Unreliable; Allies: Violation of Alliance Norms during the 1956 Suez Crisis."

30. Jones, Bremer, and Singer, "Militarized Interstate Disputes," 178.

31. Golani, *Israel in Search of a War*, viii.

32. Benny Morris, *Righteous Victims: A History of the Zionist-Arab Conflict, 1881–1999* (New York: Knopf, 1999), 276.

33. Morris, *Israel's Border Wars 1949–1956* (New York: Oxford University Press, 1993), 178–79.

34. Shlaim, *The Iron Wall*, 144.

35. Shlaim, *The Iron Wall*, 185.

36. Golani, *Israel in Search of a War*.

37. David Ben-Gurion, *Israel: A Personal History* (New York: Funk and Wagnalls, 1971).

38. See codebook for ICPSR 9905, J. David Singer and Melvin Small, *Correlates of War Project: International and Civil War Data, 1816–1992* [computer file], (Ann Arbor, MI, 1993) J. David Singer and Melvin Small [producers], Inter-university Consortium for Political and Social Research (ICPSR) [distributor], 1994. This might be simply a problem with the coding rules, but since the definitions for the terms are not provided, it becomes emblematic of the opacity of the coding process of quantitative political science generally speaking.

39. Nadav Safran, *From War to War* (Indianapolis: Pegasus, 1969), 228.

40. Jonathan Wilkenfeld, interview with author, 2001.

41. Michael Brecher, Jonathan Wilkenfeld, Sheila Moser, *Crises in the Twentieth Century*, vol. 1, "Handbook of International Crises," (Oxford: Pergamon Press, 1988), 233.

42. Brecher, Wilkenfeld, Moser, *Crises in the Twentieth Century*, 234.

43. Michael Brecher and Jonathan Wilkenfeld, *A Study of Crisis* (Ann Arbor: University of Michigan Press, 2000), CD-ROM, Case #152.

44. While Brecher and Wilkenfeld did significantly recode the case, the recoding was not the result of a review and incorporation of the critical historiography and its implications for understanding the case. Rather, the recoding was a function of a more systematic review of the entire data set that resulted in discussions of how certain cases might be more accurately coded according to the perspectives of the ICB founders. In essence, the recoding of the 1956 crises from two into one was a

"judgment call" on the part of the principal investigators. Wilkenfeld, interview with author.

45. Brecher and Wilkenfeld, *A Study of Crisis*, xx.
46. Singer, "The Incompleat Theorist," 71.
47. Wilkenfeld, interview with author, 2001.

Chapter Five

Beyond the Middle East: Recent Debates on the Historiography of Vietnam

I. INTRODUCTION

The preceding chapters have explained in some depth the problem of conducting historical inquiry into the Arab-Israeli conflict. However, it is perfectly possible that the Arab-Israeli conflict is an outlier on the spectrum of historical uniqueness. Thus, in order to give some weight to the claim that historical inquiry is a significant issue for political science in general, this chapter examines the problem of historical inquiry into the Vietnam War. Vietnam was the defining event for a generation of Americans. In tandem with public interest in the conflict, Vietnam has not gone unnoticed by political scientists, who have examined every aspect of the case from social movements to military strategy. In this chapter, I aim to evaluate the degree to which the basic historical contours of political science case studies of the Vietnam War are consistent, logically and empirically, with the historical "record" or "records" as the case may be.

In recognition of the breadth and depth of "Vietnam" as a historical case study, I have somewhat narrowed the discussion in the following pages to focus on the causes of the escalation of the war during the first sixteen months of the Johnson administration, between November 1963 and March 1965. The discussion focuses on two interrelated questions that are especially important for the shaping of political science studies that examine the case: (1) what caused the escalation of the war between November 1963 and March 1965? and (2) What are the implications of contemporary historical revisionism for political science–international relations (IR) theory in light of this case? In response to the preceding questions, the following section of the chapter surveys some of the political science literature, especially from the

subfield of IR, on the Vietnam War by introducing and explicating the acknowledged causes of the escalation as well as related theoretical claims of
import made by various authors.

   Section III presents a historiographical account of the escalation of the
Vietnam War based on new historical literature published during the past ten
years. What becomes clear from these two sections is that many of the themes
of the recent historical narrative of Vietnam differ quite significantly from
those of the political science literature. The problems that this creates for political science theorization are analyzed in more depth in chapter 6.

II. CREDIBILITY, COLD WAR, AND
VIETNAM IN THE BALANCE

Discussion of Vietnam as a historical case study in the political science literature is prolific, so much so that to effectively survey all references to the
case would be beyond the scope of a single book, let alone a single chapter.
In the pages that follow, I therefore employ a three-tiered filtering scheme to
focus on the most important and influential treatments of the case in the political science literature. The following subsections represent three subsets of
the political science literature that have discussed or employed Vietnam as a
case study: (1) General textbooks and data set compilations; (2) "classic" international relations studies that discuss Vietnam but in which the Vietnam
War is not the principal focus; and (3) monographic studies in which Vietnam
is the primary focus of inquiry.

1. General Textbooks and Data Set Compilations

Vietnam has been discussed in a number of general textbooks and data set
compilations that are used for undergraduate instruction and employed by specialists in large-n theoretical studies. For instance, the volume *Managing Interstate Conflict* indicates that "A crisis for the United States was triggered on
2 August 1964 when the American destroyer *Maddox* was attacked by North
Vietnamese torpedo boats in the Gulf of Tonkin off North Vietnam. However,
the United States' version was that a second attack was launched on 4 August
against two American destroyers. . . . The American response was prompt . . .
President Johnson ordered an air attack against North Vietnamese gunboats
and their supporting facilities, which became the trigger to a crisis for North
Vietnam." According to the account, the crisis began on August 2 and ended
by the close of the month.[1] A second crisis was triggered by the North Vietnamese attack at the U.S. army barracks at Pleiku on February 7, 1965.

An American response in the form of airstrikes followed shortly thereafter. As per the case synopsis, "For the United States, the immediate military consequences of the attack were superseded by political-diplomatic considerations related to America's commitment to maintain its influence in Southeast Asia. . . . The Pleiku Crisis may be said to have ended on 2 March 1965."[2] According to the *Managing Interstate Conflict* volume, then, the Vietnam War is seen as the sum of various component crises, each of which has a discrete beginning and endpoint. Throughout each crisis, the importance to the United States of maintaining "influence" in the region is mentioned as a significant overarching factor pertaining to the case.

The "Handbook of Foreign Policy Crises" notes that with the onset of stepped-up U.S. military advising during 1962, "the U.S. became a full-fledged party in the Vietnamese civil war." After two years, "The succession of political crises and countercoups which followed [President Ngo Dinh] Diem's overthrow during 1964–1965 prompted the U.S. to increase its military/advisory forces in the south to 148,000 by late 1965 and to assume an even more active combat role. . . . The obvious turning point in U.S. policy which escalated and widened the war occurred in August 1964 with the Gulf of Tonkin incidents."[3] In a manner similar to that employed by *Managing Interstate Conflict*, the "Handbook" views the Vietnam War as a series of stimulus-response events with several key moments, the most important of which occurred in the Gulf of Tonkin during August 1964.

Looking at more general textbooks, in his policy-oriented *Forceful Persuasion*, Alexander George asserts that "In response to recommendations from his military advisors, on March 15 [1965], the president approved more frequent, larger air strikes, and these now became part of a more deliberate" effort to coerce Hanoi to abandon support for the Viet Cong.[4] The question for George is not why the United States escalated its military involvement when and as it did, but why much more forceful measures had not been undertaken earlier. In response, George argues that "from the beginning of American military intervention in February, political-diplomatic reasons dictated considerable restraint in the use of air power as a coercive instrument." Thus, President Johnson was concerned "not to intervene militarily in ways that might be provocative and of his efforts to manage the risks of intervention. Washington's concern lest heavy air attacks against North Vietnam provoke the Soviet Union derived from the fact that Moscow had publicly agreed to provide North Vietnam with military assistance."[5] The American policy of incremental escalation was thus "essential to enable Moscow to exercise its influence" on North Vietnam to negotiate on terms favorable to the United States. According to George: "Johnson hoped this policy would motivate Moscow and at the same time allow it to play a pivotal role."[6]

George views Vietnam as a case of failed "coercive diplomacy," which entails the creation "in the opponent the expectation of costs of sufficient magnitude to erode his motivation to continue what he is doing."[7] According to George, the American effort to coerce Hanoi failed for two principal reasons. First, because American motivation to coerce Hanoi to abandon its efforts to unify Vietnam was significantly outweighed by the latter's desire to pursue that goal. Second, coercive diplomacy failed because the United States failed to "convey a sense of urgency" to North Vietnam regarding the degree of its motivation to successfully coerce.[8] For George, then, the War in Vietnam was in many respects consistent with the view articulated by many top U.S. decision makers at the time; namely, that Vietnam was one piece of a broader Cold War balance-of-power puzzle. According to this view, American decision makers at the time of the War were more concerned with systemic factors than with those on the ground in Vietnam.

In a more recently published textbook, Bruce Jentleson discusses Vietnam in the context of a chapter titled, "The Cold War Context: Lessons and Legacies." Citing the Vietnam War as "America's Most Profound Policy Setback," Jentleson asserts that "All along the main factor driving U.S. involvement in Vietnam was the belief that the credibility of American power was being tested there." Thus, "In 1965, when the decision finally was made to send in American troops, President Johnson quite explicitly articulated the need to demonstrate American credibility, as it pertained to both global allies and adversaries alike."[9] Jentleson argues that Vietnam was a failure "on all counts." The waging of the war failed to achieve peace; the power politics motivation for the war was tenuous at best; the war led to a degradation of American principles; and finally, the war damaged rather than bolstered the U.S. economy.[10] Echoing the public sentiments of President Johnson and Secretary of Defense Robert McNamara during the time of the conflict, Jentleson suggests that the Vietnam War was in large measure influenced by the American compulsion to maintain its credibility on a broader systemic level.

In another recently published textbook widely used in introductory undergraduate courses around the United States, Karen Mingst argues that "Vietnam provided a test" for the United States in the broader context of the Cold War. "To most U.S. policymakers in the late 1950s and early 1960s, Vietnam represented yet another test of the containment doctrine: communist influence must be stopped, they argued, before it spread like a chain of falling dominos though the rest of southeast Asia and beyond. . . . Thus, the United States supported the South Vietnamese dictators Ngo Dinh Diem and Nguen Van Thieu against the rival communist regime of Ho Chi Minh in the North." In the first few years of involvement in Vietnam, "the United States was fairly confident of victory—after all, a superpower with all its military hardware and technically skilled labor force could surely beat a poorly trained guerilla force."[11] Mingst essentially agrees with Jentleson that the result of this thinking was a major policy failure that resulted in "neither victory nor righteousness."[12] Mingst also agrees with Jentleson that the United States was more concerned with Vietnam for the purpose of stemming "communist influence" and, implicitly, maintaining U.S. influence in a more global sense than with regard to the specific matter of Vietnam per se.

2. "Classic" Accounts

In his landmark *Theory of International Politics*, Kenneth Waltz constructs a structural balance-of-power model of international relations based on the assumption of a constant anarchic ordering principle and juridical equality of sovereign states. Significant world events are driven by shifts in the distribution of power capabilities among states, which are in turn seen as a function of the system itself rather than of the specific policies or institutions within given states. Waltz discusses the Vietnam War in the context of his broader theoretical argument as an instance in which "One sees . . . not the *weakness* of great military power in a nuclear world but instead a clear illustration of the *limits* of military force in the world of the present as always."[13]

Waltz takes serious issue with the public statements of American officials such as President Johnson and Secretary of Defense McNamara who during the time of the war argued that global issues were at stake in Vietnam. Rather, Waltz contends that "As some saw early in that struggle, and as most saw later on, in terms of global politics little was at stake in Vietnam. The international-political insignificance of Vietnam can be understood only in terms of the world's structure. America's failure in Vietnam was tolerable because neither success nor failure mattered much internationally. Victory would not make the world one of American hegemony. Defeat would not make the world one of Russian hegemony. No matter what the outcome, the American-Russian duopoly would endure."[14] So for Waltz, Vietnam was a war driven by factors other than systemic ones and thus its outcomes, while perhaps quite significant for American domestic politics, were essentially trivial with regard to international politics. Waltz cites Senator Edward W. Brooke, who argued that "we were not . . . fighting in Vietnam 'as a necessary sacrifice to the global balance of power.'" Rather, "We were instead fighting a 'just' war to secure what is 'best for South Vietnam, and most honorable and decent for ourselves.'"[15] The Vietnam War, then, was neither indicative nor productive of a major shift in the global balance of power.

Jack Snyder in another widely-cited study discusses Vietnam as an instance of imperial, or more specifically, superpower "overstretch" on the part of the

United States. According to Snyder's theory, imperial/superpower overexpansion is the result not of the systemic balance of power but rather of logrolling coalitions that form within imperial/superpower states. Since each member of the logrolling coalition individually has an interest in continued expansion, the inertia of the logroll prevents policies of restraint from being devised when expansion exceeds thresholds beyond which continued expansion will make all worse off in the long run. According to Snyder, "The war in Vietnam was a classic example of strategic overextension, an unwinnable struggle fought for the mythical strategic purpose of maintaining the credibility of America's global commitments, a goal that fighting the war undermined."[16] Snyder argues that one of the primary factors "contributing to the Cold War consensus in favor of a globalist strategy of containment was the political competition and coalition building between 'Europe-first internationalists' and 'Asia-first nationalists'" within the U.S. Congress. A consensus on a foreign policy predicated on domino theoretic arguments was achieved by "giving both internationalists and nationalists what they wanted on the issues they cared about most." This in turn resulted in various Cold War overextensions, of which Vietnam was the most prolific.[17]

In his well-known *Why Nations Go to War*, John Stoessinger dedicates a chapter to the Vietnam War in which the main thesis "is that in Vietnam the misperceptions of five presidents transformed a tragedy of possibility into a tragedy of necessity."[18] Of the five Presidents, President Lyndon Johnson is clearly most significant to Stoessinger's account. "Johnson's ego, stubbornness, and pride destroyed his presidency and divided his people in a spiritual civil war . . . he misperceived his enemy, misled his people, and ultimately deceived himself. . . . It all began in 1964 with a memorandum to the president from the Joint Chiefs of Staff, urging him to increase the commitment in order to win the war more quickly."[19] This in turn led down a slippery slope of idiosyncratic behavior and decision making in which the specter of tragedy in Vietnam was transformed from a possibility into a certainty. Stoessinger argues that war is essentially the product of socialization: "Whereas aggression may be inherent, war is learned behavior, and as such can be unlearned and ultimately selected out entirely."[20] Within this social context, misperception, misunderstanding, and miscalculation weigh in as important aspects of Stoessinger's "common themes" of wars in the twentieth century, of which there are ten:

(1) "no nation that began a major war in this century emerged a winner;"
(2) "in the atomic age, war between nuclear powers is suicidal; wars between small countries with big friends are likely to be inconclusive and interminable; hence decisive war in our time has become a privilege of the impotent;"

(3) "In our time, unless the vanquished is destroyed completely, a victor's peace is seldom lasting. Those peace settlements that are negotiated on a basis of equality are much more permanent and durable;"

(4) "With regard to the problem of the outbreak of war, the case studies indicate the crucial importance of personalities of leaders;"

(5) "The case material reveals that perhaps the most important single precipitating factor in the outbreak of war is misperception. Such distortion may manifest itself in four different ways: in a leader's image of himself; a leader's view of his adversary's character; a leader's view of his adversary's intentions toward himself; and finally, a leader's view of his adversary's capabilities and power;"

(6) "There is a remarkable consistency in the self-images of most national leaders on the brink of war. Each confidently expects victory after a brief and triumphant campaign;"

(7) "This common belief in a short, decisive war is usually the overflow from a reservoir of self-delusions held by the leadership about both itself and the nation;"

(8) "Distorted views of the adversary's character also help to precipitate a conflict;"

(9) "When a leader on the brink of war believes that his adversary will attack him, the chances of war are fairly high. When both leaders share this perception about each other's intent, war becomes a virtual certainty;" and

(10) "A leader's misperception of his adversary's power is perhaps the quintessential cause of war. It is vital to remember, however, that it is not the actual distribution of power that precipitates a war; it is the way in which a leader thinks that power is distributed."[21]

While holding out for the possibility that social learning might in the future help to transform the frequency and nature of war, Stoessinger concludes that "In the past the anarchic nature of the nation-state system was chiefly responsible for wars."[22]

3. Vietnam Monographs

This section examines monographic studies whose primary empirical focus is on the conflict in Vietnam. In their oft-cited *The Irony of Vietnam*, Gelb and Betts suggest that the paradox of Vietnam "is that the *foreign policy* failed, but the *domestic decisionmaking system* worked. It worked as it usually does, in the way that most constitutionalists and democratic pluralists believe it should work. Vietnam was not an aberration of the decisionmaking system but a logical culmination of the principles that leaders brought with them into it." More specifically, the authors iterate three criteria by which the system worked in the case of Vietnam:

(1) the core consensual goal of postwar foreign policy (containment of communism) was pursued consistently;

(2) differences of both elite and mass opinion were accommodated by compromise, and policy never strayed very far from the center of opinion both within and outside the government;

(3) virtually all views and recommendations were considered and virtually all important decisions were made without illusions about the odds for success.[23]

According to Gelb and Betts, American involvement in Vietnam was due to top leaders' belief that Vietnam was vital to the struggle against communism. That belief was in turn reinforced by the behavior of "The presidents, Congress, public opinion, and the press all" of whom elevated "the stakes against losing and introduced constraints against winning."[24] Gelb and Betts conclude that in the case of Vietnam, the American political system did what a democracy usually does, which is to produce a policy more responsive "to the majority and the center than to the minority or the extremes of opinion."[25] In this sense then, the cause of American escalation in Vietnam can be located in the push and pull of American pluralistic politics: Vietnam was the output of a domestic political compromise among diverse societal groups and factions in response to a perceived linchpin in the global contest against communism.

In another more historically-grounded study of American involvement in Vietnam, Larry Berman contends that the documentary record of American foreign relations of the period indicates that American leaders "accepted containment of communism and the domino theory as basic premises for formulating policy and not as hypotheses for analysis."[26] Berman confesses to having "no grand theory for explaining the failure of Vietnam decision-making, nor do I believe that one is necessary. One of the lost arts in the discipline of political science is analyzing the impact of political institutions, processes, and personalities during critical turning points in history."[27] Despite the disclaimer, Berman proceeds to argue that the most important causal factor leading to American escalation resided in the individual level of the Commander-in-Chief. "In the final analysis, the president and not his advisors must accept most of the blame. Johnson was the cause of his ultimate undoing. The president was involved in a delicate exercise of political juggling" in which his ultimate goal was to "buy time" to ensure the successful fruition of his Great Society program. "Thus did Johnson commit slow political suicide."[28] So in keeping with the general view of the political science literature, Berman alludes to the importance of the broader Cold War motif in which the struggle against communism is central toward understanding American behavior in Vietnam. In contrast to that view, however, Berman stresses the individual level of analysis as the most important overall factor in explaining the causes of American behavior.

David Barrett critiques Gelb and Betts and Berman in an article that examines the decision-making context of the American escalation in Vietnam in 1965. According to Barett, Gelb and Betts as well as Berman vastly understate the scope and importance of advisors who advocated against increasing American involvement in Vietnam. Barett thus sets out to debunk two "myths" in the literature regarding President Johnson and Vietnam. The first of these is that Johnson was the victim of "groupthink;" "that is, that he did not receive wide ranging opinions from significant advisors about whether or not to intensify America's military role in Vietnam." The second is "that Johnson's personality and ego were such that he would not countenance the expression of conflicting advice that might raise the possibility that the United States would be wrong to increase its military presence in Vietnam."[29]

According to Barrett, there were at least six "significant" advisers who strongly cautioned the President against escalating the war in Vietnam in 1965. In these instances, Barrett defines "significant" as "men who had both a close personal relationship with Lyndon Johnson and/or who held a high ranking political position within Johnson administration circles."[30] The six included: Undersecretary of State George Ball, Vice President Hubert Humphrey, Chair of the Senate Armed Services Committee Richard Russell of Georgia, Chair of the Foreign Intelligence Advisory Board and later Secretary of Defense Clark Clifford; and Senators William Fulbright and Mike Mansfield. Barrett argues that President Johnson received a considerable amount of advice from these six advisors; advice that he took seriously and at times even "agonized over."

The President's decision to nonetheless proceed with escalation of the war therefore stemmed from neither cognitive closure nor a deterministic decision-making system but rather from the President's decision in the context of diverse advice. Barett suggests that while President Johnson did take the dissenters' counsel to heart, both written and spoken remarks provided by the six figures indicate that the President was heavily, perhaps unduly influenced by the so-called "whiz kids" within his administration; Robert McNamara, Dean Rusk, and McGeorge Bundy. Barett concludes by proposing further research to assess the degree to which the "whiz kids" may have influenced executive decision making during the Vietnam War.[31]

In another study of executive decision making and Vietnam, Greenstein and Burke assess the question of why both President Eisenhower in 1954 and Johnson in 1965 were faced with similar decisions regarding whether to intervene in Vietnam but that intervention was chosen in only the latter of the two cases. In their analysis of the documentary record, Greenstein and Burke argue that two factors are most salient in understanding the different decisions on intervention of the Eisenhower and Johnson administrations.[32] The first alludes to the underlying differences in the degree of formality/informality of the presidential advising system in each administration. The second regards personality: whereas President Eisenhower was more concerned with the content of policy than with politics, President Johnson instinctively took the precise opposite approach, favoring politics over policy.[33] The authors conclude that, "The president shapes the climate in which his advisers operate" and vice versa. Accordingly, neither factor can be treated as analytically or empirically more significant than the other.[34]

Michael Roskin argues that the American escalation of Vietnam was the outcome of a generationally based foreign policy orientation that is best understood in "Kuhnian" paradigmatic terms. According to this view, American foreign policy can be characterized by one of two recurring "paradigms": (1) an interventionist paradigm that favors American defense being projected abroad; and (2) a noninterventionist paradigm that suggests American defense as being limited to American territory. Roskin contends that "each elite American generation comes to favor one of these orientations by living through the catastrophe brought on by the application *ad absurdum* of the opposite paradigm at the hand of the previous generation."[35] By the late 1950s and early 1960s, the American foreign policymaking elite had come to be dominated by adherents of the "Pearl Harbor" foreign policy paradigm, which advocated strong interventionism in the face of aggression. A key component of this worldview was the adoption of a far-reaching notion of the American national interest according to which strategic offshore regions required vigorous protection. The Pearl Harbor paradigm thus demanded a forceful response to events in Vietnam regardless of circumstances unique to the conflict.

Roskin's primary evidence for the causal importance of the Pearl Harbor paradigm on Vietnam is located in the texts of speeches in which the imagery and memory of Pearl Harbor is evoked by President Johnson, Secretary of Defense McNamara, and Senators Thomas J. Dodd and Henry M. Jackson.[36] The escalation of Vietnam thus stemmed from an *ad absurdum* misapplication of policies by a generation of elites socialized according to the Pearl Harbor paradigm by virtue of having fought in and/or lived through the Second World War.

Looking at the Vietnam War from the Vietnamese perspective, King Chen points to three decisions on the part of the North Vietnamese that help to explain the escalation of the war during the mid-1960s. The first was Hanoi's decision of January 1959 to resume armed revolt in the South. The second was the decision in September 1960 to establish a general policy of "liberation" of the South and the overthrow of the Diem regime. The third was the December 1963 decision to adopt a more aggressive, offensive strategy including intensification of ground troops and material aid to the South.[37] On the basis of these decisions, Chen concludes that neither North Vietnam nor the United States specifically can be viewed as having "caused" the escalation of the Vietnam conflict. Rather, a synthesis of competing theories involving both American and Vietnamese decision making is required to explain the conflict. Thus, Chen argues that "Since the completion of the revolution had been decided as the 'sacred' mission of the Communists, a military confrontation with the United States containment policy was a foregone conclusion. Consequently, war became inevitable."[38] Chen concludes that the Vietnam War was ultimately a function of the North's view of ideological revolution as a "sacred" cause to be carried out by peaceful or violent means as prescribed by the given context. In this sense, the North did not view the situation in Vietnam as a matter of "war" vs. "peace" but rather as different tactics toward the long-term goal of completing the revolution. American decision making is relevant insofar as it established the context in which Hanoi carried out its strategic planning.[39]

In *The Vietnam Trauma in American Foreign Policy, 1945–1975*, Paul Kattenburg argues that "the United States is an 'idea' country, rather than a 'people-land' one. . . . Accordingly, principles and ideals hold a cardinal place in the U.S. national ethos and crucially distinguish U.S. performance in the superpower role."[40] Kattenburg lists three essential components of the American "idea" of the postwar "national interest":

(1) geostrategic doctrine and *realpolitik*;
(2) instruments of coercion in the form of the US military machine
(3) and the moral-ideological purpose in halting the spread of communism.[41]

In light of these three overarching components of the national interest, Kattenburg discusses six factors, which taken together, help to explain the causes of the Vietnam War. The first of these is the notion of "toughness and force" whereby the United States could not countenance involvement in a military conflict without being "tough" and "forceful" or at least conveying the appearance of being so. The second is the American premium on action, determination, and persistence in foreign policy. The third is the failure of expert analysis to separate objective from subjective factors at key junctures in the policy making process. The fourth is the triumph of the management approach to foreign policy in which managerial process and expertise was deemed to be fool-proof in its capacity to resolve political problems. The fifth factor is the perceived domestic and foreign consensus of support in favor of waging the Cold War in Vietnam. And the final factor is the closed system of decision making, which was impervious to external criticism and in which the dominance of the President in making key decisions was not adequately checked and balanced by alternative actors.[42] As a result of these factors taken together, the United States rationalized its increased involvement in Vietnam and

> conjured up theories of worldwide interlinkage of national liberation wars and the credibility of U.S. commitments. The United States invented refined deterrence and the limited-mix programmatic approach to war as an exercise in crisis management. Failing properly to review the stakes and to incorporate the critical results of objective analysis at crucial moments in the enterprise, it pursued stalemate in a closed system of decision-making in order to continue to avoid the dreaded domestic consequences of defeat or the appearance of defeat.[43]

Wallace Thies alone among the authors examined in this chapter sets out to test the basic claims of the literature on strategy and deterrence in the case of Vietnam. Accordingly, Thies argues that the Johnson Administration starting in 1964 premised its decision making in Vietnam on three crucial assumptions stemming directly from the 1960s strategic studies literature on deterrence, compellence, and "limited war." Those assumptions were: "That a program of gradually rising military pressures would induce the government in Hanoi to end its support for the insurgency in South Vietnam. . . . That the leadership would be able to 'fine-tune' the Administration's actions so as to enable it to 'orchestrate' words and deeds and 'signal' by deed as well as by word," and "That the use of force would be controllable—that is, that the pressures against the North could be turned on or off, up or down at will."[44]

According to Thies, the preceding three assumptions have never been thoroughly and systematically evaluated, either by decision makers in practice during the war or by scholars since that time. Thies contends that these assumptions are highly problematic in that they are premised on the impossible task of attempting coercion without first gaining basic information about the adversary and in particular, knowledge regarding what, if anything, is required in order to coerce her/him. In the case of Vietnam, the Johnson administration referred to the adversary simply as "Hanoi" without considering the possibility that "Hanoi" and Hanoi's core interests were both much more complicated than was commonly understood at the time.[45] This in turn led to a major failure in the United States's ability to effectively "signal" "Hanoi" and "control" events on the ground during the escalation period of 1964–1965.

Based on the American experience in Vietnam, Thies asserts "that there is no simple and direct relationship between the rate of escalation and the coercer's chances of success. Instead, it appears that the coercer's chances of success are greatest when the attempted coercion occurs before the target state's government has become firmly committed to whatever course of action the coercer seeks to prevent, and when the coercer utilizes pressure greater than those anticipated by officials in the target state."[46] In failing to comprehend this logic, the Johnson administration encountered great technical difficulties in attempting to signal Hanoi and then perpetuated the problem by failing to acknowledge its very existence. Even if the technical issues were to have been resolved, it is unlikely that U.S. policies in Vietnam would have been more successful "for the simple reason that the Administration had so little understanding of what was going on in Hanoi." From the standpoint of deterrence theory, then, Vietnam turned into a tragedy for the United States precisely because the United States never asked the crucial question: "*who* in Hanoi would have to do *what* in order to comply with American demands?"[47]

4. Conclusions

The preceding subsections reveal a voluminous and diverse political science literature pertaining to the case of Vietnam. These can be divided into two rough camps, each distinguished by a number of key themes. In the first camp, which includes data sets, textbooks, and "classic" accounts, three dominant themes recur. The first is that many American decision makers during the early 1960s viewed Vietnam a crucial piece in the broader puzzle of global competition between the United States and the Soviet Union. The second and related theme suggests that American leaders were deeply concerned, perhaps even obsessed, with the notion that Vietnam represented a pivotal test of American credibility in the eyes of the world, allies and adversaries alike. In these two senses, this first camp within the literature is more "structure-based" in its orientation toward war generally and Vietnam specifically. That is, they see the conflict as a function of the structure of the international system rather than as an outcome of a specific unit, which in this case would be the United States.[48] The third theme regards the more narrow matter of the causal sequence of the escalation of the war during 1964–1965 in which the political science literature tends to view two incidents—Gulf of Tonkin in August 1964, and Pleiku in February 1965—as critical turning points in the trajectory of the war.

The second camp, which includes the studies dedicated exclusively to Vietnam, also alludes to the importance of Cold War strategic thinking and the need and desire of the United States to prove its credibility internationally. Those themes are more weakly represented here, however, and in addition, there is a clear and dominant emphasis on the domestic decision-making process and various factors related to it. Thus, the second camp is more "agent-based" in its approach toward the question of the Vietnam War and its causes, although there remain clear references to the overarching Cold War context within which the agents maneuvered during the conflict.[49] In the following section, an account of the causes of the Vietnam War is presented based on contemporary historical scholarship on the case as presented by professional historians in light of new interviews and the most recently released archival information.

III. REVISING VIETNAM

During the past ten years, a number of new historical accounts of the Vietnam War have been published employing new archival data and an increasing degree of open and enlightening contacts between former Hanoi officials and Western scholars. While the most recent narrative of Vietnam is neither as voluminous nor unified in its claims as is the Israeli critical history discussed in the previous chapter, there are at least two consistent themes within the recent works, which taken together have important implications for Vietnam as a historical case study. The first regards the relative weight of factors for explaining the "causes" of the escalation in Vietnam during 1964–1965. The more recent literature places a heavy emphasis on the role of individual actors—especially that of President Lyndon Johnson—in determining the course of major events in the war. The second theme regards the causal sequence and timing of escalation of the war. The newer literature focuses on events and decisions in Washington during late 1963 and early 1964 as being more influential on the ultimate escalation than were the much-cited incidents on the ground in the Gulf of Tonkin and Pleiku during August 1964 and February 1965, respectively.

In a most recent and sweeping historical account, Fredrik Logevall seeks to show that the United States "chose war" over other options in its policies toward Vietnam. In doing so, Logevall stresses three overarching themes with regard to the escalation of the war in Vietnam. The first is that of contingency, by which Logevall contends that the years 1963 to 1965 were "fluid" and that no preordained U.S. policy was inevitable at that time. The second theme regards the rigidity of U.S. decision making during that period. The third regards the collective failure of the many and diverse early opponents of American involvement in Vietnam to effectively voice their opposition in a way such that policies might have been conceived of differently. "The first theme suggests that the American war in Vietnam was an unnecessary war; the second and third themes help explain why it nevertheless occurred."[50] Looking at the trajectory of executive-level decision making during the early and mid-

1960s, Logevall concludes that the key events leading to the escalation of Vietnam occurred in Washington during late 1963/early 1964, not at the time of the Gulf of Tonkin and Pleiku incidents of August 1964 and February 1965, as is generally agreed upon in the earlier literature.

Logevall cites an extensive documentary and archival record detailing Lyndon Johnson's personal views and decision processes regarding the war, often contrasting these with the much more publicized and well-known views of former Secretary of Defense Robert McNamara. In particular, by January 1964, Johnson had already stated in private on several occasions his intentions to escalate the war in Vietnam but to delay major policy shifts in order not to endanger his prospects in the upcoming November elections.[51] Thus, the day after the coup in which Nguyen Khan wrested power from Duong Van Minh in January 1964, President Johnson stated:

> Screw this neutrality, we ain't going to do business with the Communists, and get the goddamned hell out here. I'm pro-American and I'm taking over. Now it'll take him [Khan] a little time to get his marbles in a row, just like it's taking me a little time. But it's de Gaulle's loss and the neutralists' loss, not the Americans' loss, and we're going to try to launch some counterattacks ourselves. . . . We're going to touch them up a little bit in the days to come.[52]

In Logevall's view, the role of President Johnson was so great that the popular notion of "McNamara's War" is a misnomer: Vietnam was really "Johnson's War." Based on his endemic personalization of all matters pertaining to the war, President Johnson's virtual obsession with the notion of "credibility" led him to shunt aside all other factors pertaining to Vietnam.[53] President Johnson, however, in both private conversations and in written documents throughout his tenure referred to three distinct and unequal notions of "credibility." The first was American "national" credibility abroad, the second the political credibility of the Democratic Party, and the third was President Johnson's personal credibility, only the last of which was of pivotal importance. Indeed, "We may go farther," Logevall writes, "and argue that, within this three-part conception of the credibility imperative, the national part was the least important part. Geostrategic considerations were not the driving force in American Vietnam policy in The Long 1964, either before election or after; partisan political considerations were; individual careerist considerations were."[54]

According to Logevall, then, Lyndon Johnson thought of Vietnam in "Washingtonian" rather than strategic or internationalist terms. Indeed, "Neither diplomatic history nor current international politics interested [President Johnson], (as more than a few visiting diplomats were quick to notice).[55] The documentary record thus portrays President Johnson as a man fixated on the need for his "word" to be credible, especially inside of the Beltway. In this sense, the escalation of the war in Vietnam stemmed directly from the President's refusal to rethink the meaning of his personal commitment not to "lose" in Vietnam, regardless of the factors, systemic or otherwise, that might be at stake.

David Kaiser, in his recent *American Tragedy*, generally agrees with Logevall's overall perspective, with some minor but noteworthy differences. Like Logevall, Kaiser asserts and provides evidence to the effect that the weightiest decisions leading to the escalation of the Vietnam War were made in late 1963/early 1964, not in response to the later crises that unfolded on the ground. "The President," Kaiser writes,

> seems successfully to have persuaded the press and the public that he did not, in fact, decide to embark upon a major war until June and July. And so carefully did he cover his tracks and deceive even some high-level policymakers that this misconception has persisted, and even found its way into the works of various historians who have analyzed a two-part decision—first bombing, then ground forces, that never occurred. In fact the United States government made a single decision for war in principle in December 1964, decided to implement it in mid-February 1965, and began the implementation in March.[56]

According to this account, the road toward escalation led directly through the mind of Lyndon Johnson and his advisors, who filtered their major decision-making processes through a perceptual frame characterized by a strong generational consciousness. More specifically, Johnson and his chief foreign policy aides were socialized in the mode of the "G.I. generation," who were generally steadfast in the face of adversity and who had "In their youth . . . seen American firepower reduce America's enemies to rubble, and almost nothing could shake their faith that any new war must turn out the same way."[57] Accordingly, the President and his most important Vietnam architects, Secretary of Defense Robert McNamara, Secretary of State Dean Rusk, and National Security Advisor McGeorge Bundy were archetypal GI's who possessed "a vastly oversimplified view of the proper response to aggression. Essentially, because the events of the 1930s in Asia and Europe had led to world war, the GI generation had come away believing that armed aggression anywhere had to be resisted immediately, both as matter of right and because a failure to resist aggression would inevitably lead to more aggression."[58] Perhaps more important, however, was President Johnson's steadfast belief that when facing aggression, perseverance toward and faith in a desired goal will inevitably and without fail lead to a favorable outcome, as appeared to have been the case in the Great War. These factors, greatly aggravated by Johnson's proclivity to personalize politics, led to a gross misinterpretation of the actualities on the ground in Vietnam and a misunderstanding of the proper means, if any, that might have led to a successful American intervention in the conflict there.

In a unique analysis of the Vietnam War, Anne Blair examines the politics of the conflict through the perspective of two-time Ambassador Henry Cabot Lodge. While her angle into the war is different, Blair fully agrees with Kaiser and Logevall in concluding that personality and contingency appear to explain more about the escalation of the Vietnam War than system structure or military strategy. In reviewing new documentation regarding Ambassador Lodge's tenure in Saigon and his relationship with President Johnson, Blair "increasingly found that coincidence, personal style, individual ambitions, and the clash of strong wills shaped events more than explicit policy goals or the functioning of systems."[59]

Throughout her account of Lodge's tenure in Vietnam, Blair richly documents Lodge's repeated missed opportunities to publicly criticize the administration's understanding of the "situation" in Vietnam on the grounds that as Ambassador, Lodge was a "loyal" servant of the President. Instead, shortly before resigning his post in June 1964, Lodge sent a private letter to President Johnson urgently cautioning against Americanization of the war. The President proceeded to ignore the letter because Lodge was "yesterday's man."[60] President Johnson also ignored for several months Lodge's request to resign his post, "apparently on the sole ground of keeping him silent on the conduct of the war—a consideration that turned on a grave misjudgment of his ambassador's loyalty."[61] More important to Johnson, however, was the matter of pitting his advisors against one another in order to keep quiet his intent to escalate the Vietnam conflict following an electoral victory in November 1964. On the point of timing as well as of personality and contingency, Blair's account accords with those of the preceding authors in which late 1963/early 1964 was the key period during which decisions to escalate the war were made.

In his recent study on Vietnam, Lloyd Gardner too focuses on the significance of individual-level politics to the conflict, although with a slightly different twist. According to Gardner, most, if not all of Lyndon Johnson's political career and major decisions are explained as a function of his fervent "New Dealer" political identity. "Johnson," Gardner writes, "had *lived* the modernization policies his advisers prescribed for Vietnam during the New Deal and Fair Deal years."[62] Thus, the President convinced himself that "To ward off the threat to his Great Society programs . . . he had to keep conservatives happy with promises to bring back the coonskin to display on Capitol Hill. And he fantasized away public doubts, including his own, with the promise of a Mekong Valley project to surpass even the New Deal's Tennessee Valley Authority."[63]

This approach to Vietnam consisted of two related components. The first was that Johnson felt he needed to "win" Vietnam in order to secure Congressional approval for his "other war," namely the war on poverty instantiated in his Great Society legislative onslaught. Thus, "Lyndon Johnson believed he could not run away from Vietnam without giving conservatives, who did not really care much about the little brown freedom fighters in Southeast Asia, the opportunity to deny him the Great Society. When Johnson was faulted for attempting to take the Great Society to Vietnam, critics failed to add that he believed the battle for his domestic agenda turned on the outcome in Southeast Asia."[64]

The second component pertained to the President's flirtation with the notion of "bringing the New Deal to Vietnam" in the form of a $100 million TVA-style program for the Mekong Valley by means of which he could transcend the politics of the conflict as it was. After presenting this idea publicly in a speech at Johns Hopkins University on April 7, 1965, the President on the helicopter ride back to Washington declared, "Old Ho can't turn me down." As former aide Bill Moyers recollects of Johnson: "He'd say 'My God, I've offered Ho Chi Minh $100 million to build a Mekong Valley. If that'd been George Meany he'd have snapped at it!"[65] While this proposal obviously didn't bear fruit, it was indicative, in Gardner's view, of President Johnson's overall approach toward politics generally and Vietnam specifically. In this sense, then, Lyndon Johnson's political identity and personal governing style, more so than other contributing factors, explain the escalation of the war during 1964–1965.

In a study of American civil-military relations during the Vietnam era, H. R. McMaster suggests that foreign policy decision making during the Kennedy-Johnson years was causally rooted in a transformation of the relationship between the executive branch and the Joint Chiefs of Staff. Like each of the authors just discussed, McMaster places a high degree of weight on the individual level of analysis and more specifically and importantly, on the governing styles and policies of Presidents Kennedy and Johnson. "Although impersonal forces, such as the ideological imperative of containing Communism, the bureaucratic structure, and institutional priorities, influenced the president's Vietnam decisions, those decisions depended primarily on his character, his motivations, and his relationships with his principal advisors."[66] According to this account, structural changes in the National Security Council apparatus initiated under President Kennedy and consolidated under President Johnson removed the preexisting direct channel of authority between the Joint Chiefs and the President. By making such changes, Presidents Kennedy and Johnson greatly harmed the executive branch's ability to effectively assess military scenarios and to establish strategic priorities in military terms. "The relationship between the president, the secretary of defense, and the Joint Chiefs led to the curious situation in which the nation went to war without the benefit of effective military advice from the organization having the statutory responsibility to be the nation's 'principal military advisors.'"[67]

Exacerbating this situation was a high measure of personal distrust and dislike between the Joint Chiefs and their "best and brightest" civilian superiors. According to Air Force Chief of Staff Curtis Lemay, for instance, the so-called "whiz kids" were "the most egotistical people that I ever saw in my life. They had no faith in the military; they had no respect for the military at all. They felt that the Harvard Business School method of solving problems would solve any problem in the world. . . . They were better than all the rest of us; otherwise they wouldn't have gotten their superior education, as they saw it."[68] Throughout the crucial period from November 1963 to March 1965, the Joint Chiefs disagreed with Johnson's and McNamara's policies in a number of ways, at times calling for a reduced use of American force, while at others, calling for more. In particular, "the Chiefs had been united in their opposition to the Diem coup. . . . They resented the administration's disregard for their advice and the secrecy under which the coup plotting had been carried out, referring to the coup scornfully as the 'Asian Bay of Pigs.'"[69]

Unfortunately, according to McMaster's account, when it became apparent to the Joint Chiefs that their role in Vietnam was clearly subordinate to the opinions of McNamara, Bundy, and Rusk, they acquiesced in working within the strategic framework established by the political appointees. McMaster cites several reasons for this, including the professional code of military officers, which prohibits engagement in political activity, especially activity that could undermine the credibility of the government; basic loyalty to the Commander-in-Chief; and a sense that acquiescence was the best way to protect the institutional interests of the military services.[70] McMaster also cites a clearly discernable pattern of lying on the part of President Johnson and Secretary of Defense McNamara as an important secondary factor in explaining the escalation of Vietnam during the early and mid-1960s. For instance, as early as 1942, McMaster alludes to an interview in which Johnson eagerly misrepresented his record of service on a B-26 mission during World War II for the purpose of bolstering his political image.[71]

Shortly after assuming the Presidency in 1963, Johnson pledged in a New Year's greeting to President Duong Van Minh that "American military personnel can be progressively withdrawn" from Vietnam, while in reality, Johnson had already decided upon a massive future escalation of American involvement.[72] Similarly, McNamara purposefully employed the use of lies to make his case throughout the war. During a fact-finding mission to Vietnam

in December 1963, for example, McNamara reported to the President positively regarding the U.S. relationship with Saigon despite the fact that Vietnamese Vice President "Nguyen Ngoc Tho considered U.S. assistance 'unin-
telligent' and thought that the Diem regime" had alienated the public through
brutal repression.[73] During later years, McNamara gave daily press briefings
on body counts of North Vietnamese as part of a comprehensive campaign to
portray an image of American military success despite that most independent
observers "on the ground" in Vietnam conveyed a vastly divergent picture of
the war.

Echoing the views of McMaster within the narrower context of the Gulf of
Tonkin incidents, Edwin Moise depicts a similar pattern of discordant civil-
military relations to explain American behavior in Vietnam during
1963–1965. According to this reading of the Gulf of Tonkin crises, American
decision making was fraught with a major breach between the desires of political leaders and the advice of the military. Immediately following the crisis
in the Gulf of Tonkin, Maxwell Taylor, Ambassador to Saigon and a committed "Johnson man," cabled the State Department to advise that "Since any of
the courses of action" the United States might take to retaliate would "carry
a considerable measure of risk to the U.S., we should be slow to get too
deeply involved until we have a better feel for the quality of our ally." The
Joint Chiefs of Staff, in contrast, firmly disagreed with Maxwell's assessment
and recommendation, arguing that "It was too late to think of getting 'a better feel for the quality of our ally'" in light of the fact that the "The United
States is already deeply involved."[74]

On the importance of Presidential deception, Moise asserts that during the
second half of 1964, President Johnson conveyed three different and contradictory messages for three different audiences concerned with Vietnam. First,
the President sought to convince the general public that there would not be a
war between the United States and North Vietnam despite a growing consensus within the administration that this was precisely what was to occur. Second, Johnson also attempted to convince Hanoi that it would be attacked if
the RVN fell too far under communist "sway," which was a fundamental con-
tradiction of the message being sold to the American public. Third, the President sought to motivate Saigon by indicating that the United States was waiting for "the tide of battle to shift *against* the Communists in the South," when
in fact it was clear to the President that this was the reverse of how events
were unfolding on the ground.[75]

In light of the notion that Vietnam might still be won "on the cheap" using
superior American technology and strategic planning, Johnson further deceived the American public by downsizing the overall armed forces "Even
while Washington was drawing up plans for escalation."[76] Finally and per-

haps most importantly in Moise's view, it has become widely agreed among specialists that the second Gulf of Tonkin attack on August 4 was at first based on mistaken reports and then fabricated into "reality" in order to justify retaliatory air strikes. This in turn led Hanoi to react to "the apparent American decision with a significant increase in the commitment of North Vietnamese resources to war in the South (the first PAVN regiment started down the Ho Chi Minh Trail in September and October 1964, and the second in October), a major upgrading of the Ho Chi Minh trail to allow men and arms to move more easily form North to South, and an upgrading of the anti-aircraft defenses of North Vietnam."[77] Thus, executive-level deception regarding the Gulf of Tonkin helped to set in motion a sequence of events that fostered the broader escalation of the war during 1964 and 1965.

IV. CONCLUSION

This chapter presents two literatures that see Vietnam in very divergent ways. Most political scientists, with some exceptions, have tended to view the escalation of the Vietnam War in a systems theory context, with an emphasis on containment doctrine and the balance of global power during the Cold War. Interestingly, even some scholars who focus in-depth on the significance of American domestic politics still seem compelled to couch their arguments in the language of containment and deterrence. Contemporary historians, by contrast, see Vietnam in a quite different light. The most recent historiography of Vietnam depicts the rise to war as driven by factors not only internal to the United States, but very much stemming from the role of a few key executive branch officials, most significantly, the President. Does this contrast have an effect on political science theorization? That question is addressed in detail in chapter 6.

NOTES

1. Robert Lyle Butterworth, ed., *Managing Interstate Conflict* (Pittsburgh, PA: University Center for International Studies, 1976), 271.
2. Butterworth, *Managing Interstate Conflict*, 273–74.
3. Jonathan Wilkenfeld, Michael Brecher, Sheila Moser, "Handbook of Foreign Policy Crises," vol. 2, *Crises in the Twentieth Century* (Oxford: Pergamon Press, 1988), 322–23.
4. Alexander L. George, *Forceful Persuasion* (Washington DC: USIP, 1991), 40.
5. George, *Forceful Persuasion*, 42.
6. George, *Forceful Persuasion*, 43–44.

7. George, *Forceful Persuasion*, 11.

8. George, *Forceful Persuasion*, 44–45.

9. Bruce W. Jentleson, *American Foreign Policy* (New York: W.W. Norton, 2000), 140–41.

10. Jentleson, *American Foreign Policy,* 140–42.

11. Karen Mingst, *Essentials of International Relations* (New York: W.W. Norton, 1999), 50–51.

12. Mingst, *Essentials*, 51.

13. Kenneth N. Waltz, *Theory of International Politics* (New York: Random House, 1979), 189–90.

14. Waltz, *Theory*, 190–91.

15. Waltz, *Theory,* 205.

16. Jack Snyder, *Myths of Empire* (Ithaca, NY: Cornell University Press, 1991), 255–56.

17. Snyder, *Myths of Empire*, 256–57.

18. John G. Stoessinger, *Why Nations Go to War*, 5th edition (New York: St. Martins, 1990), 84.

19. Stoessinger, *Why Nations Go to War*, 99.

20. Stoessinger, *Why Nations Go to War*, 205.

21. Stoessinger, *Why Nations Go to War*, 207–13.

22. Stoessinger, *Why Nations Go to War*, 223.

23. Leslie H. Gelb with Richard K. Betts, *The Irony of Vietnam* (Washington D.C.: Brookings, 1979), 2.

24. Gelb and Betts, *The Irony of Vietnam,* 25.

25. Gelb and Betts, *The Irony of Vietnam,* 354.

26. Larry Berman, *Planning a Tragedy* (New York: W.W. Norton, 1982), 130.

27. Berman, *Planning a Tragedy*, xiii.

28. Berman, *Planning a Tragedy*, 145–46.

29. David M. Barrett, "The Mythology Surrounding Lyndon Johnson, His Advisers, and the 1965 Decision to Escalate the Vietnam War," *Political Science Quarterly*, vol. 103, no. 4 (1988): 637–38.

30. Barett, "The Mythology," 640.

31. Barett, "The Mythology," 661–63.

32. The authors then discuss seven propositions about executive decision making and the Vietnam War. Those propositions are: 1) "It is possible to illuminate the problem of presidential reality testing by identifying the types of presidential advisory systems, but classifications quickly become inadequate;" 2) "The formal organization of advising as underappreciated strengths;" 3) "The informal organization of advising has underappreciated strengths;" 4) "Multiple advocacy is not a panacea, but it may ameliorate defective process;" 5) "In presidential reality testing the buck stops in the Oval Office;" 6) "A president with a well-developed personal capacity to test reality may be able to get by without a well-developed advisory system;" 7) "But advisory systems do matter: a well-devised advisory system can mitigate the president's personal shortcomings, and a poorly devised system can exacerbate them." Fred I. Greenstein and John P. Burke, "The Dynamics of Presidential Reality Testing: Evi-

dence from Two Vietnam Decisions," *Political Science Quarterly*, vol. 104, no. 4 (1989–1990): 560–77.

33. Greenstein and Burke, "The Dynamics," 560.

34. Greenstein and Burke, "The Dynamics," 580.

35. Michael Roskin, "From Pearl Harbor to Vietnam: Shifting Generational Paradigms and Foreign Policy, *Political Science Quarterly*, vol. 89, no. 3 (Fall 1974): 563.

36. Roskin, "From Pearl Harbor," 569–70.

37. King C. Chen, "Hanoi's Three Decisions and the Escalation of the Vietnam War," *Political Science Quarterly*, vol. 90, no. 2 (Summer 1975): 240.

38. Chen, "Hanoi's Three Decisions," 243.

39. Chen, "Hanoi's Three Decisions," 257–58.

40. Paul M. Kattenburg, *The Vietnam Trauma in American Foreign Policy, 1945–75* (New Brunswick: Transaction Books, 1980), 70.

41. Kattenburg, *The Vietnam Trauma*, 75.

42. Kattenburg, *The Vietnam Trauma*, 220–28.

43. Kattenburg, *The Vietnam Trauma*, 315.

44. Wallace J. Thies, *When Governments Collide* (Berkeley: University of California Press, 1980), 9.

45. Thies, *When Governments Collide*, 220–22.

46. Thies, *When Governments Collide*, 282.

47. Thies, *When Governments Collide*, 346–47.

48. For discussion of the agent-structure relationship, see Alexander E. Wendt, "The Agent-Structure Problem in International Relations Theory," *International Organization*, vol. 41, no. 3 (Summer 1987).

49. Wendt, "The Agent-Structure Problem."

50. Fredrik Logevall, *Choosing War* (Berkeley: University of California Press, 1999), xvi.

51. Logevall, *Choosing War*, 109.

52. Cited in Logevall, *Choosing War*, 107.

53. Logevall, *Choosing War*, 390–92

54. Logevall, *Choosing War*, 388.

55. Logevall, *Choosing War*, 79. Brackets added.

56. David Kaiser, *American Tragedy* (Cambridge, MA: The Belknap Press, 2000), 410–11.

57. Kaiser, *American Tragedy*, 185.

58. Kaiser, *American Tragedy*, 409.

59. Anne E. Blair, *Lodge in Vietnam* (New Haven, CT: Yale University Press, 1995), x–xi.

60. Blair, *Lodge in Vietnam*, 139.

61. Blair, *Lodge in Vietnam*, 157.

62. Lloyd C. Gardner, *Pay at Any Price* (Chicago: Ivan R. Dee, 1995), 536.

63. Gardner, *Pay at Any Price*, xiv.

64. Gardner, *Pay at Any Price*, 98.

65. Cited in Gardner, *Pay at Any Price*, 197.

66. H. R. McMaster, *Dereliction of Duty* (New York: HarperCollins, 1997), 324.

67. McMaster, *Dereliction of Duty*, 325–26.

68. McMaster, *Dereliction of Duty*, 20.

69. McMaster, *Dereliction of Duty*, 45.

70. McMaster, *Dereliction of Duty*, 330.

71. McMaster, *Dereliction of Duty*, 51.

72. McMaster, *Dereliction of Duty*, 63

73. McMaster, *Dereliction of Duty*, 57.

74. Edwin E. Moise, *Tonkin Gulf* (Chapel Hill: The University of North Carolina Press, 1996), 245.

75. Moise, *Tonkin Gulf*, 44.

76. Moise, *Tonkin Gulf*, 246.

77. Moise, *Tonkin Gulf*, 252.

Chapter Six

Political Science's Historical Problem

I. INTRODUCTION

The most recent historical scholarship on Vietnam discussed in chapter 5 displays some very interesting insights into the causes for the escalation of the war. This begs the question: to what extent are political scientists' understandings of the war consistent with the most recent historical narratives? Of course, it is neither fair nor reasonable to expect scholars to employ sources that were not existent at the time of their research. Thus, the question just asked is important with regard to whether political science scholarship is apt to hold up well over time, both empirically and theoretically speaking. Accordingly, sections II through IV of this chapter assess political science scholarship on Vietnam in light of the new historical narrative of the war. While the results here are mixed, there is a second and more complex question regarding historical political science scholarship, which is: to what extent does the political science literature's particular approach to historical inquiry advance or hinder theoretical research in the field, regardless of the timing of the narratives employed? In section V, I examine in depth Jack Snyder's use of historical texts in his classic work, *Myths of Empire* to demonstrate the extent and seriousness of the problem of historical inquiry in political science.

II. GENERAL TEXTBOOKS AND DATA SET COMPLIATIONS

How well do data set summaries and textbook accounts of the Vietnam War fare in light of the historiography of the past ten years? We recall that

Managing Interstate Conflict and "Handbook of Foreign Policy Crises" place total reliance on the Gulf of Tonkin Crisis, beginning on August 2, 1964 as the start of the "war" in Vietnam.[1] Both accounts view the crisis as lasting "one month." *Managing Interstate Conflict* also refers to a distinct "second" crisis, triggered by the North Vietnamese attack at the U.S. army barracks at Pleiku on February 7, 1965 and cites an American "commitment to maintain its influence in Southeast Asia" as important to understanding both crises.[2] There are clearly a number of fundamental problems with these synopses, especially if one were to rely on them for the purposes of "coding" Vietnam in a large sample analysis. First, these accounts say little regarding the causes of the war other than that the crises "triggered" conflict. They say nothing about the domestic political context in the United States, much less in Vietnam, and they fail to suggest any possible alternative causes of the war.

Second, if one were to rely solely on these two accounts, one would be given the impression that the Vietnam War was in fact two distinct incidents each of which lasted approximately one month; not a protracted and escalating war that began in the 1950s and continued until 1975. The synopses further fail to give any sense of how earlier events may or may not have been influential on later events in the unfolding trajectory of the conflict, which relates to a third point. From a methodological perspective, these accounts would generate an automatic sample bias by treating the Gulf of Tonkin and Pleiku crises as separate "cases," when the latter was clearly influenced by the existence of the former. Finally, insofar as the cases are presented in a historical form, they adopt a purely systemic perspective: the crises escalated because of interstate perspectives of the adversary and because of American concern for prestige and credibility in the broader context of the Cold War. This account is at serious odds with the scholarship of contemporary historians, who place much more emphasis on American domestic politics and the individual decision making of President Johnson.

Alexander George, we recall, views the Vietnam War as an instance of failed "coercive diplomacy" in which the United States was unable to effectively persuade North Vietnam to abandon its goal of unifying Vietnam. According to George, President Johnson was most concerned lest American use of force in Vietnam become unmanageable and provoke a more serious Cold War confrontation with the Soviet Union. In George's words: "Washington's concern lest heavy air attacks against North Vietnam provoke the Soviet Union derived from the fact that Moscow had publicly agreed to provide North Vietnam with military assistance."[3] The American policy of incremental escalation was thus "essential to enable Moscow to exercise its influence" on North Vietnam to negotiate on terms favorable to the United States. According to George: "Johnson hoped this policy would motivate Moscow and at the same time allow it to play a pivotal role."[4]

While George's claim of failed coercive diplomacy commands some support (i.e., Hanoi was not "coerced"), his reasoning regarding American decision making and the escalation in Vietnam is curious in light of the historiography of the case. Recent historians make almost no mention of a serious American concern over war with the Soviet Union stemming from Vietnam. They also heavily discount the importance of working with or even considering the Soviet Union as a significant actor toward helping to resolve the conflict in Southeast Asia. In this sense, George seems to have reversed President Lyndon Johnson's strategic priorities: George portrays the President as thinking primarily in terms of Soviet-Vietnamese-U.S. relations when dealing with Vietnam, while domestic factors are unmentioned, even in passing. The recent historiography, in contrast, depicts the President as completely absorbed with inside-the-Beltway politics, with Vietnam and the Soviet Union entering the narrative as distant, almost abstract entities. Thus, it is hard to validate George's logic of coercive diplomacy based on the empirical justification for it that he provides.

The two textbooks reviewed in section I both share a theme in common with these other works: that the U.S. escalation of the conflict in Vietnam was in large measure influenced by the American compulsion to maintain its credibility at a broader systemic level. As Karen Mingst asserts: "To most U.S. policymakers in the late 1950s and early 1960s, Vietnam represented yet another test of the containment doctrine: communist influence must be stopped, they argued, before it spread like a chain of falling dominos though the rest of southeast Asia and beyond. . . . Thus, the United States supported the South Vietnamese dictators Ngo Dinh Diem and Nguen Van Thieu against the rival communist regime of Ho Chi Minh in the North."[5]

As mentioned above, this does not seem to square with the evidence provided by contemporary historical scholars of the conflict. In particular, we recall that Frederick Logevall understands President Johnson as having a complex tripartite conception of "credibility" in his decision making. The first sense of credibility: American national credibility abroad is by far the least significant according to Logevall. The second sense, the credibility of the Democratic Party in domestic politics, is more important, although this merges into the third understanding of credibility, namely that of President Johnson, the man, who was at once both leader of the party and of his own administration.[6] Logevall's view, supported by all of the other historians cited in chapter 5, is that President Johnson was far more concerned with not "losing" Vietnam than he was with any abstract notion of how the United States might or might not be perceived by either its allies or adversaries.

III. "CLASSIC" ACCOUNTS

Let us now turn attention to what the three "classic" IR accounts cited in section I impart regarding Vietnam. As mentioned in that section, it would hardly be accurate to classify *Theory of International Politics* as a work about Vietnam. Given the enormous degree to which the book has been read, however, Waltz's comments on the case cannot be ignored. We recall that Waltz asserts, "As some saw early in that struggle, and as most saw later on, in terms of global politics little was at stake in Vietnam. The international-political insignificance of Vietnam can be understood only in terms of the world's structure. America's failure in Vietnam was tolerable because neither success nor failure mattered much internationally. Victory would not make the world one of American hegemony. Defeat would not make the world one of Russian hegemony. No matter what the outcome, the American-Russian duopoly would endure."[7] This may be true, but this does not tell us much about either the cause(s) of the conflict in Vietnam specifically, or war in general.

What the recent historiography of the case indicates so vibrantly is how *little* international system structure was on the minds of key decision makers in Washington during the time of war, public pronouncements to the contrary aside. In asserting that Vietnam was unimportant in the sense that it neither made nor broke the Cold War, Waltz is implicitly dismissive of the fact that it was a major war that saw millions of lives lost and had an undeniably tremendous impact on American foreign policy. Indeed, the more recent historiography does not so much injure the internal logic of Waltz's theory as highlight how little—in terms of specific empirical cases that command widespread attention—the theory can actually explain.

Of the "classic" IR books assessed in this chapter, Stoessinger's *Why Nations Go to War* fares best when weighed against the narrative content of the newer historiography on the case. As Stoessinger puts it: "Johnson's ego, stubbornness, and pride destroyed his presidency and divided his people in a spiritual civil war . . . he misperceived his enemy, misled his people, and ultimately deceived himself. . . . It all began in 1964 with a memorandum to the president from the Joint Chiefs of Staff, urging him to increase the commitment in order to win the war more quickly."[8] Both in terms of the importance of the President-as-decision-maker and in terms of the timing of key decisions (1964 vs. 1965); Stoessinger's account is consistent, if understandably incomplete, when compared with the research of the past ten years. Where Stoessinger encounters difficulty is with regard to the internal logic of his argument. Stoessinger's contention that war is a "learned behavior" is fundamentally inconsistent with his claim that "In the past the anarchic nature of the nation-state system was chiefly responsible for wars."[9] For if war is in fact learned, then it is one among a number of possible prevailing responses to anarchy and one that is certainly not a foregone conclusion. Thus socialization—not anarchy—would be the chief causal factor behind war.[10] In either case, Stoessinger is at best unclear as to how *either* the learned behavior of war *or* anarchy was causally significant with regard to President Johnson's particular behavior and actions in leading to Vietnam.

IV. VIETNAM MONOGRAPHS

Turning to political science studies whose primary focus falls on the case of Vietnam, one of the most oft-cited works, *The Irony of Vietnam*, argues that the paradox of Vietnam "is that the *foreign policy* failed, but the *domestic decisionmaking system* worked. It worked as it usually does, in the way that most constitutionalists and democratic pluralists believe it should work. Vietnam was not an aberration of the decisionmaking system but a logical culmination of the principles that leaders brought with them into it." Thus: "the core consensual goal of postwar foreign policy (containment of communism) was pursued consistently . . . differences of both elite and mass opinion were accommodated by compromise, and policy never strayed very far from the center of opinion both within and outside the government," and "virtually all views and recommendations were considered and virtually all important decisions were made without illusions about the odds for success."[11] Let us assess these three claims in more detail in light of the current historiography of Vietnam.

First, most, if not all of the recent historians of the conflict heavily discount the importance of containment of communism as a policy goal. At best, selling to the public the appearance of not failing to contain communism was deemed by the President and his advisors as important toward maintaining their overall political effectiveness. At worst, containment was causally insignificant in respect to Vietnam. Regarding the claim that compromises were made to accommodate the differences between mass and elite opinion, there seems to be strong evidence to the contrary. According to the more recent historiography of Vietnam, President Johnson was committed to escalation of the conflict in late 1963/early 1964 at a time when he knew full well that the American general public was firmly against such a course of action. He thus spent much of a year and a half securing his political standing in order that he would be able to proceed with escalation with a minimum of political backlash. If escalation to a fighting force of 500,000 women and men was the "compromise" between two positions one of which was presumably withdrawal, then it is difficult to imagine what the other pole of the debate was arguing for. Finally, the matter of "all views being considered" is difficult to assess for a number of reasons.

First, it is unclear the degree to which dissenting views actually made their way to the President. While David Barrett argues that the President was fully apprised of opposition to escalation in Vietnam among trusted advisors, the current historiography downplays this factor and focuses on President Johnson's preconceived political proclivities.[12] Further, even if the President was given access to the dissenters, if he was under the "sway" of McNamara, Rusk, and Bundy such that he was immune to internalizing dissent, then the dissenters' access to the President is causally irrelevant. In summary, it is unclear first, the extent to which the President physically heard a diversity of views and second, when he did, the degree to which he listened to any voices other than his own. Thus, Gelb and Betts argument that the "system worked" can only be accepted if we take "system" to mean that the President can listen to whomever and ultimately decide whatever he wants in a relative vacuum of checks and balances against executive power.

Larry Berman argues that American leaders "accepted containment of communism and the domino theory as basic premises for formulating policy and not as hypotheses for analysis."[13] In addition, however, Berman also suggests that "In the final analysis, the president and not his advisors must accept most of the blame. Johnson was the cause of his ultimate undoing. The president was involved in a delicate exercise of political juggling" in which his ultimate goal was to "buy time" to ensure the successful fruition of his Great Society program. "Thus did Johnson commit slow political suicide."[14] Berman's claim that President Johnson's approach toward Vietnam can be seen as a function of his personal governing style and political preferences is very much in conformity with the conclusions of the current historiography of the case. It is odd then, that Berman would begin his argument by stressing the importance of containment and the domino theory when they are of little consequence to his own conclusions. Berman thus seems to arrive at a correct conclusion from the standpoint of contemporary historiography despite sidetracking his analysis with an inconsistent and logically misplaced discussion of containment and the domino theory.

David Barrett has an interesting perspective on Vietnam from the standpoint of political science in that he is as much concerned with new evidence about the conflict as he is with explaining the case itself. We recall that Barett seeks to dispel two "myths" in the literature regarding President Johnson and Vietnam: that Johnson was the victim of "groupthink" and that the President would not countenance advice contrary to his own views.[15] According to Barrett, there were at least six "significant" advisers who strongly cautioned the President against escalating the war in Vietnam in 1965. While this claim is interesting and his evidence for it compelling, it suffers from two major flaws.

First, Barett himself concludes that President Johnson, in spite of sincerely listening to the advice of the dissenters nonetheless proceeded to opt for different advice because he was heavily under the sway of the "whiz kids" McNamara, Rusk, and Bundy. If this is the case, then the absence or presence of the dissenters is causally inconsequential to American decision making regarding Vietnam. Second, even if this were not the case, Barett utterly fails to explain why, in spite of strong advice to the contrary from trusted advisors; President Johnson proceeded so uncautiously ahead with the escalation of the war, other than the notion that the "whiz kids" "advised him" to do so. But this still doesn't explain why either the whiz kids or the President wanted to escalate the war. Clearly, they did want to do so, so toward that effect Barrett provides an interesting complement to the historiography of the Vietnam War. However, a compelling explanation for the war is otherwise absent in his analysis.

Greenstein and Burke argue that there are two keys to understanding the different decisions on intervention of the Eisenhower and Johnson administrations. The first alludes to the underlying differences in the degree of formality/informality of the presidential advising system in each administration. The second regards personality: whereas President Eisenhower was more concerned with the content of policy than with politics, President Johnson instinctively took the precise opposite approach, favoring politics over policy.[16] The authors conclude that, "The president shapes the climate in which his advisers operate" and vice versa, such that one factor can not be treated as either analytically or empirically dominant over the other.[17] Greenstein and Burke, like Barett, suffer from the problem of not necessarily getting the historiography of the case wrong but nonetheless failing to arrive at a worthwhile theoretical conclusion in light of that historiography. In short, the claim that presidents influence their advisors and vice versa reveals quite little about when, why, and how important foreign policy decisions are made. It is not surprising, then, that Greenstein and Burke have little definitive to say regarding the ostensible focus of their study: namely why President Lyndon Johnson decided in late 1963/early 1964 to escalate the war in Vietnam.

Michael Roskin, we recall, argues that the American escalation of Vietnam is explained as an outgrowth of a generationally-based foreign policy orientation that can be understood in "Kuhnian" paradigmatic terms. According to this view, the Pearl Harbor paradigm of foreign policy orientation held by American leaders required a forceful response to events in Vietnam. The escalation of Vietnam was thus the result of an *ad absurdum* misapplication of policies suggested by the Pearl Harbor paradigm. Roskin bases this claim on the use of Pearl Harbor imagery and discourse in the speeches of several key figures, including President Johnson, Secretary of Defense McNamara, and Senators Thomas J. Dodd and Henry M. Jackson.[18]

The clearest link between Roskin's work and the contemporary historiography of Vietnam is with David Kaiser's discussion of the importance of generational outlook to executive decision making. However, Kaiser makes the more narrow and defensible claim that Presidents Kennedy and Johnson, as products of the GI generation, adopted a resilient attitude in the face of "aggression" within a broader domestic political context. Kaiser does not suggest, as per Roskin, that American policy toward Vietnam writ large was based on an *ad absurdum* application of the lessons of Pearl Harbor. Further, whereas Roskin attempts to explain American foreign policy in light of references to a sample of speech texts, Kaiser deliberately *shows*, via an extensive documentary record, that President Johnson behaved the way the GI role-type would expect him to. In order for Roskin's argument to hold, he would have to show not only that key leaders engaged in discourse indicative of the Pearl Harbor paradigm, but also that the conceptual framework of that paradigm actually *influenced* the key decisions of top decision makers, the most important of which was clearly President Johnson. The recent historiography, including the work of David Kaiser, indicates that President Johnson was far more concerned with his domestic political agenda and personal political standing than he was with halting aggression. To the extent that defending Vietnam was important, it was as a means toward the end of enhancing the President's domestic political position, not an end in itself.

Alone among all of the political scientists who have written on Vietnam, King Chen looks at the conflict from the perspective of Hanoi. Looking at three key strategic decisions taken by the North between 1959 and 1963, Chen argues that the escalation of the conflict is a function of the North's irrevocable commitment to the goal of unifying Vietnam.[19] Once the United States came into the path of that goal, war became inevitable, although only as a means toward the end of unification of the country, not as an end in itself. Like several of the authors just discussed, Chen's problem is not so much with the historiography of the case as with his interpretation of it. That the North wished to unite Vietnam is not questioned by the recent historiography. However, insofar as the United States thwarted that goal and, in so doing, made escalation of the war inevitable, an additional and ultimately separate explanation is required to explain how the United States came to occupy such a position. Toward that effect, Chen has little to say and thus his discussion of the view from Hanoi ultimately fails to explain the causes of the escalation of the war in Vietnam, since it appears that escalation was more motivated by the United States than by North Vietnam.

Paul Kattenburg's account of the Vietnam War is an interesting and complex one that dares to take the role of ideas seriously in understanding world politics. In light of the recent historiography of the case, Kattenburg is certainly "validated" in his claim that the crucial role of the President in decision making was unchecked and occurred in what he refers to as a "closed system." The principal problem with Kattenburg's account is that it substitutes description for theory. Kattenburg's six factors leading to Vietnam when taken together *are themselves a historical account* of the war rather than a causal explanation for it. While Kattenburg's basic "historiography" fares well insofar as it goes, there is no relative weighting of factors, from the role of ideas to the role of bureaucratic politics to the role of the Commander-in-Chief. In this sense, Kattenburg's problem is not one of getting the case "wrong," but of assuming that the case "speaks for itself" and thereby provides an effective substitute for theory.

We recall that Wallace Thies, the sole deterrence theorist among the authors discussed, argues that the Johnson Administration based its Vietnam strategy and policy on three core assumptions: "That a program of gradually rising military pressures would induce the government in Hanoi to end its support for the insurgency in South Vietnam . . . that the leadership would be able to 'fine-tune' the Administration's actions so as to enable it to 'orchestrate' words and deeds and 'signal' by deed as well as by word," and "that the use of force would be controllable—that is, that the pressures against the North could be turned on or off, up or down at will."[20] Thies's claim that the Johnson administration grossly oversimplified the character of "Hanoi" and its interests is certainly not inconsistent with the more recent historiography of the case, which argues that decisions on Vietnam were to a much greater extent a function of politics in Washington than they were of events in the theater of conflict. Further, the notion that the United States never asked the key question of *who* in Hanoi would have to do *what* in order to attain the results the United States sought is similarly compatible with current literature.

That said, it is difficult to evaluate Thies's theoretical commitments in light of the present chapter for the reason that Thies does not directly respond to the question "what caused the war?" Rather, Thies is concerned with evaluating the core operating assumptions of the Johnson administration during the war as well as the strategic theoretical premises on which they were based. Toward that end, Thies's effort is logically consistent and persuasive. *In the context of a conflict whose causes are given,* Thies convincingly demonstrates that compellence will fail absent a firm understanding of precisely who would have to do what in order to gain a desired result. Insofar as this type of knowledge is very difficult to command, compellence is an exceedingly risky enterprise and one that should be undertaken only with a high regard for caution. That said, it is not clear that the knowledge gained from Thies's study can be used to understand the causes of a conflict in the first place. In the case of Vietnam, Thies can explain why the United States's attempt at compellence failed, but he can explain neither the motivations for that attempt nor those of the Vietnamese, without which there would have been no war from the outset.

V. HISTORICAL REVISIONISM, SELECTION BIAS, AND JACK SNYDER'S VIETNAM

This section analyzes the way in which Jack Snyder created his Vietnam case-study, which he used to support his argument about the *Myths of Empire*.[21] As was the case with many of the studies just examined, Snyder's interpretation of Vietnam is somewhat at odds with the way most contemporary historians see the matter, which should not be overly surprising. As mentioned earlier, it is not sensible to expect scholars to predict new historical narratives prior to their creation. However, a deconstruction of Snyder's Vietnam to its constituent sources reveals a deeper problem with regard to Snyder's approach toward historical inquiry. By looking in more depth at the sources Snyder had available to him, we find that his selective treatment of those sources calls into question the appropriateness of the claims he makes for the *Myths of Empire* in light of Vietnam. This in turn indicates that the problem of historical inquiry in political science goes beyond merely keeping up to date with the most recent historical revisions *du jour*: the way in which scholars go about interpreting history has a profound impact on the cogency and utility of political science theories.

According to Snyder's theory of the myths of empire, imperial or superpower overexpansion is the result not of the systemic balance of power, as many previous scholars argued, but rather of logrolling coalitions that form within imperial and superpower states. Due to the particularistic interest that each member of the logrolling coalition has individually in continued expansion, the inertia of the logroll prevents policies of restraint from being devised when expansion exceeds thresholds beyond which continued expansion will make all worse off in the long run. According to Snyder, "The war in Vietnam was a classic example of strategic overextension, an unwinnable struggle fought for the mythical strategic purpose of maintaining the credibility of America's global commitments, a goal that fighting the war undermined."[22] Snyder argues that one of the primary factors "contributing to the Cold War consensus in favor of a globalist strategy of containment was the political competition and coalition building between 'Europe-first internationalists' and 'Asia-first nationalists'" within the U.S. Congress. A consensus on a foreign policy predicated on domino theoretic arguments was achieved by "giving both internationalists and nationalists what they wanted on the issues they cared about most." This in turn resulted in various Cold War overextensions, of which Vietnam was the most prolific.[23] In his construction of the case, Snyder makes two crucial historiographical claims based on his reading of the Vietnam historiography. The first is that John F. Kennedy and more importantly, Lyndon Johnson, were sensitive to domestic criticism, as evidenced by the Presidents' discussions of that criticism. The second is that President Johnson escalated American involvement in Vietnam in order to preserve his "true love," namely, the Great Society domestic policy package.

Let us see how Snyder's interpretation fares in light of the new historiography of the case. At the most general level, Snyder argues that America's escalation of the Vietnam War resulted from "giving both internationalists and nationalists what they wanted on the issues they cared about most." Absent from his case study, however, is a specification of *who*, specifically, had the power to "give" the logrollers what they wanted and thus in the process of giving to influence the repertoire of possible choices with regard to Vietnam policy. The answer to these crucial questions is provided very clearly in the new historiography on Vietnam: President Lyndon Johnson. While Congressional coalitions may have been a prerequisite for Johnson to attain the Gulf of Tonkin resolution, it is difficult to imagine the escalation of the war in Vietnam as a function of Congressional policy making, especially considering the opposition to the war of a number of influential Senators. Thus, the logrolling coalitions to which Snyder alludes were at best a necessary condition for the escalation of the Vietnam conflict. Even then, it is not clear, in light of the strong opinions and preferences of President Johnson and his key advisors, especially Robert McNamara, that logrolling coalitions had much effect on the conflict. Indeed, even some earlier scholars have noted that President Johnson repeatedly ignored the advice of powerful leaders in the Senate who vocally opposed escalation of the war in Vietnam, including Chair of the Senate Armed Services Committee Richard Russell and Senators William Fulbright and Mike Mansfield.[24] To the extent that the President paid heed to Congress at all with regard to escalating the war, Snyder's own account refers only to Johnson's concern over fallout that might have harmed his Great Society programs, not to proactive logrolling coalitions pertaining to foreign policy.[25]

Regarding Snyder's more specific claim that Lyndon Johnson was sensitive to domestic criticism, Frederick Logevall writes: "it would be wrong to overemphasize the importance of the Great Society in the decision to escalate the conflict—that is, to give too much weight to the idea that LBJ took the nation to war because of fears that if he did not, Republicans and conservative

Democrats would oppose and possibly scuttle his beloved domestic agenda."[26]
Logevall quotes McGeorge Bundy, who says:

> I think if [Johnson] had decided that the right thing to do was to cut our losses, he
> was quite sufficiently inventive to do that in a way that would not have destroyed
> the Great Society. It's not a dependent variable. It's an independent variable.

Logevall goes on to assert that "In Bundy's view, Johnson saw achieving victory in Vietnam as important for its own sake, not merely as necessary to ensure the survival of some domestic agenda. LBJ vowed steadfastness in Vietnam in his very first foreign-policy meeting in November 1963 and had
adhered to that line at all points thereafter."[27] Like Logevall, David Kaiser
emphasizes that the "American decision in late 1964 and early 1965" to wage
war in Vietnam "after declining to do so in 1961–1962, shows the influence
of both personality and chance."[28] Similarly, Anne Blair concludes that "co-
incidence, personal style, individual ambitions, and the clash of strong wills
shaped events more than explicit policy goals or the functioning of systems."[29] Neither Kaiser nor Blair denies that President Johnson was concerned with the status of his domestic agenda, as any President would have
been. However, their accounts reveal no crucial linkage between the war and
the Great Society and to the contrary, Kaiser in particular contends that his
"book shows clearly that" when President Johnson escalated the war in Vietnam in February-March 1965, "he was implementing one basic decision for
a major war that had been reached in December 1964"—a decision that had
been reached regardless of its potentially large negative impact for the
prospects of the Great Society. Kaiser continues, "The Johnson administration did not decide upon the war out of fear of right-wing backlash, or because of a belief that Congress or the American public demanded it, or as a
means of saving the Great Society."[30] Rather, the decision to escalate the war
in 1964–1965 was the product of the particularistic generational outlook of
the "GI generation" of leaders, most importantly, Lyndon Johnson, who "contained no doubts about the wisdom or the success of the enterprise" of the war
in Vietnam.[31]

In contrast to Logevall and Kaiser, Lloyd Gardner is more sympathetic to
Snyder's claim that President Johnson was adamant on Vietnam out of fear of
losing ground in Congress on the Great Society. "Lyndon Johnson," Gardner
writes,

> believed he could not run away from Vietnam without giving conservatives,
> who did not really care much about the little brown freedom fighters in South-
> east Asia, the opportunity to deny him the Great Society. When Johnson was
> faulted for attempting to take the Great Society to Vietnam, critics failed to add

that he believed the battle for his domestic agenda turned on the outcome in Southeast Asia.[32]

Indeed, the central theme of Gardner's account is that the President could not distinguish his approach toward Vietnam from that toward his domestic political program. Ideally, according to Gardner, Johnson, the committed New Dealer, wished to bring the Great Society to Vietnam as a means of transcending the conflict. Thus, in a speech at the Johns Hopkins University on April 7, 1965, the President proposed a $100 million TVA-style program for the Mekong Valley.[33] But when it became clear that this approach to Vietnam would fall on deaf ears in Hanoi, he was left with only the American facet of his Great Society program on which to focus.

It is neither surprising nor especially problematic that Snyder's account is divergent from the new historiography on Vietnam insofar as new interpretations are always bound to arise on historical questions. Less predictable, however, are the questions that arise regarding Snyder's theory as result of analyzing the highly selective way in which he employed the sources he had available to him. The first source Snyder invokes is Daniel Ellsberg, who in Snyder's words "argues that domestic politics created a 'stalemate machine' whereby no president could risk either the political repercussions of losing Vietnam to communism or the risk of provoking Chinese intervention by taking the war decisively to the North." While Snyder acknowledges that Ellsberg's claim is "exaggerated," he nonetheless asserts that subsequent historical accounts back up the notion that fear of domestic criticism was "discussed among Kennedy and Johnson administration officials."[34] Toward that effect, Snyder cites five authors as follows:

In reference to a Rusk-McNamara memo of November 1961, George McT. Kahin says that the fall of Vietnam:

> would stimulate bitter domestic controversies in the United States and would be seized upon to divide the country and harass the Administration.[35]

Doris Kearns is cited for indicating Lyndon Johnson's fear of a:

> mean and destructive debate. . . . "There would be Robert Kennedy out in front leading the fight against me, telling everyone that I had betrayed John Kennedy's commitment to South Vietnam.[36]

Kearns and Kahin are again cited as indicating that:

> Both John Kennedy and Johnson have been quoted as saying that they thought the loss of Vietnam would bring a revival of McCarthyism in America.[37]

Ellsberg is cited for his quote of the Pentagon Papers in which McGeorge Bundy, referring to the 1965 escalated reprisal campaign, remarked to President Johnson that:

> even if it fails, the policy will be worth it. At a minimum it will damp down the charge that we did not do all that we could have done, and this charge will be important in many countries, including our own.[38]

George Herring is cited for his reference to a McGeorge Bundy memorandum to the President of July 1965 in which Bundy warns that the "Goldwater crowd," who would slam Johnson if he withdrew from Vietnam,

> were more numerous, more powerful and more dangerous than the fleabite professors.[39]

Snyder acknowledges that there is an argument counter to the preceding claims, namely that of Greenstein and Burke, who suggest that Johnson could have pulled the United States out of Vietnam after having trounced Barry Goldwater in the 1964 Presidential contest.[40] But in order for this argument to hold, Snyder argues, Johnson would apparently have had to feel unaffected by Congressional opposition to his Vietnam policies as they might relate to the success of his more cherished domestic political priorities. This, Snyder argues, was not the case, and to the contrary, the President believed that "abrupt action"—either escalating too quickly in or pulling out of Vietnam would "kill the woman I really loved—the 'Great Society.'"[41] Thus, Snyder concludes that "A broad consensus of historians believes that Johnson's preoccupation with the Great Society led him to do the minimum not to lose the war, in order to postpone attacks from both hawks and doves until the domestic program had passed."[42] Once Johnson established his Vietnam policy of graduated escalation, "the habits and practices of the Cold War consensus helped keep the public debate to a minimum. Senator William Fulbright agreed to push through the Gulf of Tonkin resolution and deflect questions."[43] while "Richard Russell, Johnson's mentor and a skeptic about escalation, agreed not to criticize" Johnson's decision to mobilize vastly increased forces to Vietnam.[44] Congress, as well as the media and the U.S. Army itself helped allow Johnson's "whitewash" of his Vietnam policy so that the Cold War consensus could "get what it wanted" out of American involvement in Vietnam.[45]

Let us see how a more comprehensive analysis of Snyder's sources might alter the conclusions one could reach about Vietnam on the basis of those sources. According to Snyder, Daniel Ellsberg "argues that domestic politics created a 'stalemate machine' whereby no president could risk either the political repercussions of losing Vietnam to communism or the risk of provoking

Chinese intervention."[46] In his essay, "The Quagmire Myth and the Stalemate Machine," Ellsberg indeed argues that the "stalemate machine" of American Vietnam policy stemmed from two rules of executive decision making: "Rule 1 of that game is: *Do not lose the rest of Vietnam to Communist control before the next election. . . .* Rule 2, which asserts among other things: *Do not commit U.S. ground troops to a land war in Asia, either.*"[47] However, nearly all of the evidence that Ellsberg cites indicates just how U.S. military policy in Vietnam was predicated on these "rules"—*not how Congressional politics, as supported by empirical evidence, actually did or did not influence Executive decision making.* Thus, Ellsberg *assumes* that domestic politics matter to Presidents and that this in turn affects military policy but he does not seek to assess the verisimilitude of the former claim. The bulk of Ellsberg's empirical analysis, then, pertains to the effects of the stalemate machine on Vietnam military policy; not the political process and not the Congressional logrolling coalitions that may (or may not) have produced the logic of stalemate in the first place. Interestingly, Ellsberg's stalemate thesis is itself a rebuttal of the earlier "quagmire myth," which was propounded most notably by Arthur Schlesinger Jr. According to the quagmire myth, American Presidents, especially Kennedy and Johnson, naively stumbled into the quagmire of Southeast Asia. Thus, the myth helps to exonerate Kennedy's and Johnson's policies by presuming "Presidential *unawareness* . . . ignorance *is*, after all, an excuse."[48] The stalemate machine, in contrast, shows how U.S. Presidents purposefully devised American policy toward Vietnam and were thus hardly ignorant and more importantly, fully responsible for the tragedy that ensued. Thus, the quagmire myth seemed plausible to the public because "Presidents themselves choose to foster impressions, when new crises and requirements emerge, that their past Vietnam decision-making has been subject to a quicksand process." Instead of risking candor, "Presidents prefer the risks of concealment and deception. . . . All very calculated, this."[49] Considering, then, this broader context of Ellsberg's argument, Ellsberg's views appear more in line with those of the revisionists Logevall, Kaiser, and Gardner than with those of Snyder. That is to say that both Ellsberg and the revisionists stress to a significant degree the personal policy making style and power of the President. Whereas Snyder employs Ellsberg to show that legislative logrolling coalitions matter, an impartial inquirer might find more evidence for the importance of the executive decision structure and personality from Ellsberg's account. Had Snyder employed a less stylized reading of Ellsberg from the outset, he might possibly have averted some of the injury that the revisionist historiography does to the account of Vietnam in *Myths of Empire*.

Another of Snyder's crucial points is that "A broad consensus of historians believes that Johnson's preoccupation with the Great Society led him to do the minimum not to lose the war, in order to postpone attacks from both hawks and doves until the domestic program had passed."[50] It is undoubtedly the case that the nine "historians" he cites provide evidence to that effect and thus Snyder has engaged in positive triangulation, or drawing upon a common theme from otherwise disparate sources. However, Snyder's point here is perhaps too subtle for its own good: on the one hand, he is claiming that losing Vietnam would have put Lyndon Johnson in a precarious domestic situation. On the other hand, however, too much in the way of escalation might be equally damaging. While this is indeed the stalemate machine Ellsberg discusses (see above), it creates a curious state of unfalsifiability for Snyder: evidence that Johnson escalated the war out of fear that losing would harm his Great Society will support Snyder equally as well as evidence to the contrary—that escalating too dramatically in Vietnam would hurt Johnson's domestic political program and so the President proceeded with caution. This situation is untenable not only because it is unfalsifiable, but also because only one side of the stalemate machine could reasonably support Snyder's theory: Snyder's theory regards overexpansion, not overcaution, so only the notion that fear of losing Vietnam pushed Johnson to escalate the war more than he otherwise might have could conceivably support Snyder's argument. Evidence that Johnson actually proceeded more cautiously than he otherwise might have would in fact hurt Snyder's claim. A closer look at the two "historians" Snyder most oft cites in fact yields evidence only for the latter view.

Doris Kearns, based on verbatim notes she took while working as a Fellow in the Johnson White House, cites the President having told her that "moving step by step [on Vietnam] was not only the best way to plan the budget, it was the best way to save the Great Society."[51] However, as is made clear in the pages preceding and following the quote cited by Kearns and recited in Snyder, "save" in this context is in reference to the economic tradeoffs brought about by increased military spending on Vietnam. Thus Kearns's quote cited above is prefaced by the following passage: "In the absence of either wage and price controls or a tax increase, the Great Society became the sacrificial lamb of rising inflation. . . . When the inflation set it . . . the centers of power in the Congress responded with a conventional call to cut the budget."[52] In this aspect of Kearns's narrative, Congressional opposition mattered to the President, but not in the sense of placating a foreign policy logrolling coalition trying to push for more expansion in Vietnam. To the contrary, the coalitional politics in Kearns's account pushed Johnson to proceed "step by step" so as not to alarm fiscal watchdogs in Congress over the ever-escalating expense of the war.

The other historian most oft cited by Snyder, George McT. Kahin, makes several mentions of the stalemate dynamic and its importance for President

Johnson's Great Society package. In one instance, Kahin alludes to the "enormous political backlash he [Johnson] expected would follow a Saigon collapse"[53] while later, Kahin asserts that the President in fact held back the pace of escalation in order to placate Congressional opposition to the war. Kahin himself relies in part for the latter claim on a quote of Doris Kearns, who wrote:

> By pretending there was no major conflict, by minimizing the level of spending, and by refusing to call up the reserves or ask Congress for an acknowledgment or acceptance of the war, Johnson believed he could keep the levers of control in his hands. He had worked hard to reach the position where he could not only propose but pass his Great Society Legislation. . . . "I was determined to keep the war from shattering that dream," Johnson later said, "which meant I simply had no choice but to keep my foreign policy in the wings. I knew the Congress as well as I know Lady Bird, and I knew that the day it exploded into a major debate on the war, that day would be the beginning of the end of the Great Society.[54]

Again, the context of the passage is revealing. Kahin precedes the above quote with a discussion of how a majority in Congress were relieved by and approved of the President's public announcement on July 28, 1965 that he would not call up reserves and that he would be willing to consider negotiations with Hanoi.[55] Thus again, as was the case with Kearns, Kahin's allusion to the President's concern over the Great Society's fate in light of Vietnam depicts the Congress as pushing Johnson for more caution, not more expansion. While Snyder and his sources agree that Lyndon Johnson cared passionately about the Great Society and that the President often alluded to that fact in discussing Vietnam, a more careful reading of his sources leads to an unsettling conclusion.

In a very important respect, Snyder's treatment of Vietnam is stylized so much so that it stretches the bounds of logical consistency. We recall that Snyder's original argument is that "The war in Vietnam was a classic example of strategic overextension, an unwinnable struggle fought for the mythical strategic purpose of maintaining the credibility of America's global commitments, a goal that fighting the war undermined."[56] The reason for this self-defeating policy was due in large measure to the strength of a "Cold War consensus" that emerged from Congressional coalitions each getting what they wanted out of American foreign policy.[57] In his reconstruction of Vietnam, however, Snyder's logic is as follows:

1. President Johnson was concerned with domestic criticism of his policies.
2. President Johnson was concerned that controversy over Vietnam might harm his Great Society domestic program.

3. Ergo: "a broad consensus of historians believes that Johnson's preoccupation with the Great Society led him to do the minimum not to lose the war, in order to postpone attacks from both hawks and doves until the domestic program had passed."[58]

There is a major problem here, however, in that the conclusion that Snyder logically draws from the evidences he cites (#3 above) is not the one for which he ostensibly argues. Thus:

> A broad consensus of historians believes that Johnson's preoccupation with the Great Society led him to do the minimum not to lose the war, in order to postpone attacks from both hawks and doves until the domestic program had passed.[59]

—is a fundamentally different claim from:

> American involvement in Vietnam resulted at least "in part from a tacit logroll—organized by Republican internationalists like John Foster Dulles— between Europe-first internationalists and Asia-first nationalists of both parties. Foreign policy consensus and harmony within the Republican party were achieved by giving both the internationalists and nationalists what they wanted on the issues they cared about most."[60]

This breakdown in logic leads to an obvious question: Where was the foreign policy "logroll" in the development of Vietnam policy? The answer seems to be that it is indeed missing from the sources Snyder had at his disposal when he wrote *Myths of Empire*. The more recent historiography of Vietnam, as discussed earlier, only compounds the problem.

VI. CONCLUSION

This chapter suggests several conclusions regarding the problem of historical inquiry for political science theorization and research. Regarding the case of Vietnam specifically, all of the subsets of political science literature reviewed in this chapter convey to a greater or lesser extent an emphasis on the international system and the perceived American concern with the global balance of power during the Cold War. Within the political science literature, however, there is a clearly discernable variation in that emphasis. The data set compilations, textbooks, and policy-oriented texts stress systemic or structural dynamics almost to the exclusion of all other factors. The Vietnam-centric studies, especially those on foreign policy decision making, incorporate other factors and in particular, the role of domestic politics. This is somewhat intuitive: research focused on decision-making structures is inherently more apt to pay heed to factors associated with those structures. Thus, foreign policy is seen as being made within the context of a domestic political policy establishment, and so on. What is peculiar about the decision-making literature on Vietnam, however, is that even with overwhelming evidence indicating the importance of domestic politics, especially executive-level decision making, several authors remained committed to the significance of containment doctrine and systemic anarchy as causal factors despite a lack of empirical support for that assertion. As was the case with the Arab-Israeli conflict, it appears that some scholars see system-structure in the historical record prior to analyzing the history.[61]

A second conclusion is that the propensity for data sets and textbooks to include incomplete or misleading historical interpretations is troubling for the simple reason that these types of scholarship tend to be more widely-cited and read than monographs and specialized theoretical studies. As pointed out in chapter 4, if a single case synopsis in a large-n data set is flawed, then every study employing that data set will reproduce that flaw and potentially generate misguided and even dangerous theoretical conclusions. The potential detriment to undergraduate students and policy analysts stemming from flawed textbooks and policy guides is perhaps less easily measured but certainly no less significant.

A third conclusion is that, as with the case of the Arab-Israeli conflict, I would caution against interpreting the current chapter's findings as a "victory" for first- and second-image – that is, individual and societal factors — over third-image — or international systemic—analysis in international relations.[62] Clearly, the historians examined in this chapter weigh individual and social factors as being far more causally significant than the global balance of power or the doctrine of containment. However, this appears to be the historical consensus *for this case*. It is certainly possible that systemic factors might be more significant in other cases. The main lesson here is that the best political science theorization should proceed by taking a broad and deep look into history without preconceived notions of how history will or will not reinforce particular theoretical interpretations of the world.

Finally and most importantly, the problem of historical inquiry is not merely a matter of keeping up to date with the latest trends in historiography, though that is in itself an important point. As the analysis of Jack Snyder's *Myths of Empire* shows, there is a temptation, whether conscious or not, among political scientists to find what they seek within historical texts. Stylized interpretation and unrefined culling of historical data are apt to produce flawed scholarship. This has far-reaching implications for political science theorization. Put differently, historical interpretation is not just an issue for historians; it is at crucial problem for both empirical and theoretical political science scholarship. In chapter 7, I suggest that a pragmatist approach to historical inquiry can greatly help political science to respond to this problem.

NOTES

1. Butterworth, ed., *Managing Interstate Conflict*, 271 and Wilkenfeld et. al., "Handbook of Foreign Policy Crises," 322–23.
2. Butterworth, *Managing Interstate Conflict*, 273–74.
3. Alexander L. George, *Forceful Persuasion* (Washington D.C.: USIP, 1991), 42.
4. George, *Forceful Persuasion*, 43–44.
5. Karen Mingst, *Essentials of International Relations* (New York: W.W. Norton, 1999), 50–51.
6. Fredrik Logevall, *Choosing War* (Berkeley: University of California Press, 1999), 388.
7. Kenneth N. Waltz, *Theory of International Politics* (Reading, MA: Addison-Wesley, 1979), 190–91.
8. John G. Stoessinger, *Why Nations Go to War*, 5th edition (New York: St. Martins, 1990), 99.
9. Stoessinger, *Why Nations Go to War*, 223.
10. For an elaboration on this point, see Alexander Wendt, *Social Theory of International Politics* (New York: Cambridge University Press, 2000).
11. Leslie H. Gelb with Richard K. Betts, *The Irony of Vietnam* (Washington D.C.: Brookings, 1979), 2.
12. See David M. Barrett, "The Mythology Surrounding Lyndon Johnson, His Advisers, and the 1965 Decision to Escalate the Vietnam War," *Political Science Quarterly* vol. 103, no. 4 (1988).
13. Larry Berman, *Planning a Tragedy* (New York: W.W. Norton, 1982), 130.
14. Berman, *Planning a Tragedy*, 145–46.
15. Barrett, "The Mythology Surrounding Lyndon Johnson," 637–38.
16. Fred I. Greenstein and John P. Burke, "The Dynamics of Presidential Reality Testing: Evidence from Two Vietnam Decisions," *Political Science Quarterly* vol. 104, no. 4 (1989–1990): 560.
17. Greenstein and Burke, "The Dynamics," 580.
18. Michael Roskin, "From Pearl Harbor to Vietnam: Shifting Generational Paradigms and Foreign Policy, *Political Science Quarterly* vol. 89, no. 3 (Fall 1974): 569–70.
19. King C. Chen, "Hanoi's Three Decisions and the Escalation of the Vietnam War," *Political Science Quarterly* vol. 90, no. 2 (Summer 1975).
20. Wallace J. Thies, *When Governments Collide* (Berkeley: University of California Press, 1980), 9.

21. The full case study is on the American Cold War Consensus; Vietnam is a component of the larger whole, although it is treated, in Snyder's words, as a "classic example" of the dynamic in which he is interested. Jack Snyder, *Myths of Empire* (Ithaca, NY: Cornell University Press, 1991).

22. Snyder, *Myths of Empire*, 255–56.

23. Snyder, *Myths of Empire*, 256–57.

24. See Barrett, "The Mythology Surrounding Lyndon Johnson."

25. It could be argued that Snyder has a general theory of logrolling that neither could nor should be expected to explain every aspect of American foreign policy. This is certainly a reasonable point, but if it is so, then it begs the question of why Snyder alludes to Vietnam as "a classic example of strategic overextension, an unwinnable struggle fought for the mythical strategic purpose of maintaining the credibility of America's global commitments, a goal that fighting the war undermined." Snyder, *Myths of Empire*, 255–56.

26. Logevall, *Choosing War*, 391.

27. McGeorge Bundy interview with Logevall, New York City, 15 March 1994, cited in Logevall, *Choosing War*, 391.

28. David Kaiser, *American Tragedy* (Cambridge, MA: The Belknap Press, 2000), 3.

29. Anne E. Blair, *Lodge in Vietnam* (New Haven: Yale University Press, 1995), x–xi.

30. Kaiser, *American Tragedy*, 5, 5–6.

31. Kaiser, *American Tragedy*, 6.

32. Lloyd C. Gardner, *Pay at Any Price* (Chicago: Ivan R. Dee, 1995), 98.

33. Gardner, *Pay at Any Price,* 197.

34. Snyder, *Myths of Empire*, 300. Snyder does not provide a page citation for his characterization of Ellsberg quoted above.

35. George McT. Kahin, *Intervention* (New York: Alfred A. Knopf, 1986), 138, cited in Snyder, *Myths of Empire*, 300.

36. Doris Kearns, *Lyndon Johnson and the American Dream* (New York, 1976), 252–53, cited in Snyder, *Myths of Empire*, 300.

37. Kahin, *Intervention*, 147, and Kearns, *Lyndon Johnson,* 282, cited in Snyder, *Myths of Empire*, 300.

38. Daniel Ellsberg, *Papers on the War* (New York: Simon and Schuster, 1972), 91, cited in Snyder, *Myths of Empire*, 300.

39. Herring, *America's Longest War*, 1st edition, (New York: Wiley, 1979), 141–42, cited in Snyder, *Myths of Empire*, 300.

40. John Burke and Fred I. Greenstein, *How Presidents Test Reality* (New York: Russell Sage, 1991), 146–49, 167, 192–94, cited in Snyder, *Myths of Empire*, 301.

41. Kearns, *Lyndon Johnson*, 251, cited in Snyder, *Myths of Empire*, 301.

42. Snyder, *Myths of Empire*, 301.

43. Herring, *America's Longest War*, 2nd edition, 123; and Kahin, *Intervention*, 219–25, cited in Snyder, *Myths of Empire*, 301.

44. Burke and Greenstein, *How Presidents Test Reality*, 249, cited in Snyder, *Myths of Empire*, 301.

45. Snyder, *Myths of Empire*, 301–302.

46. Snyder, *Myths of Empire*, 300.

47. Ellsberg, "The Quagmire Myth and the Stalemate Machine," in *Papers on the War*, 102. Emphasis in original.

48. Ellsberg, "The Quagmire Myth," 49. Emphasis in original.

49. Ellsberg, "The Quagmire Myth," 115–16.

50. Snyder, *Myths of Empire*, 301. Snyder's claim of a consensus among "historians" is itself problematic. Of the nine "historians" cited by Snyder as representative of the historical consensus, only one (Kahin) is in fact a historian by either training or vocation. Of the rest, four—Richard Berman, Richard Betts, John Burke, and Fred Greenstein—are political scientists. George Ball was undersecretary of state during much of the Vietnam period. Peter Braestrup was Saigon bureau chief for *The Washington Post* from 1968–1973. Leslie Gelb is currently president of the Council on Foreign Relations and formerly a Pentagon staffer and *New York Times* editor. Doris Kearns was White House Fellow under President Johnson prior to writing the biographical *Lyndon Johnson and the American Dream*.

51. LBJ/DHK, cited in Kearns, *Lyndon Johnson*, 298, cited in Snyder, *Myths of Empire*, 301. Brackets added.

52. Kearns, *Lyndon Johnson*, 297, 298.

53. Kahin, *Intervention,* 320, cited in Snyder, *Myths of Empire*, 301.

54. Kearns, *Lyndon Johnson*, 296–96, cited in Kahin, *Intervention*, 398, cited in Snyder, *Myths of Empire*, 301.

55. Kahin, *Intervention*, 398.

56. Snyder, *Myths of Empire*, 256–57.

57. Snyder, *Myths of Empire*, 256–57.

58. Snyder, *Myths of Empire*, 301.

59. Snyder, *Myths of Empire*, 301.

60. Snyder, *Myths of Empire*, 256–57.

61. See esp., Larry Berman, *Planning a Tragedy*, and Stoessinger, *Why Nations Go to War*. I would attribute the emphasis on systemic factors and anarchy to the dominance of neorealist and in particular, Waltzian structural approaches within the political science subfield or IR. If this is correct, one might suggest the emergence of a "discursive norm" in which IR research must proceed by way of mentioning system-structure and anarchy, even when such factors have little or even no relationship to the research in question.

62. For an elaboration on the IR images, see Kenneth N. Waltz, *Man, the State and War* (New York: Columbia University Press, 1959).

Chapter Seven

Solving the Historical Problem: History, Methodology, and Political Research

I. INTRODUCTION

The preceding three chapters have demonstrated, hopefully with some success that the problem of historical inquiry is indeed a profound one for political science research. The present chapter seeks a pragmatist response to the problem of historical inquiry in the sense of developing practical strategies political scientists can adopt to produce more sophisticated historical research. The following section discusses the current state of the art of political science methods in order to ascertain the extent to which the problem of historical inquiry may have already been somewhat addressed, if not definitively resolved. Section III attempts to move beyond current understandings of historical research methodology to suggest mechanisms and modes of thinking that may help alleviate the problem of historical inquiry in political science research. Alleviating and accounting for historical bias via new methodological techniques is important and useful. However, the implications of a pragmatist approach to historical inquiry are more significant than simply tweaking standard political science research methods. A pragmatist approach enables political scientists so see that the way in which we interpret history can have profound effects on both political science theories as well as important "real-world" political issues. That is, some historical interpretations are better at solving problems—both theoretical and political—than are others. Section IV of this chapter demonstrates that in the case of the Arab-Israeli conflict, the critical history is in fact better at resolving old problems than is the older narrative of the conflict.

II. THE PROBLEM OF HISTORICAL INQUIRY AND POLITICAL SCIENCE METHODOLOGY

What does the state of the art of contemporary political science methodology say about how to conduct empirical research? The most oft-cited work of political science research methodology and design during the past decade is King, Keohane, and Verba's *Designing Social Inquiry*. The text argues that both quantitative and qualitative social scientific inquiry can and should operate according to a single, unified logic of inference, namely, a scientific one. Of particular concern to the present discussion is the manner in which the authors address issues pertaining to historical inquiry, which is perhaps the most common type of qualitative research in political science. King, Keohane, and Verba define scientific research in the social sciences in terms of four characteristics. The first is that the goal of such research is inference; either descriptive inference: "using observations from the world to learn about other unobserved facts;" or causal inference, which the authors define as "learning about causal effects from the data observed." The second is that the procedures of inquiry are public. The third is that the conclusions are uncertain; knowledge with perfect certainty in the social sciences is not realistic. The final characteristic is that the content of research is the method. That is to say, social science (and all science, for that matter) is a set of rules and logic that can be applied to any subject matter, so the content of the inquiry is predicated not on the material but on the method used to study it.[1]

While the methods of data manipulation are the main focus of *Designing Social Inquiry*, the authors do speak at some length regarding the nature of data accumulation and data itself. "Data," according to the authors, "are systematically collected elements of information about the world."[2] King, Keohane, and Verba suggest a number of guidelines for improving data quality, several of which are significant to the present discussion. The first is that "*in order better to evaluate a theory, collect data on as many of its observable implications as possible*. This means collecting as much data in as many diverse contexts as possible." The second is that researchers are encouraged to maximize the validity of their measurements; that is, political scientists should strive to measure as accurately as possible what they presume to be measuring. The third is to ensure reliable methods of collecting data, by which the authors intend "that applying the same procedure in the same way will always produce the same measure." Finally, King, Keohane, and Verba would have that all social scientific research be replicable whereby a "new researcher should be able to duplicate our data and trace the logic by which we reached our conclusions."[3]

According to King, Keohane, and Verba, the process of data accumulation and manipulation is fraught with tension produced by two interrelated dichotomies: general/specific and simple/complex. On the one hand, there are scholars who study highly complex and detail-specific small samples of data through the use of interpretative methods, such as Geertz's thick description.[4] On the other hand are scholars who collect and examine large samples of data in which each individual datum appears in simplified form and from which generalizations about broader populations of similar data can be drawn. King, Keohane, and Verba assert that the method of inference, whether using one case rendered in all of its complexity or many cases rendered in a simplified fashion, is the same. The authors thus take issue with researchers in the interpretivist tradition who "believe that they would lose their ability to explain the specific if they attempted to deal with the general."[5] Rather, King, Keohane, and Verba suggest that the specific complexity of thickly-described cases is very useful when "disciplined" by analytical categories relevant to the particular research program.

The authors thus endorse the use of what Alexander George calls "structured, focused, comparison," which entails "systematic collection of the same information—the same variables—across carefully selected units." Scholars must therefore "stress the need for theoretical guidance—for asking carefully thought-out explanatory questions—in order to accomplish this systematic description."[6] "Our descriptions of events should be as precise and systematic as possible. This means that when we are able to find valid quantitative measures of what we want to know, we should use them." King, Keohane, and Verba also discuss the matter of summarizing historical information: "After data are collected, the first step in any analysis is to provide summaries of the data. . . . Summarization is necessary." Thus, political scientists should follow the lead of their counterparts in history: "Good historians understand which events were crucial, and therefore construct accounts that emphasize essentials rather than digressions."[7]

King, Keohane, and Verba's treatment of history and data—or history-as-data—runs into precisely the same problem as that encountered by the quantitative data sets analyzed in chapter 4. That is to say, the methods for manipulating data that King, Keohane, and Verba advocate are hypothetically sound if the data to be manipulated could ever be discretely held constant, or at least seen as unproblematic. But so long as the problem of historical inquiry is unresolved, this cannot be the case. The authors define data as "systematically collected elements of information about the world." But in a world of potentially unlimited information, some data will ultimately be collected and most will be ignored. The criterion for distinguishing significant from irrelevant data is predicated on the notion of "being systematic." But what determines the criteria for being systematic? King, Keohane, and Verba suggest that an *a priori* "theoretical guidance" is required in order to attain systematic description. However, this seems to be a tautology: In order to test a theory, we need to select relevant data. But in order to determine which data are relevant and which are not, we must rely on theoretical guidance. This tautology alludes to a second and related problem.

What, specifically, does "theoretical guidance" mean? While King, Keohane, and Verba do not explicitly say, they suggest that theoretical guidance is something along the lines of: "a set of conceptual categories which one may use for the purpose of coding and sorting data into classes and cases." The authors rightly allude to the fact that qualitative scholars in the interpretivist tradition oppose this type of data organization because they question the basis for *a priori* categorization of cases. That is, interpretivists in the Geertzian tradition stress the uniqueness of specific cases and are hence skeptical of developing abstract, general categories that could allude *with equal propriety* to many otherwise distinct cases. King, Keohane, and Verba state that interpretivists fear that they "would lose their ability to explain the specific if they attempted to deal with the general." But this is not an altogether fair assessment: what the interpretivists are saying is that the conceptual categories social scientists give to classes of cases are apt to distort the cases as they see them and thereby weaken, rather than improve our general understanding of the world.

Moving this discussion into the terrain of historical research, King, Keohane, and Verba argue that in order to test theories in light of historical cases, cases should be constructed by summarizing the data with a focus on the relevant information culled from the historical record. Like "good historians," good historical social scientists too should "understand which events were crucial, and therefore construct accounts that emphasize essentials rather than digressions." However, the only way in which researchers can separate the historical wheat from the chaff is to employ theoretical guidance, or a reliance on *a priori* classification schemes for coding classes of events and cases. In the instance of historical research, this goes beyond tautology and into the realm of blatant selection bias: scholars create categories of cases according to criteria that are independent of the actual past as it may or may not have been. Those categories are then labeled as representative of the "easy" and "hard" cases that could be used to test their theories. This would not be problematic were it not for the fact that there is no foundation on which this process of categorization rests: the theory determines the categories and then the categories determine the extent to which theory is supported by the evidence.

Scholars employing this logic of inference will invariably find what they seek in the historical record. The reason for this, to reiterate from the previous chapter, is that King, Keohane, and Verba and like-minded positivists conceive of history as an unproblematic database: they assume that historical events are like carbon and hydrogen—discrete, unchanging facts waiting to be classified. As this book has gone to some length to demonstrate, historical events are not of this nature and history is not an unproblematic database.

In order to make this point more clear, let us provide a hypothetical example with regard to the case of the 1956 Arab-Israeli war. Suppose a scholar were to test the effects of the international system on Israeli decision making with regard to whether or not to go to war in 1956.[8] The scholar first "collects data" by exploring the "historical record" ("database") regarding the case. Upon completing the process of data collection, the scholar proceeds to "summarize" the data by emphasizing the most significant historical events: (1) the Fedayeen terrorist raids on Israel; (2) the blockade of Israeli shipping; and (3) the Czech arms deal. In the process of data summary, the scholar discards less relevant information: the weather during 1956, what music was popular in Cairo and Tel Aviv, etc. But what criteria were used to distinguish the data that is relevant from that which is not? In order to answer this question, we need to know more about the operating assumptions of the investigator. We would scarcely be surprised to learn that our investigator assumes: (1) that there is, in fact, an international system; (2) that states are primarily concerned with security within that system; and (3) that states will be especially sensitive to shifts and changes in the balance of power in system. By making these assumptions—provided by the theoretical guidance of the investigator—our investigator logically chose to focus on the traditional three factors that are widely cited within the political science literature to have been causes of the 1956 Arab-Israeli war. But by doing so, this hypothetical scholar produced a perfectly biased historical study. The reason for this is that because the investigator was theoretically guided away from exploring domestic, cultural, or alternative systemic factors,[9] she found what she was looking for in the historical record (database) and thus affirmed the importance of systemic factors in understanding the Arab-Israeli conflict.

This type of problem is quite common in historical political science research. We need look no further than Steven Van Evera's *Guide to Methods in Political Science* to find a similar example. In Van Evera's discussion of case study methodology, he defines process tracing as the exploration of "the chain of events or the decision-making process by which initial case conditions are translated into case outcomes."[10] To illustrate his point, Van Evera discusses a hypothetical process-tracing test of Kenneth Waltz's proposition that bipolar distributions of power in the international system "cause peace." According to Waltz (as per Van Evera), bipolarity "causes the following pacifying phenomena: less false optimism by governments about the relative power of opponents;

easier cooperation and faster learning by each side about other . . . faster and more efficient internal and external moves by each side to balance growth in the other's power . . . causing deterrence; and the selection of fewer inept national political leaders."[11] In order to test Waltz's proposition, "A process-tracing test would look for evidence of these phenomena in cases of bipolarity (for example, the cold war, 1947–1989) and, if they are found, for evidence that they stemmed from bipolarity."[12] However, the notion that any given historical period is bipolar will be heavily informed by the "theoretical guidance" endowment of a particular theoretic perspective. That is, only a systems theorist such as Waltz would read polarities into historical accounts in order to test propositions about his systems theory. Polarity is not a given, fixed attribute of the historical record; it does not exist within the past-as-it-was.[13]

Both of the preceding examples stem from a positivist approach toward the problem of historical inquiry. To reiterate, positivism suggests that there is a set of basic facts in the historical record that antecedently exists and needs only be collected by an aspiring scholar. Once collected, the facts are then ordered systematically to account for which variables seem most salient in historical cause-effect relationships.[14] As mentioned above, this understanding of historical research is fundamentally flawed because the very process by which facts are ordered is a function of the theoretical disposition and operating assumptions of the researcher. Even if this were not the case, there is still another problem endemic to historical social science research for which King, Keohane, Verba, and Van Evera provide little assistance. That is, even if one were to accept the propriety of the classes social scientists use to order their historical facts, by what process do scholars select the sources from which to cull those facts? This question is obviously a crucial one with regard to the notion of producing a thorough and unbiased set of facts.

As many of the studies cited in this book suggest, there are two time-tested methods by which scholars tend to choose their historical sources. The first is what may be termed "reference to the authoritative record." To elaborate, most political scientists, unless they have a particular regional expertise in the case they are studying, will refer to authoritative texts in the field to gain information on historical events. This is usually done the way professional sports leagues pick their all-star teams—through some combination of reputation based on accomplishment and popularity with the fans. The appeal of choosing sources this way is obvious: by referring to the "best" names in a given field, a political scientist can feel confident that she has employed sources that are deemed worthy by the time-tested standards of peer review and professional achievement.

This practice is, however, highly problematic. The reason for this is that with any historical problem, there are always apt to be a wide range of theoretical and ideological perspectives with regard to the events in question. But not all perspectives are heard equally across time and space. Thus, for instance, if one were to select the "top ten" historical works written on any topic by American historians during the 1950s; it would be unlikely, in light of the influence of McCarthyism, that any Marxist perspectives would be found. Thus, the authoritative record is not an unbiased one and in many instances, it may reveal only a narrow range of interpretations within the historical field.

A second approach toward source selection in the production of historical case studies is similarly problematic. This approach is essentially what Collingwood called "scissors and paste" history—the cutting and pasting of convenient citations or "mining for quotes" from an otherwise diverse and problematic historical record in order to tell a story that is favorable to the theoretic perspective of the social scientist.[15] This approach can take on a number of forms, which we can think of as running along two parallel continua. The first continuum can be conceptualized in terms of depth of factual bias. On one hand, the bias can be as simple as petty "cutting and pasting"— a stringing together of small quotes and citations that tell a convenient story. At the other extreme, the bias could be as in depth as reviewing a relatively large number of historical texts written from highly divergent perspectives and choosing to cite only those whose theoretic commitments happen to fall in line with those of the social scientist.

The second continuum can be thought of terms of "degree of guilt." That is, in the instance of petty cutting and pasting of minor facts, the social scientist may very well be genuinely unaware of the bias entailed in her historical research. At the other extreme, however, is the scholar who has reviewed a broad range of historical literature and selectively omitted those texts that are theoretically at odds with the investigator's theoretic commitment. Since the scholar was fully aware of a substantial body of historical literature that would problematize her claim but yet chose to ignore it; the "degree of guilt" in this instance is quite high. Both of the practices just discussed—reference to the authoritative record and scissors and paste historical research—stem from the positivist tendency to treat the historical record as an unproblematic database. That is, if the historical record is comprised solely of unwinnowed data, then it doesn't really matter from where a political scientist culls their quotes and sources because the only concern is to get "just the facts." As has been discussed now at length, a pragmatist approach toward the problem of historical inquiry rejects this mode of historical thinking and research. Pragmatism, in contrast to positivism, views history not as an unproblematic database but rather as a dynamic terrain where interpretation and fact are constantly reinventing one another. This returns to the question: given a pragmatist historical epistemology, how, specifically, can we improve our lot with regard to historical social scientific research? A response to that question is the subject of section III.

III. PRACTICAL SOLUTIONS TO THE PROBLEM OF HISTORICAL INQUIRY IN POLITICAL SCIENCE RESEARCH

The previous section of this chapter indicates that very little, if any effort has been made to reconcile responses to the problem of historical inquiry with mainstream political science methods. Efforts to grapple with the question of how to do historical political science given a pragmatic approach toward the problem of historical inquiry are few in number, but at least one example is most promising. In a recent *APSR* article that is particularly relevant here, Ian Lustick makes quite clear the notion that history is not an unproblematic grab bag from which to pluck convenient citations. Given that this is the case, Lustick suggests a new and alternative way for political scientists to approach historical literatures. Rather than take the traditional positivist view in which history is raw, undifferentiated data, we can instead conceptualize history as represented by a variety of different implicit theoretical perspectives embedded within the historical texts that political scientists use as the main sources for historical case studies.

In epistemological terms, this calls for abandoning the notion that the single, correct, and human-independent truth of historical events could be captured by scratching ever closer to that truth, at least so far as social science research is concerned. While the correct truth may very well be out there, all political scientists have to rely on are historical texts, and once this is acknowledged, then the dividing line between historical fact and interpretation has been irrevocably crossed. In an important sense, this is a very pragmatist perspective insofar as it assumes that: (1) there is no human-independent means of producing a single, correct historical case study; (2) despite this first point, we can nonetheless use methodological devices to overcome the practical problem of making sense out of the past for the purpose of a present endeavor, which in this instance is social science research.

Given this pragmatist epistemology, Lustick identifies four methodological procedures that can be employed to overcome the notion that history is a database of fixed, discrete facts ready to be culled and ordered. The first procedure is to be overt and clear about the theoretic and normative nature of the sources being utilized in historiographical reconstruction or what Lustick terms being "true to your school." In many instances, basic disagreement among historians of certain subjects may be so prolific and the body of scholarship so diverse that it is infeasible to piece together a synthesized account that roundly represents the breadth of the literature and range of perspectives within it. Thus, one can instead identify a subset of the literature whose approach is most persuasive to the researcher and in so doing, make explicit in the context of the study the precise nature of that historiographical subset's theoretic commitments and biases.[16] Note the crucial word choice here of "persuasive;" not "useful" or "favorable." It could thus be added to Lustick's point that the scholars should employ that historiography which seems least objectionable with regard to quality and *explicitly not* that which most conveniently and readily supports the social science theory in question. To the extent that the historiographical school is in theoretic accordance with the social science theory in question, the biases and assumptions common to each should be clearly stated at the outset.

A second procedure afforded to historically minded social scientists is to commit some effort toward explaining variance within the historiographical record, such as it appears. This can be done by assuming that there is a standard distribution of implicit theoretical commitments within a given historiography. Methodologically speaking, the greater the body of historiographical literature, the more standard such a distribution is likely to be. In proceeding from this standpoint, the researcher is somewhat empowered to place significance on regularities within the distribution of theoretical commitments that appear in spite of the differences that otherwise distinguish the breadth of the literature.[17] Such regularities can then be used to form the common threads of a reconstructed narrative—or more commonly, a historical case study for use in theory testing. Thus, in the case of the old Israeli history, the center of the bell curve of explanations for the second Arab-Israeli war refers to three factors as most significant: (1) Fedayeen raids; (2) blockades and closure of the Suez Canal; and (3) the Czech arms deal. This is not to say that there couldn't be additional, less well-known explanations within the older literature. To the extent that there are, then variance must be explained. It is thus important to note that theoretical regularities do not and cannot be an unfiltered representation of the historiographical record and toward that effect, use of this technique should be explained overtly and clearly. Perhaps more important, it is a distinct possibility that the most "regular" theoretic commitment within the historiography may run counter to the theory held by the social scientist. The social scientist is then left to choose either to respond to this discordance or to reconsider her original theoretic commitment.

A third procedure is in some sense the opposite of being true to your school. Thus, rather than identify the most persuasive among competing schools within the historiography, one might attempt what Lustick terms "quasi triangulation," or assembling a background narrative from otherwise diverse claims made by different historians who consult different archival

sources and/or espouse different theoretic commitments.[18] In an important regard this approach is superior to being true to one school in that it attempts
the best of all worlds. That is, by triangulating—or constructing a single narrative from two or more distinct accounts—one can alleviate each of the possible selection biases that would otherwise occur by selecting only one or two
"true schools." Again, using the Israeli case as instructive, if one relied solely
on the old historiography of the case, one would process trace the second
Arab-Israeli war as a function of systemic factors. If one relied solely on the
critical historiography, the narrative would see domestic factors as more
salient in leading to the war. A triangulated account would seek to reconcile
the two narratives and place an emphasis on consistencies that appear in both
the old and critical historiographies.

A final technique available to the historical social sciences is the regular
use of discursive annotation to reveal the existence of competing theoretical
debates within the historiography. The historically minded social scientist can
engage in "explicit triage" by being sure to cite not only those sources whose
theoretic commitments correspond to her/his own, but also the competing
sources as well.[19] The use of this triage technique fully acknowledges the regularity of historical revisionism within the historiography and demonstrates
the researcher's effort to avert blatant bias that would ensue if only sources
based on the criterion of theoretic convenience were cited.

These four measures represent a vast improvement over the contemporary
state of thinking about historical inquiry in the social sciences. But there are
several issues that remain unresolved. First, the way in which the problem
orientation of social scientists unalterably affects their predisposition toward
their research needs to be incorporated into the discussion. Second, there are
still nagging questions that many political scientists will certainly ask;
namely, given these exciting ways of thinking, how do I "do"—in the most
literal and mundane sense—historical research. And finally, still unaddressed
is the matter of practical reform of the quantitative methods in light of the
pragmatist historical epistemology advocated in this project. Each of these
matters is addressed in the remainder of this chapter.

1. Problem Orientation and Bias

Most political scientists, whether qualitative or quantitative, structuralist or
constructivist, agree that the best way to commence a research project is to
ask an interesting question, one that alludes to a problem of widespread concern to a significant audience.[20] For instance, in a symposium of some of the
top specialists in comparative politics, symposium chair Atul Kohli asserts
that there is a strong consensus among leading experts in the field "that com-

parative politics is very much a problem-driven field of study. What motivates the best comparative politics research are puzzles of real-world significance."[21] Others, such as James Kurth, have issued stinging criticism of academic scholarship precisely for its move away from a practical problem orientation. Lamenting the poor quality of contemporary IR scholarship, Kurth writes "that in most American universities in the future, the study of international relations will be even more uninteresting and irrelevant than it is now."[22] A pragmatist would agree in full with these sentiments.

However, from this basic starting point of agreement the pragmatist approach will quickly depart from conventional wisdom. That is, the traditional positivist perspective advocated by King, Keohane, and Verba and others dictates that scholars must suspend all personal, political, or other concerns for the problems on which they are drawn to work. In chapter 1 of this project, I argue that this notion of social scientific inquiry is empirically flawed and logically problematic. Empirically, it is impossible for humans to operate like automatons. Logically, it is impossible to separate a theoretical position from its normative basis.

Given that this is the case, how should scholars proceed? After developing a particular problem orientation, scholars should be encouraged to ask two crucial questions: (1) how will I be likely to read the history of this problem in certain historical cases? (2) Toward which types of accounts am I most likely to be most/least sympathetic? In asking these important questions, it is useful to think of historical research as being as much an instance of personal critical introspection as it is an exercise in examining events in history. Operating in this manner, scholars are empowered to adopt a more critical and powerful perspective toward the historical literatures that they will encounter. By asking and reflecting on the preceding questions prior to commencing their review of historical literatures, researchers are able to respond to the problem raised by Lustick of ascertaining which accounts are most ideologically/theoretically supportive of certain positions and for what reasons. Scholars are then more strongly positioned to undertake steps such as the explicit triage suggested by Lustick and discussed in the preceding section. In this sense, I would argue that all social scientific scholarship is biased, but a distinction can be drawn between "pragmatically" *versus* negatively biased scholarship.

Negatively biased scholarship is of the type discussed in the previous section of this chapter. This type of work ignores historical materials and texts that adopt perspectives inconvenient or injurious to the theoretical position of the political science researcher. Negatively biased scholarship will tend to produce highly stylized renderings of historical cases without reference to the problems of interpretation that exist within the historical literatures on those cases and without explication of the fact that the historical narrative in question could be re-created differently. Pragmatically biased scholarship does precisely the opposite: it acknowledges at the outset the particular problem orientation of the researcher *as well as* the normative implications of that orientation. Having first laid these issues out on the table, pragmatically biased historical work will then elaborate on the specific way in which a historical narrative was produced, accounting for problems and countervailing perspectives within the historical literature. This again highlights the distinction between the positivist versus the pragmatist approach. Whereas the former expects scholars to suspend their beliefs for the purpose of objective analysis, the latter concedes that all social scientists are biased but that some are simply more aware of and honest about it.

2. Locating Historical Literatures

A second question is certainly crucial for any historical political science researcher: how can historically minded political scientists locate the appropriate historical literatures with which to work in the production of historical studies? After all, if scholars rely only on literature familiar to them they are likely to end up producing a "scissors and paste" negatively biased narrative-of-convenience. Alternatively, many scholars may have no familiarity whatsoever with any of the literatures on particular historical events—especially when scholars are producing multiple case studies drawn from different regions. One particularly useful way to begin the process of locating historical literatures is simply to consult an area studies or historical expert from among a political science, history, or an area studies department. This can be particularly helpful for a number of reasons.

First, if the expert consulted is a sophisticated scholar, she will already be aware that there are multiple competing interpretations within the historical literature pertaining to a given topic and may thus be able to recommend useful representative texts drawn from various ideological and theoretical perspectives. Second, the expert may herself be a known partisan in a particular debate on a topic related to the historical event in question. She may thus recommend only "authoritative" texts that happen to conveniently coincide with her particular point of view of the topics at hand. If this is the case, it should be relatively easy to identify the competing protagonists in these debates and begin the process of delineating where the interpretative fault lines on the problem of historical inquiry are situated. Third, the regional expert may identify herself at the outset as a partisan in a particular debate and then do the political scientists' job for them by listing the reputable and discredited works in the field on the historical question. With a little bit of clever interpretation, "reputable" and "discredited" may be recoded to read as "works with which the expert agrees" and "works with which she takes issue." This will quite readily yield a set of multiple competing historical narratives of the matter at hand.

3. Reading Historical Literatures

Once historical literatures on the topics in question are located, the next step is to delineate the appropriate corresponding narratives of the given historical question. This could be a tricky process insofar as it runs into the problem discussed above regarding King, Keohane, and Verba's approach toward organizing data. That is, political scientists don't want to create competing historical narratives that the historians being classified would neither recognize nor accept. This is not to say that there is ever a single, discrete, and appropriate set of categories that exists as defined by historians who belong to them. But at a minimum, *someone* in the historical discipline should acknowledge that these narratives exist. In order to ascertain in the fairest way the existence of and boundaries between competing historical narratives, again, consultation with area studies and historical experts may be quite useful.

Once the competing narratives within the literature are identified, the process of researching a historical problem entails two interrelated and inseparable questions: (1) what happened? (2) What do the competing narratives on the topic say happened and how do their ideological/theoretic commitments affect their narratives? In order to respond to these questions, the employment of triangulation suggested by Lustick may prove quite useful. That is, the historical political scientist can ask on what areas of historical fact do the various perspectives agree, despite their otherwise divergent perspectives on the topic in question? As Lustick rightly points out, however, it may be difficult to triangulate questions beyond simple matters of agreement, such as names and dates. What about issues that cannot be triangulated; that is, what does one do when the narratives utterly fail to agree? A pragmatist political scientist will respond to this difficulty not in terms of the quest for ultimate historical truth, but in terms of which narratives can address the most historical problems. Put differently, some narratives may be able to address the problems of their competitors but also respond to anomalies and problems that other narratives cannot speak to. This point is elaborated upon in the context of the Arab-Israeli conflict below.

4. Quantitative Historical Research

Quantitative historical research is at once a frustrating and a promising area in which a response to the problem of historical inquiry discussed in this project may bear fruit. On the one hand, the quantitative research program has generally adopted a highly oversimplified approach toward historical questions insofar as the need to develop uniform codes for complex historical events seems to obscure more than it reveals. On the other hand, quantitative data sets, due to their very nature, may be better empowered to respond to historical revisionism than any other area of political science research. There are two points that are of most interest and potential in this regard. The first is that unlike most singly-authored qualitative historical studies, quantitative data sets tend to have a more ongoing and incomplete character about them. That is to say, qualitative small-n studies are generally conducted toward the end of a book that will in turn be scheduled for publication at the time of a targeted deadline. While second and revised editions are not uncommon, there is nonetheless a sense that projects are complete upon publication. In contrast, quantitative projects that produce data sets, especially those with long term funding streams and large staffs of coders, need not ever have a point of completion. Thus the second point is that quantitative IR projects are perhaps best enabled to address the problem of historical inquiry insofar as they can continue to revise, update, and incorporate dynamic changes in the basic narratives pertaining to the cases within data sets. Some research projects, such as the ICB, have begun to adopt this approach in a preliminary fashion, but the limits on continuous updating and multiple narrative incorporation are only hypothetical. Presumably, a project with a ten-year budget and a dozen or more research assistants could incorporate far more historical interpretations than a lone scholar attempting to publish a new small-n study every five to seven years.

Were quantitative research projects to adopt the mode of continuous updating and modification suggested here, a basic change in the nature of the data set compilation would also have to be made in order to make the data more effective. Three discrete steps are in order here. First, quantitative researches could never think in terms of a completed data set; data sets would by definition always be works-in-progress seeking to incorporate new and yet-to-be identified sources of historical interpretation. This would have to produce corresponding changes in the methods of coding. Coding procedures would have to be made much more complex to account for changes as they occur within the ongoing process of historical research and inquiry. Second and accordingly, quantitative scholars will have to drop the position advocated by J. David Singer that there is or can conceptually be a sharp distinction between fact and interpretation.[23] Rather, in acknowledging the notion that fact and interpretation continuously reinvent one another, the data in data sets would need to be complexified to account for the problem of multiple interpretation.

Third, quantitative data sets would need to be reconfigured to account for multiple interpretation over both space (horizontally) and time (diachronically). To date, projects such as the ICB have worked solely on the latter of these problems. That is, they have sought to address vertically the problem of multiple interpretation over time by incorporating critical historical sources as they become available. However, there is the additional problem of accounting horizontally for the existence of competing interpretations regarding crucial historical events as they exist at the same time. Thus, coded data pertaining to the Arab-Israeli conflict should have some mechanism for accounting for the sharp divergence among Arab and Jewish perspectives on the Arab-Israeli wars, even prior to the emergence of the critical historians. The same would be the case for the Indo-Pakistani and Serbo-Croatian-Bosnian conflicts, and so on.

This notion of accounting for heterogeneity has been acknowledged in other areas of quantitative research, most notably with regard to study of ethnic politics. In a recent symposium on this topic, a number of leading scholars discussed the problem of multiple identity over space—that is, individuals often wear many hats—as well as over time in instances of ethnic conflict. While some participants defended the notion that identities are relatively fixed and essential, others such as David Laitin, disagreed: "If we want to build better models of the relationship between ethnic diversity and economic growth or political stability or the quality of governance, it is essential to commit ourselves, as a discipline, to the collection of data that validly represents the multiple dimensions of ethnic diversity found in each country, and does so over time."[24] The relevance of these comments to the problem of historical inquiry discussed here is remarkable. In both instances, whether speaking of multiple ethno-political identity or hybridity of historical interpretation over both time and space, the problem created for data sets that assume data points to be static is the same. The comprehensive research design of a new data set or revision of an existing one to incorporate new ways of thinking about the coding of data is beyond the scope of the present discussion and outside of the expertise of the current author. But insofar as the problem of historical inquiry is indeed a major problem for quantitative political science, the preceding preliminary points represent an important start on the path toward a truly dynamic approach to historical problems and one that may help researchers to cope with the problem of multiple historical interpretation and revisionism.

IV. THE ARAB-ISRAELI CONFLICT: OLD PROBLEMS, NEW SOLUTIONS

Is the Israeli critical history truer, more accurate, or "better" than the old? As with all matters of historical truth, it depends upon whom you ask.[25] In

attempting to evaluate historical narratives, there are traditionally two
rather tired approaches to the matter. The first is the debate over historical
objectivity, or whether and how it is possible to discover the truth of history. While there have been many interesting perspectives on the matter, the
view of this author, speaking as a political scientist, is that much of the discussion fluctuates somewhere between what Patomaki and Wight term the
boundaries of "boredom" and "negativity," the former of which devolves
into self-referentialism and the latter of which approaches radicalism for its
own sake.[26] The second approach toward historical evaluation is to let
purely normative commitments guide the inquiry such that historical objectivity becomes essentially a matter of good *versus* bad. Thus, from the old
historical perspective, the Israeli critical history is fundamentally "bad" because it denigrates the legitimacy and moral authority of the state of Israel.
The old narrative of Ben-Gurion, Eytan, Eban, and Allon thus provides a
"good" account of the Arab-Israeli conflict by portraying Israel in a more
flattering light.[27]

I suggest here the importance of a pragmatist approach toward history, as
discussed earlier in chapter 2. Rather than thinking in terms of true/untrue or
good/bad history, we should instead evaluate the degree to which historical
programmes, or narratives, can resolve problematic situations. This entails
two interrelated aspects: First, historians and political scientists would want a
history that can provide a more complete package of answers to questions in
which researchers and society more broadly are interested. Second and related, we might seek a historical interpretation that is most likely to resolve
"real" political problems.

1. History as Arbitrator for Political Science

In terms of historical inquiry, the older historical narrative certainly answers
a number of important questions: (1) Why is there an Arab-Israeli conflict?
(2) Who started the conflict? (3) What are the causes of the Arab-Israeli wars?
According to the older narrative, the main reason for the Arab-Israeli conflict
rests with the unwillingness of the Arab states and leaders to accept the partition of Palestine and the existence of a Jewish state in the region. That intransigence produced in turn a systemic condition of acute strategic insecurity under which Israel was forced to exist as a "state under siege," constantly
fearful of and preparing to defend against imminent war and even total annihilation. The old historical narrative thus clearly depicts the Arab-Israeli conflict as having been started by and continued at the behest of the Arabs. Focusing for illustrative purposes on 1956 war, the causes of the war, as listed
by both the old historians and many IR scholars are clear: increasing *feday-*

een terrorist raids; the blockade of the Straights of Tiran; and the Czech arms deal, all of which perpetuated the ongoing state of war between Israel and the Arabs and served to further increase Israel's strategic vulnerability. This in turn readily yields support for a structural realist political science analysis of the Arab-Israeli conflict. That is, Israel's wars with the Arabs can be seen as a small and insecure state's response to an unfavorable balance of power in the subsystemic context Middle East. As discussed earlier, that is precisely what well-known structural realists like Randall Schweller and Stephen Walt conclude.

However, it is certainly fair to ask, which problems are left unresolved in account? Two major questions come to mind. Firstly, if Israel was so strategically insecure, how was it capable of defeating the Arab armies convincingly in 1948 and devastatingly in 1956 and 1967? Didn't the same Israeli leaders who were writing the history of that time know the "real" military balance between themselves and the Arabs? Clearly, there is a piece to this puzzle that is missing in the old accounts: barring miracles of a biblical nature, Israel could not be *both* David *and* Goliath at the same time. A second important question is, if Israel "cried out" to make peace with the Arabs continuously since 1948, why was it unable to do so during the late 1950s/ early 1960s when: (a) it had won not just one, but two smashing military victories; (b) it enjoyed a preponderance of military power relative to the Arabs; (c) the Middle East generally and Israel's borders specifically were in a phase of relative calm? The old Israel narrative cannot really respond to this question other than to reiterate the ongoing theme of Arab intransigence. But in light of the conditions just listed, this explanation is at best unfulfilling.

As one might suspect, I would argue that the Israeli critical history can explain all that is accounted for in the old history as well as the anomalous questions just raised. In short order, the Israeli critical history is quite clear that the Arab states refused to accept the UN partition plan. But the critical history also shows that Israel valued territory and power at least as much, if not more than peace with the Arabs. The Israeli strategy toward territorial consolidation and strategic advantage manifested itself in the struggle between the Ben-Gurionists and the followers of Moshe Sharett within the ruling Mapai Party. Ben-Gurion believed that the choice between his approach and that of Sharett was one of raising Israeli "cowards" *versus* "warriors." Closely associated with this struggle was the institutionalization of a distinct militarism within the Israeli state and society. As a result, military solutions to political problems were given preference over other viable alternatives. Thus, the Arab-Israeli conflict generally and the 1956 and 1967 wars specifically were the result of multiple causation: Arab intransigence *plus* Israeli militarism and desire for strategic gain both played critical roles. The Israeli critical history also thus takes serious issue with the older narrative over the question of "who started" the second and third Arab-Israeli wars. Whereas the latter viewed the wars as iterations of a war that was already in-progress, the critical historians are of a clear mind on the matter: Israel started it.

In terms of political science paradigms, the newer interpretation of the conflict reveals more of a "second-image" or liberal analysis of conflict, in which the role of domestic political actors and institutions is crucial toward understanding the decisions that states make. Indeed, Israeli critical history scholars such as Yagil Levy and Motti Golani make a point of arguing specifically that Israeli policy was decidedly *not* a response to systemic threats and to an extent the policy-making process proceeded according to its own internal logic of militarism and the language of force. In sum, then, I suggest that the Israeli critical history is "better" than the old history, but not because the older account is objectively false. Rather, I argue that the Israeli critical history can answer the same questions as does the older narrative plus those that the latter cannot, and that it can do so in ways that are logical and compelling, if not definitive.

Does this suggest that the critical history is the final word on the Arab-Israeli conflict? I would hesitate to say as much. There are certainly questions we can ask regarding the new interpretations. For one, why would a generation of Israeli historians write texts that are so unflattering to Israel? Many nasty things have been said about this on Zionist websites and chat rooms, but needless to say, no one has presented a compelling answer to that question. Thus, while the critical history may not be the end of the story, so to speak, it is the most useful, least problematic story we have for now.

2. Historical Interpretation and Solving "Real" Political Problems

Taking this argument one step further, I suggest that the historical narrative one chooses can play an important role in "real" politics. For one matter, the Israeli critical historians have had a deep impact on Israeli politics and society in ways that are readily observed. For example, the largest overhaul of public school history texts in Israeli history, initiated by then-Education Minister Yossi Sarid, was widely covered internationally for its use of the critical historians' scholarship.[28] The critical historians also interact in very public and influential ways with high-ranking regional leaders. Thus, when the late King Hussein of Jordan gave his final, widely-cited interview in the *New York Review of Books*, Avi Shlaim sat in the interviewer's chair. More recently, Benny Morris interviewed former Prime Minister Ehud Barak in a much-discussed article, also published in the *New York Review*.[29] Even Morris's personal politics have been a matter of international controversy.[30]

Thinking in terms of a pragmatist understanding of historical inquiry, I would argue that the specific manner in which we write the past can have important effects on the politics of the present and future. In the case of Israel, the way this process plays itself out is relatively easy to see. Internalization of the older historical narrative shows Israel as a weak, insecure state, surrounded by hostile enemies and continuously struggling for survival, despite its critical victories. What kind of politics does this engender? Specifically, it informs the very policies of most Likud party leaders. Take for instance, former Prime Minister Benyamin Netanyahu, for whom the Palestinian-Israeli peace process is a *strategic* rather than a political problem. "Given the specifics of the West Bank," Netanyahu contends, "the slogan 'land for peace' is singularly inappropriate: To achieve a sustainable peace, Israel must maintain a credible deterrent long enough to effect a lasting change in Arab attitudes. It is precisely Israel's control of this strategic territory that has deterred all-out war and has made eventual peace more likely."[31]

Alternatively, the Israeli critical history yields a totally different form of politics, one that is encapsulated in the political platforms of the Left wing of the Labor Party and the Leftist Meretz Party. Like the critical historians, leaders such as current Labor Party Chair Shimon Peres have concluded that military power and strategic considerations will ultimately fail to resolve the Arab-Israeli conflict: "To achieve peace, the basic problems of the Middle East need to be approached realistically. First and foremost, we must all acknowledge the futility of war: the Arabs cannot defeat Israel on the battlefield; Israel cannot dictate the conditions of peace to the Arabs."[32] Peace, in Peres' view is a political rather than a strategic problem. Informed by a more cosmopolitan historical perspective, Peres argues that, "the key to maintaining an equitable and safe regional system is in politics and economics. . . . True power—even military power—is no longer anchored in the boot camp, but on the university campuses. Politics should pave the way from pure military strategy to an enriched political and economic repertoire."[33]

While we shouldn't overstate the case that history drives politics, it is nonetheless important to acknowledge that all historical inquiry is initiated in response to contemporary stimuli.[34] In the case of Israel, the acute tension caused by the ongoing conflict with the Palestinians is the problematic situation that drives the need to interpret the past. However, as the examples discussed in the book demonstrate, variation in the way the story is told can suggest and inform very different political positions and policies.

NOTES

1. Gary King, Robert O. Keohane, and Sidney Verba, *Designing Social Inquiry* (Princeton University Press, 1994), 7–9.

2. King, Keohane, and Verba, *Designing Social Inquiry,* 23.

3. King, Keohane, and Verba, *Designing Social Inquiry,* 24–26. Emphasis in original.

4. See Clifford Geertz, *An Interpretation of Cultures* (New York: Basic Books, 1973), esp. chapter 1, "Thick Description: Toward an Interpretive Theory of Culture," 1–27.

5. King, Keohane, and Verba, *Designing Social Inquiry,* 42.

6. See Alexander L. George and Timothy J. McKeown, "Case Studies and Theories of Organizational Decision Making," *Advances in Information Processing and Organizations*, vol. 2 (1985).

7. King, Keohane, and Verba, *Designing Social Inquiry,* 45, 44, and 53.

8. And let us put aside, for the sake of simplicity and since it is not significant to this example, the additional problem posed by the old versus the critical historiography of the case.

9. It should be emphasized that "second-image" factors are not the only alternative to the systemic approach provided in this example. There is of course an alternative systemic explanation that could be derived by looking at the case from an Arab perspective. According to this alternative systemic view, Arab actions may have been strategic responses to Israeli challenges in the form of massive "retaliation" raids. Again, the perspective of the investigator drives the choice of historical "facts" or "data" that are examined.

10. Stephen Van Evera, *Guide to Methods for Students of Political Science* (Ithaca, NY: Cornell University Press, 1997), 64.

11. See Kenneth N. Waltz, Theory of International Politics (Reading, MA: Addison-Wesley, 1979), 161–76, cited in Van Evera, *Guide to Methods*, 64–65.

12. Van Evera, *Guide to Methods,* 65.

13. The point here is not to dispute whether polarity-in-anarchy is a useful device for understanding international politics. Rather, it is to stress that the notion of polarity-in-anarchy is just that: a device, or what Ankersmit would call a "narrative substance," which is created and employed in order to make sense and order out of history, but *not something that could be literally located or understood within the past itself.* See Frank Ankersmit, "Reply to Professor Zagorin," *History and Theory*, vol. 29, no. 3 (1990), 277–82, discussed in Keith Jenkins, *Why History?* (New York: Routledge, 1999).

14. It should be reiterated: I do not claim that *all* positivists view the process of inquiry in this fashion. However, taking King, Keohane, and Verba as the "vanguard" of contemporary positivism, this is indeed the way they view historical inquiry and data and the way they encourage aspiring young scholars to also view it.

15. R. G. Collingwood, *The Idea of History* (New York: Galaxy, 1963 (1946)), 257–58.

16. Ian S. Lustick, "History, Historiography, and Political Science: Multiple Records and the Problem of Selection Bias," *American Political Science Review*, vol. 90, no. 3 (September 1996): 616.

17. Lustick, "History," 616.

18. Lustick, "History," 616.

19. Lustick, "History," 616.

20. See King, Keohane, and Verba, *Designing Social Inquiry*, 14–19; and Van Evera, *Guide to Methods*, 97–99.

21. Kohli, conclusion to "The Role of Theory in Comparative Politics: A Symposium." (Atul Kohli, Peter Evans, Peter J. Katzenstein, Adam Przeworski, Susan Hoeber Rudolph, James C. Scott, Theda Skocpol) *World Politics*, vol. 48, no. 1 (October 1995), 46.

22. Kurth, "Inside the Cave: The Banality of I.R. Studies," *The National Interest*, no. 53 (Fall 1998), 13 (internet version).

23. J. David Singer, "The Incompleat Theorist: Insights without Evidence," in K. Knorr and J. N. Rosenau, eds., *Contending Approaches to International Politics* (Princeton University Press, 1969), 71.

24. David Laitin, "The Implications of Constructivism for Constructing Ethnic Fractionalization Indices," in "Symposium: Cumulative Findings in the Study of Ethnic Politics," *APSA Comparative Politics Section Newsletter* (Winter 2001), 15 (preliminary version). Perhaps not surprisingly, Laitin's and the other constructivists' most ardent opponent in the symposium was Stephen Van Evera. Contrary to the constructivist claim that political identity is highly volatile across both space and time, Van Evera argued that ethnic identities can be "hardened" by a number of factors, reducing the salience of horizontal and vertical hybridity. Van Evera, "Primordialism Lives!" in *Symposium: Cumulative Findings in the Study of Ethnic Politics*, 20–24 (preliminary version).

25. On that note, it is interesting to peruse amazon.com reader reviews of Avi Shlaim's *The Iron Wall*, perhaps the most widely-read critical history text. One favorable reader writes: "If you are the type of person to view an objective and accurate history of Israel as somehow 'pro-Arab' or 'revisionist at its worst' then this book will surely anger you. But if you are a fan of accuracy and objectivity, like myself, then you will applaud Shlaim's work." On the opposite end of the spectrum, a critic writes: "It reads like a mediocre piece of homework by an adolescent, endlessly listing rehearsed anti-Israeli propaganda, with no interesting conclusion other than a shallow look into the angry and confused mind of the author. http://www.amazon.com/exec/obidos/tg/detail/-/0393321126/ref=cm_rev_next/002-4102486-5236057?v=glance&s=books&vi=customer-reviews&show=-submittime&start-at=21 (January 2002).

26. Heikki Patomaki Colin Wight, "After Postpositivism? The Promises of Critical Realism, *International Studies Quarterly*, vol. 44, no. 2 (2000): 214. For reference to significant contributions to that debate, see n4.

27. While this may seem facile to some, it is surprising how many people adopt this approach to the history of the Arab-Israeli conflict, and not just readers who contribute to the reviews on amazon.com. For a telling example, see the editorial of the inaugural issue of *Azure* (Polisar 2000), a journal dedicated to reinvigorating Zionism

and specifically committed to challenging what the editors perceive to be the "corrosive" views of the critical historians.

28. *New York Times*, August 14, 1999, A1; *New York Times*, November 14, 1999, Section 7, 6.

29. Avi Shlaim, "His Royal Shyness: King Hussein and Israel" (interview with King Hussein), *New York Review of Books*, July 15, 1999; Benny Morris, "Camp David and After: An Exchange (An Interview with Ehud Barak)," *New York Review of Books* 49 (10), June 13, 2002.

30. See Benny Morris, "Peace? No Chance," *Guardian,* February 21, 2002, http://www.guardian.co.uk/israel/comment/0,10551,653594,00.html (June 2004).

31. Benjamin Netanyahu, *Durable Peace: Israel and Its Place among the Nations* (New York: Warner Books, 2000), 319.

32. Shimon Peres, *The New Middle East* (New York: Henry Holt, 1993), 49.

33. Peres, *The New Middle East*, 34–35.

34. John Dewey, *Logic: The Theory of Inquiry* (New York: Holt, Rinehart, and Winston, 1938), 32–239.

Conclusion

What is History? E. H. Carr posed the question in his classic 1961 text. Just as the subject matter of history is multifaceted and contested, so too is the answer to Carr's most complicated question. This study may not have definitively answered Carr's query nor conclusively resolved the problem of historical inquiry posed to social science. However, the preceding chapters have sought to break fundamentally new ground in revealing that the basic historical character of political science research is as problematic as it is fundamental to the production of new knowledge in the field. Insofar as this is the case, and I argue that it is very much the case, then the problem of historical inquiry and the particular position adopted to deal with it is of critical importance. To date, it seems that academic political science has not moved very far afield from an unreconstructed positivist position, which though it may not be reflective of each individual political scientist or even all those who identify themselves as "positivist," is nonetheless widespread. So it is that most political science scholarship fails to acknowledge the socially constructed character of history.

Whereas positivism may be criticized for staking out a naively uncritical position on the question of history, postmodernism adopts an almost diametrically opposing perspective. The postmodern mode of historical inquiry calls for the subversion of any and all means that might arbitrate or manage the production of historiography. While many postmodernists claim otherwise, none has offered a convincing argument that can explain how Derrida's "hyperpoliticization" or Lyotard's "incredulity" avoid a devolution into radical relativism. In response to this unsatisfying state of affairs, I argue that the pragmatist alternative offered by John Dewey avoids the obvious flaws in each of these two positions. A Deweyan perspective allows us to view history as the dynamic, complex phenomenon that it is. Insofar as understanding the past will help to resolve contemporary theoretical and political problems, pragmatism also compels us to seek better methods to interpret history. In addition, the Deweyan approach suggests that rigorous methods need an ethical compass so as to maintain a healthy problem orientation within the field. Perhaps most important, Deweyan pragmatism allows political scientists to see that some histories are in fact better than others, but not in the sense of being more objectively accurate or true. Rather, some histories can help to solve theoretical as well as "real-world" political problems better than others. This is a new and important contribution to political science.

Though the problem addressed in this book is partly an epistemological one, its existence and importance most certainly can be examined empirically, for it is in the realm of empirical research that its effects are most keenly felt. This project has thus undertaken to reveal those effects looking at the historical revisionist movement spurred by the Israeli critical historians. By examining in some depth the way in which various generations have written the history of the Arab-Israeli conflict, I have shown that the basic question of what happened is an intricate one that cannot be resolved via cursory examination. Further, through a critical analysis of both qualitative and quantitative political science treatments of the conflict, we can see that the failure to acknowledge and cope with the problem of historical inquiry as instantiated in historical revisionism results in both empirical inconsistencies and a weakening of important theoretical claims within the literature. The additional demonstration of this problem in the case of the Vietnam War suggests that the problem of historical inquiry is not solely a matter for students of the Middle East.

Two final points are in order, one with regard to political science and one with regard to politics. First, by now, it is hoped that readers will agree that historical bias—a ubiquitous problem in the field—results from the inability to see that all historical texts have embedded normative and theoretical commitments. By adopting a pragmatist approach toward historical research, we can see that history is indeed constructed, but what is critically important is not the degree of objectivity of the texts we use, but rather their usefulness in helping us to answer questions and anomalies left unaddressed by other sources and accounts. Rather than search for the "best" or most accurate historical texts, political scientists should assume multiple competing historical schools and seek to delineate their respective answers to important research and political questions. I argue further that uncritical reliance on a single narrative is likely to produce biased and skewed research that fails to adequately explain historical causation in a rigorous and accurate manner.

Second, accounting for historical bias is not only a matter for political scientists. As philosophical pragmatists such as John Dewey persuasively argued and this examination of the Arab-Israeli conflict affirms, historical inquires can and do have in impact upon "real-world" politics. A more expansive discussion of the policy implications of this last point is beyond the scope of this book, but at least one conclusion is worth noting. The type of history used as a backdrop for understanding the present will lend itself to quite different political platforms. If Israel has in fact been a weak and vulnerable "state under siege" for so many decades, then the notion of a neighboring Palestinian state as a harbor for terror and violence seems more real. If, however, Israeli rhetoric regarding its victim-hood is rather a façade for its expansionist state-building aspirations, then the need to make serious compromises with the Palestinians from a position of strength becomes a more logical option. Thus, it is not surprising that contemporary Israeli leaders like current and former Prime Ministers Ariel Sharon and Ehud Barak, respectively, see both the past and the present of the Arab-Israeli conflict in such different terms. Whereas the former talks of Israeli "survival" in the harsh confines of the Hobbesian Middle East, the latter sought to bring about a final and complete "end to the conflict" with the Palestinians. Of course, during the past year or two, Barak has begun to sound more like Sharon. Sharon, with his plan to disengage from Gaza and a small portion of the northern West Bank, sounds more like Barak. But this only goes to show that history, like everything in politics, is fluid.

The approach toward history contained in this book should help scholars to acknowledge the common flaws found in much historical political science scholarship. More importantly, this study has sought to provide some new ways of addressing those flaws by suggesting a more nuanced understanding of history and highlighting practical methodological and procedural measures that will help to alleviate the problem of historical inquiry as it pertains to political science research. Toward that effect, it is hoped that scholars are emboldened to be more patient and rigorous in their approach toward historical questions and cases. Equally important, I invite scholars to begin to chip away at the stigma associated with discussing normative considerations in political science research and to break down the apartheid of ethical from social scientific questions through the production of more critical and self-reflective scholarship. In so doing, it is my hope that scholars interested in historical problems not proceed with the question of "which is the real story about the past?" but rather with the much more interesting and important question of "what kind of future do we want and what type of story is most useful in helping to lead us there."

References

C. Alexander, L. George, and Timothy J. McKeown, "Case Studies and Theories of Organizational Decision Making," in Robert F. Coulam and Richard A. Smith, eds., *Advances in Information Processing in Organizations*, vol. 2. (Greenwich, CT: JAI Press, 1985)

Yigal Allon, *Shield of David* (London: Weidenfeld and Nicolson, 1970)

http://www.amazon.com (January 2002)

Frank Ankersmit, "Reply to Professor Zagorin," *History and Theory* vol. 29, no. 3 (1990)

The Associated Press, "Dayan Reveals Regrets over Golan, Hebron in Newly Disclosed Interview," May 11, 1997.

David P. Auerswald, "Inward Bound: Domestic Institutions and Military Conflicts," *International Organization* vol. 53, no. 3 (Summer 1999)

Azure, journal published by the Shalem Center (Washington, DC, and Jerusalem, 1996)

David A. Baldwin, ed., *Neorealism and Neoliberalism* (New York: Columbia University Press, 1993)

Loren Baritz, *Backfire* (New York: W. Morrow, 1985)

Mordechai Bar-On, *The Gates of Gaza* (New York: St. Martins, 1994)

David M. Barrett, "The Mythology Surrounding Lyndon Johnson, His Advisers, and the 1965 Decision to Escalate the Vietnam War," *Political Science Quarterly* vol. 103, no. 4 (1988)

Andre Beaufre, *The Suez Expedition 1956* (London: Faber & Faber, 1964)

Uri Ben-Eliezer, *The Making of Israeli Militarism* (Bloomington: Indiana University Press, 1998)

David Ben-Gurion, *Israel: A Personal History* (New York: Funk and Wagnalls, 1971)
——, *Israel: Years of Challenge* (New York: Holt, Rinehart, and Winston, 1963)

Robert F. Berkhofer, Jr., *Beyond the Great Story* (Cambridge, MA: Belknap Press, 1995)

Larry Berman, *Planning a Tragedy* (New York: W.W. Norton, 1982)

Richard K. Betts, "Surprise Despite Warning: Why Sudden Attacks Succeed," *Political Science Quarterly* vol. 95, no. 4 (Winter 1980–1981)

Anne E. Blair, *Lodge in Vietnam* (New Haven: Yale University Press, 1995)

Michael Brecher, *Decision's in Israel's Foreign Policy* (New Haven: Yale University Press, 1975)

Michael Brecher, "Turning Points: Reflections on Many Paths to Knowledge," in Joseph Kruzel and James N. Rosenau, eds., *Journeys through World Politics* (Lexington, MA: Lexington Books, 1988)

Michael Brecher, Jonathan Wilkenfeld, Sheila Moser, *Crises in the Twentieth Century* vol. 1 "Handbook of International Crises," (Oxford: Pergamon Press, 1988)

Michael Brecher and Jonathan Wilkenfeld, *A Study of Crisis* (w. CD ROM) (Ann Arbor: University of Michigan Press, 2000)

Hedley Bull, "International Theory: The Case for a Classical Approach," in K. Knorr and J. N. Rosenau, eds., *Contending Approaches to International Politics* (Princeton University Press, 1969)

John Burke and Fred I. Greenstein, *How Presidents Test Reality* (New York: Russell Sage, 1991)

Robert Lyle Butterworth, ed., *Managing Interstate Conflict* (Pittsburgh, PA: University Center for International Studies, 1976)

Barry Buzan and Richard Little, "The Idea of 'International System': Theory Meets History", *International Political Science Review* vol. 15, no. 3 (1994)

——, "Reconceptualizing Anarchy: Structural Realism Meets World History," *European Journal of International Relations* vol. 2, no. 4 (1996)

David Campbell, *Writing Security*, revised edition (Minneapolis: University of Minnesota Press, 1998)

E. H. Carr, *What is History* (New York: Vintage Books, 1961)

King C. Chen, "Hanoi's Three Decisions and the Escalation of the Vietnam War," *Political Science Quarterly* vol. 90, no. 2 (Summer 1975)

Molly Cochran, *Normative Theory in International Relations* (Cambridge: Cambridge University Press, 1999)

Charles G. Cogan, "From the Politics of Lying to the Farce at Suez: What the U.S. Knew," *Intelligence and National Security* vol. 13, no. 2 (Summer 1998)

R. G. Collingwood, *The Idea of History* (New York: Galaxy, 1963 (1946))

Moshe Dayan, *Diary of the Sinai Campaign* (Jerusalem: Steimatzky's Agency, 1965)

——, *Story of My Life* (New York: William Morrow and Company, Inc., 1976)

James Der Derian, Post-Theory: The Eternal Return of Ethics in International Relations," in *New Thinking in International Relations Theory*, Michael W. Doyle and G. John Ikenberry, eds., (Boulder: Westview, 1997)

Jacques Derrida, "Remarks on Deconstruction and Pragmatism" in Simon Critchley, Jacques Derrida, Ernesto Laclau, and Richard Rorty, *Deconstruction and Pragmatism* (London: Routledge, 1996)

Daniel Deudney, "The Philadelphian System: Sovereignty, Arms Control, and Balance of Power in the American States-Union, Circa 1787–1861," *International Organization*, 49 (Spring 1995)

John Dewey, *Outlines of a Critical Theory of Ethics* (1891), in *The Early Works of John Dewey, 1882–1898* vol. 3 (Carbondale: Southern Illinois University Press, 1969)

———, "Lecture Notes: Political Philosophy" (1892), Dewey Papers, Special Collections, Morris Library, Southern Illinois University, Carbondale, IL.

———, *How We Think*, in *The Middle Works, 1899–1924*, Jo Ann Boydston, ed. (Southern Carbondale: Illinois University Press, 1976–1983)

———, *John Dewey: Lectures in China, 1919–1920*, Robert W. Clopton and Tsuinchen Ou, eds. (Honolulu: University Press of Hawaii, 1973)

———, *Reconstruction in Philosophy* (Boston: Beacon Press, 1948 (1920))

———, *The Public and Its Problems* (Denver: Alan Swallow, 1954 (1927))

———, *Logic: The Theory of Inquiry* (New York: Holt, Rinehart, and Winston, 1938)

John Dewey and James H. Tufts, *Ethics*, revised edition (New York: Henry Holt and Company, 1932 (1908))

Abba Eban, *My People* (New York: Random House, 1968)

———, *My Country* (New York: Random House, 1973)

Daniel Ellsberg, *Papers on the War* (New York: Simon and Schuster, 1972)

Walter Eytan, *The First Ten Years* (London: Weidengeld and Nicolson, 1958)

Mathew Festenstein, *Pragmatism and Political Theory* (Cambridge, UK: University of Chicago Press, 1997)

Herman Finer, *Dulles over Suez* (Chicago: Quadrangle, 1964)

Martha Finnemore, *National Interests in International Society* (Ithaca, NY: Cornell University Press, 1996)

Simha Flapan, *The Birth of Israeli: Myths and Realities* (New York: Pantheon, 1987)

Forum on the New Institutionalism, *Polity* vol. 28, no. 1 (Fall 1995)

John Lewis Gaddis, *Strategies of Containment* (Oxford: Clarendon Press, 1982)

Lloyd C. Gardner, *Approaching Vietnam* (New York: W.W. Norton, 1988)

———, *Pay at Any Price* (Chicago: Ivan R. Dee, 1995)

Clifford Geertz, *An Interpretation of Cultures* (New York: Basic Books, 1973)

Leslie H. Gelb with Richard K. Betts, *The Irony of Vietnam* (Washington D.C.: Brookings, 1979)

Alexander L. George, *Forceful Persuasion* (Washington D.C.: USIP, 1991)

Alexander L. George and Timothy J. McKeown, "Case Studies and Theories of Organizational Decision Making," *Advances in Information Processing and Organizations*, vol. 2 (1985)

Robert Gilpin, *War and Change in World Politics* (New York: Cambridge University Press, 1981)

Motti Golani, *Israel in Search of War* (Portland, OR: Sussex, 1998)

Fred I. Greenstein and John P. Burke, "The Dynamics of Presidential Reality Testing: Evidence from Two Vietnam Decisions," *Political Science Quarterly* vol. 104, no. 4 (1989–1990)

Stephen H. Haber, David M. Kennedy, and Stephen D. Krasner, "Brothers under the Skin: Diplomatic History and International Relations," *International Security* vol. 22, no. 1 (Summer 1997)

Muhammad Hasanayn Haykal, *Al-Urush wa'l-juyush: kadhalik infajara al-sira'a fi filastin* vol. 1 [Thrones and Armies: Thus Erupted the Struggle in Palestine (Cairo, 1998)]

Yoram Hazony, *The Struggle for Israel's Soul* (New York: Basic Books, 2000)

B. Healy and A. Stein, "The Balance of Power in International History: Theory and Reality," *Journal of Conflict Resolution*, 17 (1973)

George C. Herring, *America's Longest War*, 1st edition, (New York: Wiley, 1979)

——, *America's Longest War*, 2nd edition (Philadelphia, Temple University Press, 1986)

Steven Heydemann, "Revisionism and the Reconstruction of Israeli History," in Ian S. Lustick and Barry Rubin, eds., *Critical Essays on Israeli Society, Politics, and Culture* (Albany, NY: SUNY Press, 1991)

Thomas R. Hietala, *Manifest Design* (Ithaca, NY: Cornell University Press, 1985)

Gertrude Himmelfarb, *Critical History and the Old* (Cambridge, MA: Harvard University Press, 1987)

——, "Some Reflections on the Critical History," *American Historical Review*, 94 (June 1989)

Stanley Hoffman, *Gulliver's Troubles* (New York: McGraw-Hill, 1968)

Francis W. Hoole and Dina A. Zinnes, "Introduction," in Francis W. Hoole and Dina A. Zinnes, eds., *Quantitative International Politics* (New York: Praeger, 1976)

http://www.amazon.com/exec/obidos/tg/detail/-/0393321126/ref=cm_rev_next/002-4102486-5236057?v=glance&s=books&vi=customer-reviews&show=-submittime&start-at=21

Georg G. Iggers, *Historiography in the Twentieth Century* (Hanover, NH: Wesleyan University Press, 1997)

G. John Ikenberry, *After Victory: Institutions, Strategic Restraint, and the Rebuilding of Order after Major Wars* (Princeton: Princeton University Press, 2000)

"Israeli Historiography Revisited," *History and Memory* vol. 7, no. 1 (Spring/Summer 1995)

Israel Office of Information, *Israel's Struggle for Peace* (New York: Israel Office of Information, 1960)

Keith Jenkins, *The Postmodern History Reader* (London: Routledge, 1997)

——, *Why History?* (New York: Routledge, 1999)

Bruce W. Jentleson, *American Foreign Policy* (New York: W.W. Norton, 2000), 140–42.

Robert Jervis, *Perception and Misperception in International Politics* (Princeton University Press, 1976)

Brian L. Job and Charles W. Ostrom, "An Appraisal of the Research Design and Philosophy of Science of the Correlates of War Project," in Francis W. Hoole and Dina A. Zinnes, eds., *Quantitative International Politics* (New York: Praeger, 1976)

Lyndon B. Johnson, *The Vantage Point: Perspectives of the Presidency* (New York: Holt, Rinehart, and Winston, 1971)

Daniel M. Jones, Stuart A. Bremer, and J. David Singer, "Militarized Interstate Disputes, 1816–1992: Rationale, Coding Rules, and Empirical Patterns," *Conflict Management and Peace Science* vol. 15, no. 2 (1996)

George McT. Kahin, *Intervention* (New York: Alfred A. Knopf, 1986)

Miles Kahler, "Inventing International Relations: International Relations Theory after 1945," in Doyle and Ikenberry, eds., *New Thinking in International Relations Theory* (Boulder, CO: Westview Press, 1997)

David Kaiser, *American Tragedy* (Cambridge, MA: The Belknap Press, 2000)

Morton A. Kaplan, "The New Great Debate: Traditionalism vs. Science in International Relations," in K. Knorr and J. N. Rosenau, eds., *Contending Approaches to International Politics* (Princeton University Press, 1969)

Efraim Karsh, *Fabricating Israeli History: The "Critical Historians"* (London: Frank Cass, 1997)

Paul M. Kattenburg, *The Vietnam Trauma in American Foreign Policy* (New Brunswick, NJ: Transaction Books, 1980)

Dorris Kearns, *Lyndon Johnson and the American Dream* (New York, 1976)

Robert O. Keohane, ed., *Neorealism and its Critics* (New York: Columbia University Press, 1986)

Walid Khalidi, *Al-Sihyunniyya fi mi'at 'am*, 1897–1997 [A Century of Zionism] (Beirut, 1998)

Walid Khalidi, ed., *All That Remains: The Palestinian Villages Occupied and Depopulated by Israel in 1948*, research and text, Sharif S. Elmusa, Muhammad Ali Khalidi (Washington, DC: Institute for Palestine Studies, 1992)

Walid Khalidi, ed., *From Haven to Conquest: Readings in Zionism and the Palestine Problem until 1948* (Washington, DC: Institute for Palestine Studies, 1987 (1971))

Walid Khalidi and Jill Khadduri, eds., *Palestine and the Arab-Israeli Conflict: An Annotated Bibliography* (Beirut: Institute for Palestine Studies, 1974)

Fred J. Khouri, *The Arab Israeli Dilemma*, 3rd edition, (Syracuse: Syracuse University Press, 1985)

Elizabeth Kier, *Imagining War: French and British Military Doctrine between the Wars* (Princeton: Princeton University Press, 1998)

Baruch Kimmerling, "Academic History Caught in the Cross-Fire: The Case of Israeli-Jewish Historiography," *History and Memory* vol. 7, no. 1 (Spring/Summer 1995)

Gary King, Robert O. Keohane, Sidney Verba, *Designing Social Inquiry* (Princeton: Princeton University Press, 1994)

David Kinsella, "Conflict in Context: Arms Transfers and Third World Rivalries during the Cold War," *American Journal of Political Science* vol. 38, no. 3 (August 1994)

Jonathan Kirshner, *Currency and Coercion* (Princeton, NJ: Princeton University Press, 1995)

Henry Kissinger, *Diplomacy* (New York: Random House, Simon and Shuster, 1994)

Atul Kohli, "Conclusion," in "The Role of Theory in Comparative Politics: A Symposium." (Atul Kohli, Peter Evans, Peter J. Katzenstein, Adam Przeworski, Susan Hoeber Rudolph, James C. Scott, Theda Skocpol) *World Politics* vol. 48, no. 1 (October 1995)

Joseph Kruzel and James N. Rosenau, eds., *Journeys through World Politics* (Lexington, MA: Lexington Books, 1988)

Thomas S. Kuhn, *The Structure of Scientific Revolutions* (The University of Chicago Press, 1962)

Charles Kupchan, *The Vulnerability of Empire* (Ithaca, NY: Cornell University Press, 1994)

James Kurth, "Inside the Cave: The Banality of I.R. Studies," *The National Interest* no. 53 (Fall 1998)

Keith Kyle, *Suez* (New York: St. Martin's, 1991)

David Laitin, "The Implications of Constructivism for Constructing Ethnic Fractionalization Indices," in "Symposium: Cumulative Findings in the Study of Ethnic Politics," *APSA Comparative Politics Section Newsletter* (Winter 2001)

Christopher Layne, "The Unipolar Illusion," *International Security* vol. 17, no. 4 (Spring 1993), reprinted in Sean M. Lynn-Jones and Steven E. Miller, eds., *The Cold War and After* (Cambridge: MIT Press, 1993)

Daniel Levy, "The Future of the Past: Historiographical Disputes and Competing Memories in Germany and Israel," *History and Theory* vol. 38, no. 1 (February 1999)

Jack S. Levy, "Too Important to Leave to the Other: History and Political Science in the Study of International Relations," *International Security* vol. 22, no. 1 (Summer 1997)

Jack S. Levy and Joseph R. Grochal, "Democracy and Preventive War: Israel and the 1956 Sinai Campaign," Paper presented at the Annual Meeting of the American Political Science Association (APSA), September 2–5, 1999.

Yagil Levy, *Trial and Error* (Albany, NY: SUNY, 1997)

Fredrik Logevall, *Choosing War* (Berkeley: University of California Press, 1999)

Wm. Roger Louis and Roger Owen, eds., *Suez 1956: The Crisis and its Consequences* (Oxford: Clarendon, 1989)

Kennet Love, *Suez: The Twice-Fought War* (New York: McGraw-Hill, 1969)

Ian S. Lustick, "History, Historiography, and Political Science: Multiple Records and the Problem of Selection Bias," *American Political Science Review* vol. 90, no. 3 (September 1996)

——, "Israeli History: Who is Fabricating What?" *Survival* (Autumn 1997)

Jean-Francois Lyotard, *The Postmodern Condition: A Report on Knowledge* (Minneapolis: University of Minnesota Press, 1979)

S. L. A. Marshall, *Sinai Victory* (New York: William Morrow, 1958)

C. Behan McCullagh, *Justifying Historical Descriptions* (Cambridge: Cambridge University Press, 1984)

——, *The Truth of History* (London: Routledge, 1998)

Rose McDermott, *Risk-Taking in International Politics* (Ann Arbor: The University of Michigan Press, 1998)

Terrence J. McDonald, ed., *The Historic Turn in the Human Sciences* (Ann Arbor: The University of Michigan Press, 1996)

H. R. McMaster, *Dereliction of Duty* (New York: HarperCollins, 1997)

Militarized Interstate Dispute (MID) Version 2.1, http://pss.la.psu.edu/MID_DATA. HTM (September 2001)

Karen Mingst, *Essentials of International Relations* (New York: W.W. Norton, 1999)

Edwin E. Moise, *Tonkin Gulf* (Chapel Hill: The University of North Carolina Press, 1996)

Barrington Moore, *Social Origins of Dictatorship and Democracy: Lord and Peasant in the Making of the Modern World* (Boston: Beacon, 1966)

Benny Morris, *The Birth of the Palestinian Refugee Problem* (New York: Cambridge University Press, 1987).

———, *1948 and After: Israel and the Palestinians* (New York: Oxford University Press, 1990)

———, *Israel's Border Wars 1949–1956* (New York: Oxford University Press, 1993)

———, "The New Historiography," lecture given at the University of Pennsylvania, Philadelphia, PA, January 21, 1997.

———, *Righteous Victims: A History of the Zionist-Arab Conflict, 1881–1999* (New York: Knopf, 1999)

———, "Peace? No Chance," *Guardian*, February 21, 2002, http://www.guardian.co .uk/israel/comment/0,10551,653594,00.html (June 2004)

———, "Camp David and After: An Exchange (An Interview with Ehud Barak)," *New York Review of Books* 49 (10), June 13, 2002

Murray G. Murphey, *Our Knowledge of the Historical Past* (New York: Bobbs-Merill Company, 1973)

———, *Philosophical Foundations of Historical Knowledge* (Ithaca, NY: SUNY Press, 1994)

Benyamin Netanyahu, *A Durable Peace* (New York: Time Warner, 2000)

Richard E. Neustadt and Ernest R. May, *Thinking in Time* (New York: The Free Press, 1986)

New York Times, "History Textbooks Replace Myths with Facts," August 14, 1999, A1

New York Times, "Israel: The Revised Edition," November 14, 1999, sec. 7, 6

Peter Novick, *That Noble Dream* (New York: Cambridge University Press, 1988)

Anthony Nutting, *No End of a Lesson* (New York: Clarkson N. Potter, 1967)

Edgar O'Ballance, *The Arab-Israeli War 1948* (New York: Praeger, 1957)

Michael Oakeshott, *Experience and Its Modes* (Cambridge: Cambridge University Press, 1933)

Karren Orren and Stephen Skowronek, "Beyond the Iconography of Order: Notes for a 'New Institutionalism,'" in Lawrence C. Dodd and Calvin Jillson, eds., *The Dynamics of American Politics* (Boulder, CO: Westview, 1994)

Robert E. Osgood and Robert W. Tucker, *Force, Order, and Justice* (Baltimore: The Johns Hopkins Press, 1967)

Ilan Pappé, *Britain and the Arab-Israeli Conflict*, 1948–1951 (London: MacMillan, 1988)

———, "Critique and Agenda: The Post-Zionist Scholars in Israel," *History and Memory* vol. 7, no. 1 (Spring/Summer 1995)

———, ed., *The Israel/Palestine Question* (London: Routledge, 1999)

Heikki Patomaki and Colin Wight, "After Postpositivism? The Promises of Critical Realism," *International Studies Quarterly* vol. 44, no. 2 (2000), 213–37

T. V. Paul, *Asymmetric Conflicts: War Initiation by Weaker Powers* (Cambridge University Press, 1994)

Shimon Peres, *The New Middle East* (New York: Henry Holt, 1993)

Daniel Polisar, open solicitation letter for *Azure: Ideas for the Jewish Nation* (undated)

Donald J. Puchala, "The Pragmatics of International History," *Mershon International Studies Review* no. 39 (1995)

Hilary Putnam, *Realism with a Human Face*, James Conant, ed. (Cambridge: Harvard University Press, 1990)

——, *Renewing Philosophy* (Cambridge: Harvard University Press, 1993)

Willard Van Orman Quine, "Two Dogmas of Empiricism," in *From a Logical Point of View* (Cambridge: Harvard University Press, 1980 (1953))

Thomas Risse-Kappen, *Cooperation among Democracies*, (Princeton: Princeton University Press, 1995)

Terrence Robertson, *Crisis* (London: Hutchinson, 1964)

David Rodman, "War Initiation: The Case of Israel," *The Journal of Strategic Studies* vol. 20, no. 4 (December 1997)

Richard Rorty, *Philosophy and the Mirror of Nature* (Princeton: Princeton University Press, 1979)

——, *Objectivity, Relativism, and Truth* (New York: Cambridge University Press, 1991)

Gideon Rose, "Neoclassical Realism and Theories of Foreign Policy," *World Politics* 51 (October 1998)

Michael Roskin, "From Pearl Harbor to Vietnam: Shifting Generational Paradigms and Foreign Policy, *Political Science Quarterly* vol. 89, no. 3 (Fall 1974): 569–70.

Gunther E. Rothenberg, *The Anatomy of the Israeli Army* (London: B. T. Batsford, 1979)

Routledge Encyclopedia of Philosophy, www.rep.routledge.com/philosophy/articles/ -entry/ N/N044/N044.html (September 2000)

Routledge Encyclopedia of Philosophy, www.rep.routledge.com/philosophy/articles/ -entry/R/R017/R017.html (September 2000)

Bruce Russett, "Foreword," in Francis W. Hoole and Dina A. Zinnes, eds., *Quantitative International Politics* (New York: Praeger, 1976)

Howard M. Sachar, *A History of Israel* (New York: Alfred A. Knopf, 1993 (1979))

Nadav Safran, *From War to War* (Indianapolis: Pegasus, 1969)

Brian C. Schmidt, *The Political Discourse of Anarchy* (Albany, NY: SUNY Press, 1998)

Paul W. Schroeder, "A Final Rejoinder," *Journal of Conflict Resolution* vol. 21, no. 1 (March 1977)

——, "Quantitative Studies in the Balance of Power," *Journal of Conflict Resolution* vol. 21, no. 1 (March 1977)

——, "Historical Reality vs. Neo-Realist Theory," *International Security* vol. 19, no. 2 (Summer 1994)

Randall L. Schweller, "Domestic Structure and Preventive War," *World Politics* vol. 44, no. 2 (1992)

Theda Skocpol, "Sociology's Historical Imagination," in Skocpol, ed., *Vision and Method in Historical Sociology* (New York: Cambridge University Press, 1984)

——, "Emerging Agendas and Recurrent Strategies in Historical Sociology," in Skocpol, ed., *Vision and Method in Historical Sociology* (New York: Cambridge University Press, 1984)

Theda Skocpol and Margaret Somers, "The Uses of Comparative History in Macrosocial History," in Skocpol, *Social Revolutions in the Modern World* (New York: Cambridge University Press, 1994)

Anita Shapira, *Land and Power: The Zionist Resort to Force, 1881–1948* (New York: Oxford, 1992)

——, "Politics and Collective Memory: The Debate over the 'Critical Historians' in Israel," *History and Memory* vol. 7, no. 1 (Spring/Summer 1995)

Moshe Sharett, *Personal Diary*, Reprinted in Livia Rokach, *Israel's Sacred Terrorism: A Study Based on Moshe Sharett's Personal Diary* (Belmont, MA: Association of Arab-American University Graduates, Inc., 1980)

Gabriel Sheffer, *Moshe Sharett* (New York: Oxford University Press, 1996)

Jonathan Shimshoni, *Israel and Conventional Deterrence* (Ithaca, NY: Cornell University Press, 1988)

Avi Shlaim, *Collusion across the Jordan* (Oxford: Clarendon, 1988)

——, "The Debate about 1948," *International Journal of Middle East Studies* vol. 27, no. 3 (1995)

——, "The Protocol of Sevres, 1956: Anatomy of a War Plot," *International Affairs* vol. 73, no. 3 (1997)

——, "His Royal Shyness: King Hussein and Israel" (Interview with King Hussein), *New York Review of Books*, July 15, 1999

——, *The Iron Wall* (New York: Norton, 2000)

Avi Shlaim and Eugene L. Rogan, eds., *The War for Palestine* (Cambridge University Press, 2001)

John R. Shook, *Dewey's Empirical Theory of Knowledge and Reality* (Nashville: Vanderbilt University Press, 2000)

J. David Singer, "The Incompleat Theorist: Insights without Evidence," in K. Knorr and J. N. Rosenau, eds., *Contending Approaches to International Politics* (Princeton University Press, 1969)

——, "The Correlates of War Project: Continuity, Diversity, and Convergence," in Francis W. Hoole and Dina A. Zinnes, eds., *Quantitative International Politics* (New York: Praeger, 1976)

——, "Individual Values, National Interests, and Political Development," in J. David Singer, ed., *Correlates of War, Volume I* (New York: The Free Press, 1979)

——, "Introduction," in J. David Singer, ed., *Correlates of War, Volume I* (New York: The Free Press, 1979)

——, "The Making of a Peace Researcher," in Joseph Kruzel and James N. Rosenau, eds., *Journeys through World Politics* (Lexington, MA: Lexington Books, 1988)

J. David Singer and Melvin Small, *Correlates of War Project: International and Civil War Data, 1816–1992* [Computer file], (Ann Arbor, MI, 1993) J. David Singer and

Melvin Small [producers], Inter-university Consortium for Political and Social Research (ICPSR) [distributor], 1994

Jerome Slater, "The Significance of Israeli Historical Revisionism," in Walter P. Zenner and Russell A. Stone, eds., *Critical Essays on Israeli Social Issues and Scholarship* (Albany, NY: SUNY Press, 1994)

Rogers Smith, "Science, Non-Science, and Politics," in Terrence J. McDonald, ed., *The Historic Turn in the Human Sciences* (Ann Arbor: The University of Michigan Press, 1996)

Thomas W. Smith, *History and International Relations* (London: Routledge, 1999)

Jack Snyder, *Myths of Empire* (Ithaca, NY: Cornell University Press, 1991)

Social Science Research Council (SSRC), *Theory and Practice in Historical Study: A Report of the Committee on Historiography*, Bulletin 54 (New York: Social Science Research Council, 1946)

Social Science Research Council (SSRC), *The Social Sciences in Historical Study*, Bulletin 64 (New York: Social Science Research Council, 1954)

William Stafford, Review of McCullagh's *The Truth of History*, in *The English Historical Review* vol. 114, issue 457 (June 1999)

Ernest Stock, *Israel on the Road to Sinai* (Ithaca, NY: Cornell, 1967)

John G. Stoessinger, *Why Nations Go to War*, 5th edition (New York: St. Martins, 1990)

Martin Stuart-Fox, "Can History be True? A Review Essay," *The Australian Journal of Politics and History* vol. 44, issue 1 (March 1998)

"Symposium: History and Theory," *International Security* vol. 22, no. 1 (Summer 1997)

David Tal, "Israel's Road to the 1956 War," *International Journal of Middle East Studies* no. 28 (1996)

Kathleen Thelen and Sven Steinmo, "Historical Institutionalism in Comparative Politics," in Steinmo, Thelen, and Frank Longstreth, eds., *Structuring Politics* (New York: Cambridge University Press, 1992)

Wallace J. Thies, *When Governments Collide* (Berkeley: University of California Press, 1980)

Hugh Thomas, *Suez* (New York: Harper and Row, 1966)

Charles Tilly and David S. Landes, eds., *History as Social Science* (Englewood Cliffs, NJ: Prentice-Hall, 1971)

Charles Tilly, *As Sociology Meets History* (New York: Academic Press, 1981)

——, "War Making and State Making as Organized Crime," in Peter Evans et al., *Bringing the State Back In* (Cambridge, MA: Cambridge University Press, 1985)

——, *Coercion, Capital, and European States* (Cambridge, MA: Blackwell, 1992)

Selwyn Ilan Troen and Moshe Shemesh, eds., *The Suez-Sinai Crisis 1956* (New York: Columbia University Press, 1990)

Stephen Van Evera, *Guide to Methods for Students of Political Science* (Ithaca, NY: Cornell University Press, 1997)

——, "Primordialism Lives!" in "Symposium: Cumulative Findings in the Study of Ethnic Politics," *APSA Comparative Politics Section Newsletter* (Winter 2001)

Stephen M. Walt, *The Origins of Alliances* (Ithaca, NY: Cornell University Press, 1987)

——, *Revolution and War* (Ithaca, NY: Cornell University Press, 1996)

Kenneth N. Waltz, *Theory of International Politics* (Reading, MA: Addison-Wesley, 1979)

——, "America as a Model for the World? A Foreign Policy Perspective," *PS*, December 1991

Alexander E. Wendt, *Social Theory of International Politics* (Cambridge, MA: Cambridge University Press, 1999)

Robert B. Westbrook, *John Dewey and American Democracy* (Ithaca, NY: Cornell University Press, 1991)

Hayden White, *Tropics of Discourse* (Baltimore, MD: The Johns Hopkins University Press, 1978)

Jonathan Wilkenfeld, Interview by Jonathan B. Isacoff, University of Maryland, June 15, 2001

Avner Yaniv, *Deterrence without the Bomb* (Lexington, MA: D.C. Heath, 1987)

Norman R. Yetman, Introduction to "The Murphey Symposium: Murray G. Murphey and the Philosophical Foundations of American Studies," *American Studies* vol. 37, no. 2 (Fall 1996)

Index

1948–1949 Arab-Israeli war, 10, 17n32, 42, 50, 52, 57, 71, 83, 169, 180–81
1956 Arab-Israeli war, 11–12; critical history of, 59–71; old history of, 51–59; planning of, 67–71; political science scholarship on, 77–94; quantitative coding of, 105–12. *See also* Sinai Campaign
1967 Arab-Israeli war, 181

Acton, Lord, 20
Allon, Yigal, 52, 55, 65, 73n10
American Political Development (APD), 4–5
American Political Science Association (APSA), 3, 15n11
Ankersmit, Frank, 27, 44n34, 184n13
APD. *See* American Political Development
APSA. *See* American Political Science Association
Ashkenazi, 66, 75n74, 84, 97n22
Auerswald, David, 79, 96n8

Ball, George, 127, 163n50
Barak, Ehud, 182, 186n29, 189
Barrett, David, M., 127, 140n29, 148–49, 162n15, 162n24
Beard, Charles, 3

Ben-Gurion, David, 11, 68, 70, 71, 73n6, 73n8, 81–82, 84–86, 89–90, 92–93, 108, 117n37, 180, 181; competition with Moshe Sharett, 60–65. *See also* Israel, militarism of
Berman, Larry, 126–27, 140n26, 148, 162n13, 163n50
Betts, Richard K., 96n10, 125–27, 140n23, 148, 162n11, 163n50
Blair, Anne E., 135, 141n59, 154, 163n29
Brecher, Michael, 83, 91–92, 97n44, 101, *111*, *112*, 116n13, 117n41, 117n43, 117n44, 139n3
Bremer, Stuart A., 102, 107, 115n1
Brooke, Edward W., 123
Bull, Hedley, 5, 6, 16n17
Bundy, McGeorge, 127, 134, 137, 148–49, 154, 156, 163n27
Burke, John P., 127, 140n32, 149, 156, 162n16, 163n40, 163n50

Campbell, David, 35
Carr, E. H., 19–20, 43n2, 187
Chen, King C., 128–29, 141n37, 150, 162n19
Clark, Sir George, 20
Clifford, Clark, 127
Clinton, Bill, 1

Smith, Rogers, 5, 16n14
Smith, Thomas W., 7, 16n24, 20, 43n5,
115n1, 116n16
Snyder, Jack, 13, 14n4, 123–24,
140n16, 152–60
Social Science Research Council
(SSRC), 3–4, 15n7, 15n8
Soviet Union, 1, 78, 80–81, 84, 92, *105*,
106–9, 112, 121, 131, 144–45
SSRC. *See* Social Science Research
Council
Stoessinger, John, 124–25, 140n18,
146–47, 162n8
Straights of Tiran, 11, 56, 59, 80, 86, 91,
113, 181
structural realism, 2, 94, 123, 160,
164n61
Suez Crisis, 57–58, 67, 70, 72n5,
78–79, 86, 106–8

Taylor, Maxwell, 138
thick description, 167, 184n4
Thies, Wallace J., 130, 141n44, 151–52,
162n20
Tilly, Charles, 95, 97n21
Tucker, Robert W., 90–91, 97n43
Tufts, James, 39

UN. *See* United Nations
United Nations (UN), 17n32, 52, 61, 65,
92, 181

United States, 42, 50, 78, 96n5, 106–9;
involvement in Vietnam, 120–24,
127, 129–32, 134, 138–39, 144–45,
150–52, 155–56
University of Michigan, 6, 99, 100

Van Evera, Stephen, 14, 18n34, 169,
184n10, 185n24
Verba, Sidney, 14, 18n34, 166–70, 175,
177, 184n1
Vermars, 58–59, 70–71, 74n49
Vietnam, 13, 188; historical scholarship
on, 132–39; political science
scholarship on, 119–32, 143–62
Von Ranke, Leopold, 2, 20, 42n1

Walker, R. B. J., 6, 16n19
Walt, Stephen, 80–82, 181
Waltz, Kenneth N., 35, 123, 140n13,
146, 162n7, 164n62, 169–70,
184n11
Wendt, Alexander, 3, 15n5, 162n10
West Bank, 183, 189
White, Hayden, 27, 42, 44n32
whiz kids, 127, 137, 149
Wight, Colin, 36, 44n26, 180, 185n26
Wilkenfeld, Jonathan, 101, 103, *111*,
112, 115, 116n22, 117n41, 117n43,
117n44, 162n1

Yaniv, Avner, 90

About the Author

Jonathan B. Isacoff is Assistant Professor of Political Science at Gonzaga University. He worked previously as a Confidential Assistant to Governor Mario M. Cuomo of New York and as a consultant for the MeretzUSA organization in New York. Professor Isacoff has published articles and book chapters on international security, historical interpretation, the Arab-Israeli conflict, the Iraq War, and the political thought of John Dewey. His most recent articles have appeared in *Perspectives on Politics*, *Millennium: Journal of International Studies*, and *International Relations*.